ABOUT BECKETT

The Playwright and the Work

John Fletcher

faber and faber

First published in 2003
by Faber and Faber Limited
3 Queen Square London WC1N 3AU
This edition published in 2006

Typeset by Faber and Faber Limited
Printed in England by Bookmarque Ltd, Croydon

A CIP record for this book
is available from the British Library

ISBN 978-0-571-23011-2
ISBN 0-571-23011-3

2 4 6 8 10 9 7 5 3 1

To my sons Hilary and Edmund

Contents

Editors' Note

There are few theatre books which allow direct access to the playwright or to those whose business it is to translate the script into performance. These volumes aim to deal directly with the writer and with other theatre workers (directors, actors, designers and similar figures) who realize in performance the words on the page.

The subjects of the series are some of the most important and influential writers from post-war British and Irish theatre. Each volume contains an introduction which sets the work of the writer in the relevant historical, social and political context, followed by a digest of interviews and other material which allows the writer, in his own words, to trace his evolution as a dramatist. Some of this material is new, as is, in large part, the material especially gathered from the writers' collaborators and fellow theatre workers. The volumes conclude with annotated bibliographies. In all, we hope the books will provide a wealth of information in accessible form, and real insight into some of the major dramatists of our day.

Abbreviations

For full references, see the Select Bibliography p. 215.

Texts Used

The Complete Dramatic Works (Faber and Faber) is the reference text for Beckett's plays, and for his other writings the editions published by John Calder.

Chronology

1906	Samuel Barclay Beckett born at Foxrock, near Dublin, on 13 April, second son of William Frank Beckett, a quantity surveyor, and his wife Mary, *née* Roe. Kindergarten: Miss Ida Elsner's Academy, Stillorgan. Prep. school: Earlsfort House School, Dublin. Public school: Portora Royal, Enniskillen.
1923–27	Trinity College, Dublin; top first in French and Italian; large gold medal.
1928	Spends first two terms teaching at Campbell College, Belfast.
1928–30	Exchange lector at the École Normale Supérieure in Paris. Meets James Joyce. First poems published.
1930–32	Assistant lecturer in French, Trinity College, Dublin. Resigns after four terms.
1932–37	Years of study and travel, mainly in Germany.
1937	Settles permanently in Paris.
1942	Resistance group in which Beckett is active is betrayed to the Gestapo; Beckett escapes to the south of France.
1942–45	Lives in hiding in the village of Roussillon (Vaucluse department).
1945–46	Works as storekeeper and interpreter with the Irish Red Cross hospital in Saint-Lô (Normandy).
1946	Back in Paris, writes *Waiting for Godot* in French.
1953	Première in Paris of *Waiting for Godot*.
1955	Première in London of *Waiting for Godot*.
1957	*All That Fall* broadcast by BBC radio; première in London of *Endgame* in French.

1958   Première in London of *Endgame* in English and of *Krapp's Last Tape*.

1961   Première in New York of *Happy Days*.

1963   Première in Germany of *Play* [*Spiel*].

1966   *Eh Joe* broadcast on BBC2.

1969   Nobel Prize for Literature.

1972   Première in New York of *Not I*.

1976   Première in London of *Footfalls*.

1989   Dies in Paris; buried in Montparnasse cemetery.

Introduction

When Samuel Beckett died, in December 1989, the event was overshadowed by the momentous happenings in Romania that were occurring at the same time. As part of the collapse of Communism that was sweeping through the whole of Eastern Europe, the people of that country overthrew their tyrants, the Ceauşescu family; the hated dictator and his wife were summarily tried and executed. Mr Ceauşescu's obituary appeared in *The Times* on the same day as Beckett's – 27 December; but even then it was clear whose death held significance: the article about the dramatist (which I had been asked to write) took up the top half of the page, and the politician's was relegated to the space beneath it.

For, as history teaches us, kings, princes and other potentates come and go, but artists live for ever. Who would now remember the name of the Archbishop of Salzburg for whom Mozart worked in the 1770s if the great composer had not fallen out with him? How much would we know – or care – about the little princesses who lived at the Spanish court in the 1650s if the great painter Velasquez had not been commissioned to do their portraits? So, long after the Ceauşescus have been relegated to a footnote in the history books, Beckett's plays will still be performed around the world and studied in schools and universities everywhere. Even as I write, Channel 4 is screening specially made television versions of the complete dramatic works, and this means, of course, that they will reach a mass audience for the first time.

This book aims to explain why Beckett's work is so significant and why it will last. Already, when he died at the age of eighty-three, he was seen as one of the truly great literary figures of the twentieth century; his writings for the theatre in particular had made him famous, and the plays that I shall be focusing on here – *Waiting for Godot, Endgame, Krapp's Last Tape, Happy Days, Play* and *Not I* – had become part of the standard repertoire in theatres all over the world. These and his novels were already considered classics of modern literature and as naturally a part of an educated person's experience as the works of Proust or Kafka or James Joyce. 'I put him among the top writers: Proust, Joyce, Kafka and Beckett, the top four of the century,' declared lifelong friend Georges Pelorson, and John Calder, another close associate, agreed, adding that because Beckett 'encapsulated the other three in his own work and did it so brilliantly, he will ultimately be seen as the greatest of the twentieth-century writers' (*BD*, pp. 117–18).

Although he once declared, in an arresting phrase, 'the artist who gambles his being comes from nowhere and has no brothers', Samuel Barclay Beckett (to give him his full name) did have a biography, even if he was discreet and self-effacing about personal matters. His deep pessimism – something to which I shall return – led him to consider his birth (at Foxrock, near Dublin, on Good Friday, 13 April 1906) a 'calamity', and yet his childhood was happy enough. His father, William Frank Beckett, was a respected and prosperous Dublin businessman; he and his wife Mary (née Roe) were very fond of their second son, and he of them: their deaths, in 1933 and 1950 respectively, grieved him deeply.

'Willie' Beckett, as the father was affectionately known in Irish business and professional circles, was a cheerful, plump man who much enjoyed taking long walks and sharing jokes with his young son, whose outstanding sporting and academic record, first at school and then at university, made him, an early school-leaver himself, immensely proud. Though like all the family a regular church-goer, Beckett senior was less passionate in his Protestant belief than either his wife or his elder son Frank, who succeeded him at the head of the family firm. As for young Samuel's faith, this did not survive his student days, but

Christian mythology was to remain a haunting motif behind his writing from first to last, as we shall see when we come to look more closely at the plays, *Waiting for Godot* in particular.

Willie and Mary Beckett, like all caring parents, wanted the best possible education for their child. He was sent first to Miss Ida Elsner's Academy, a kindergarten near where they lived, and when he was a bit older he commuted by rail to Earlsfort House preparatory school in Dublin. He was to remember this regular journey on the old steam train, mocked by local wits as the 'Dublin Slow and Easy', many years later in his first and finest play for radio, *All That Fall* (1957). The people who have come to meet their loved ones at the little station at Foxrock that Beckett knew so well are starting to get anxious over the fact that the 12.30 from the city is running strangely late, and so they look to the station-master for an explanation:

MRS ROONEY Before you slink away, Mr Barrell, please, a statement of some kind, I insist. Even the slowest train on this brief line is not ten minutes and more behind its scheduled time without good cause, one imagines . . .

MR TYLER [*Reasonably.*] I do think we are owed some kind of explanation, Mr Barrell, if only to set our minds at rest.

MR BARRELL I know nothing. All I know is there has been a hitch. All traffic is retarded.

(*CDW*, pp. 186–7)

When the time came for the young Samuel to start his secondary education, his parents decided to send him to one of the top fee-paying establishments in Ireland, Portora Royal, a Protestant boarding school in County Fermanagh (now part of Northern Ireland). From there he went, loaded with academic and sporting honours, to university in Dublin, winning a scholarship to read French and Italian at Trinity College, the great Protestant foundation that dates back to the reign of Queen Elizabeth I. Here again he enjoyed an active extra-curricular life, notably in amateur dramatics and in the chess, golf and cricket clubs. He is, in fact, the only winner of the Nobel Prize for Literature to have played in first-class cricket: *Wisden* records his participation in the Northamptonshire vs. Dublin University match in July 1927. In his finals he got the top 'first' of his year and was awarded the distinction of a large gold medal. Some fifty years before him the same prize had been won by another great Irish playwright, Oscar Wilde, who refused to part with the precious object even when poverty-stricken and on his death bed in Paris.

As one would expect of such a brilliant student, Beckett was marked out by his teachers for an academic career and, as the first step in this direction, he was chosen to represent Trinity in the regular scheme for exchanging lectors with the prestigious École Normale Supérieure in Paris. He filled the two-term interval between his finals and the start of his French contract by accepting a temporary teaching post at Campbell College in Belfast. Although he was a Protestant in a majority Protestant community – since by then Ireland had been partitioned – he was not happy in the North, and could not wait to escape to Paris. In fact, his family's religion was never an issue when it came to his national identity. To the end of his life he kept his Republic of Ireland passport and never had any doubts that he was a (southern) Irishman to the core. He had reservations about such things as the dominance of the Roman Catholic Church in the young Republic, not because it was Catholic (his best friend in Ireland, Thomas McGreevy, was a devout Roman Catholic), but because it was (in his view) an institution that did nothing to discourage the new state from adopting such illiberal and philistine policies as the censorship of books. He was, in other words, a thoroughly patriotic Irishman who found it more congenial to live abroad and return home for family visits.

Beckett took up his post at the École Normale in October 1928. A near-contemporary at the school was the brilliant philosopher and founder of French existentialism, Jean-Paul Sartre, but the two men had little contact. On the other hand, Beckett formed a close friendship with a student of English there, Alfred Péron, whose death later in a German concentration camp affected him deeply. But the major event of his two years at the École was the meeting with James Joyce, a fellow-Dubliner who had settled in Paris.

Joyce was old enough to be Beckett's father, and was a Catholic (albeit a lapsed one) of distinctly lower-class origins, so nothing in their background suggested that they would get on. Moreover, the older man had an exuberant, outgoing temperament, whereas the younger was inclined to be taciturn and withdrawn; but Joyce was a genius, and Beckett recognized this at once. He became Joyce's devoted friend and helper (Joyce suffered from very poor eyesight and needed people to read things for him). Although never his secretary, Beckett gave him a lot of assistance in his work, and his own writing (which began when he moved to Paris) was for a time influenced by that of the older master. He was particularly impressed by Joyce's single-minded dedication to his art and came to share it, although his own path as a writer soon diverged from his friend's.

On the expiration of his Paris contract, in 1930, he returned to Dublin to take up a post as assistant in French to Professor Thomas B. Rudmose-Brown, a cultivated and widely read man who had had a decisive role in forming his literary tastes as an undergraduate. He began publishing literary criticism – his book on the great French novelist Marcel Proust appeared in 1931 – and seemed safely launched on the academic career that his intellectual ability made him appear eminently suited for and that his father very much hoped he would make a success of. An echo of this can be heard in a later novel that he decided to leave unfinished, *From an Abandoned Work*:

> Fortunately my father died when I was a boy, otherwise I might have been a professor, he had set his heart on it. A very fair scholar I was too, no thought, but a great memory. One day I told him about Milton's cosmology, away up in the mountains we were, resting against a huge rock looking out to sea, that impressed him greatly.
>
> (p. 142)

However, Beckett soon found that he had no vocation for, and little skill at, university teaching; as he later put it, with characteristic self-deprecation, 'I could not bear the absurdity of teaching others what I did not know myself.' The crisis came during the Christmas vacation of 1931, when he was visiting friends in Germany, and he telegraphed his resignation. Irresponsible as the act appeared to his family and friends at the time, it was decisive in cutting the umbilical cord with Trinity and the Dublin literary circles in which a lesser man might have been content to accept the pre-eminent place his talents granted him. Not that Beckett ever lost his respect for those Irish painters and poets, such as Jack B. Yeats, Denis Devlin and Thomas McGreevy, whose work he praised in print whenever he was given the opportunity.

The years that followed his abrupt departure from academe were lonely and often unhappy, but they were not wasted. Beckett travelled widely in Europe – in Germany in particular – making himself an expert in the visual arts (he later used his connoisseurship to champion neglected painters whom he had befriended, such as Henri Hayden and Bram van Velde) and in the major European languages and literatures. He even lived for a time in London, in Chelsea, where he set his first major novel, *Murphy*, published in 1938. Although he tried subsequently to repudiate most of his early work, Beckett still considered this book the foundation stone of his literary output. Its publication was hardly a triumph, but a few were affected by it – notably the novelist Iris Murdoch, who read it as an undergraduate at Oxford and later paid affectionate homage to it in her own first novel, *Under the Net* (1954).

In 1937 he ended his years of wandering and made Paris his permanent home, settling in the Montparnasse area. Appropriately he is buried close to the places he haunted for the best part of his life, in Montparnasse cemetery, alongside many other famous artists and writers, including the greatest of all French poets, Charles Baudelaire. Until the royalties from *Waiting for Godot* made him wealthy, he eked out the annuity that his father had left him by doing literary translations, his skill in this art being highly valued by editors.

The outbreak of the Second World War in 1939 found him vacationing with his family in Dublin; he got back to France just in time, preferring, as he later put it, 'France in war to Ireland in peace'. Because the Irish Republic had declared itself neutral, his citizenship would have protected him from molestation in German-occupied Paris, but influenced by his friend Alfred Péron and his own distaste for Nazism (which he had seen at first hand in Germany in the mid-1930s), he chose to join the French resistance. His group was infiltrated by a double agent and betrayed to the Gestapo. Beckett narrowly escaped arrest and eventually found his way to a small village in the south of France, where he went into hiding. He later joined the local resistance group and, among other things, hid weapons and explosives for them. Had he been caught with this compromising material in his possession, his Irish passport would not have saved him from the firing squad. Traces of this dangerous occupation (for which he was decorated after the war by General de Gaulle), and of the general anxiety of living every day with the stress of clandestinity and secrecy, survive in the unease that the heroes of his later novels express about 'writing their report'. This is Moran speaking, in the novel *Molloy*, published in 1951, six years after the war ended:

> A letter from Youdi, in the third person, asking for a report. He will get his report . . . One day I received a visit from Gaber. He wanted the report . . . I have spoken of a voice telling me things . . . It told me to write the report . . . Then I went back into the house and wrote, It is midnight. The rain is beating on the windows. It was not midnight. It was not raining.
>
> (pp. 175–6)

The contradiction in the last four sentences betrays the ambivalence Beckett felt about the activities that he was called upon to engage in and that he later self-deprecatingly dismissed as 'boy-scout stuff'. General de Gaulle evidently did not share his opinion of this wartime work.

The liberation of France in 1944 enabled Beckett eventually to resume his Paris existence. There he wrote, almost in an inspired trance, those works in French (later self-translated into English) on which his reputation will permanently rest: the trilogy of novels *Molloy*, *Malone Dies* and *The Unnamable*, and the play *Waiting for Godot*. The burst of creative energy that produced these works petered out in 1950. Nothing he wrote later, with the exception of the plays *Endgame* and *Krapp's Last Tape*, and the late autobiographical prose poem *Company* (1980), was quite to equal the works of the late 1940s in profundity, originality and imaginative power.

In *profundity*, because the trilogy and *Waiting for Godot* probe the big questions of human existence: who are we and why are we here? In *originality*, because Beckett evolved a style that succeeds in balancing comedy and tragedy, the grotesque and the sublime; in fiction it made him the greatest experimenter since Joyce, in the theatre the most influential dramatist since Ibsen. In *imaginative power*, finally, because his finest work attains almost effortlessly to the status of universal myth: the outcast heroes of his novels, like his two clowns waiting on a roadside for Godot, the elusive benefactor who never arrives, strike a chord in all of us in this age of doubt and anxiety when none of the age-old certainties of class, family and religion hold sway any longer.

In later years, while still continuing to write new drama and prose, and even the occasional poem, Beckett took an increasing interest in the direction of his own plays. His productions of *Waiting for Godot* and *Krapp's Last Tape* at the Schiller Theater in Berlin and of *Happy Days* at the Royal Court in London were the first of many that offered fresh, authoritative readings of works that he simplified and stylized in ways other directors would not have dared. The influence that he has exerted over the modern theatre, both as a writer and director, is immense. Figures as pre-eminent as the playwright Harold

Pinter and the director Peter Hall acknowledge the enormous debt they owe him; indeed, theatre people the world over revere him as the greatest modern master of their age-old art.

However, though universally admired and much written about (Beckett studies quickly became an academic growth industry, somewhat ironically in the light of Beckett's own misgivings about the efficacy of higher education), he accepted surprisingly few honours and then (the 1969 Nobel Prize in particular) only with reluctance. A modest and unassuming man, he was courteous and generous with people whom he trusted, and he was an extremely loyal friend.

Two examples will suffice to illustrate this. When he received the Nobel Prize money, he promptly gave it all away to institutions and people who, he felt, needed and deserved it more than he did. One of them was his first French director, Roger Blin, about whom I will have a lot more to say in the pages that follow. The note accompanying the gift said that Blin was not to refuse it or express gratitude either – a nice pun on the French word *merci*, which can mean both 'thank you' and 'no thanks'. Years later, when he attended his friend's funeral, he 'sobbed bitterly' (*DF*, p. 696).

An even more remarkable example of loyalty was his attitude to someone I mentioned earlier, Georges Pelorson. A graduate of the École Normale Supérieure, Pelorson (b. 1909) was three years younger than Beckett. Their paths first crossed during Beckett's time in Paris; they met up again when the Frenchman arrived at Trinity College as the École's appointee to the exchange-lector post during Beckett's period as a lecturer there, and they became close friends. Politically speaking, Pelorson stood at the opposite end of the ideological spectrum from Beckett's other École Normale friend, Alfred Péron, and therefore from Beckett himself. We tend to think of this prestigious school as being exclusively left-wing, if only because of famous alumni of Marxist persuasion such as Jean-Paul Sartre, but people of the extreme right went there too.

Pelorson was one such. Later on, during the German occupation of France, he worked for the puppet Vichy government, where he was assistant to the person responsible for youth movements. Some elements in that collaborationist régime wished to see such organizations remodelled on Nazi lines in order to create a French equivalent of the Hitler Youth. The country was liberated before this could be accomplished, but Pelorson was compromised, so when he embarked on a career as a literary journalist after the war, he wrote under the name 'Georges Belmont'. When I asked Beckett if Georges Belmont, the author of newspaper articles about his work (including, as we shall see, a review of the London première of the French *Endgame*), and Georges Pelorson the college friend and co-author of *Le Kid* (of which more below) were one and the same person, he said they were, but that there was no need for me to mention the fact in the bibliography I was preparing. This put me in a quandary. I wanted to respect his wishes, but academic integrity dictated that the information in the scholarly work of reference that I was compiling had to be as full and as accurate as possible. The compromise solution I adopted was to say nothing about this in the text but to include cross-references to 'Belmont, Georges' and 'Pelorson, Georges' in the index (*FF*, pp. 358 and 367).

It was characteristic of Beckett that he remained loyal to Belmont in spite of *alter ego* Pelorson's problems with the French authorities at the Liberation. This showed real magnanimity on the great writer's part, for while Pelorson had been living in safety on an official salary in one part of occupied France, Beckett had been experiencing danger and some hardship in another.

He could be difficult, not to say intransigent, only when it came to upholding standards of production and translation of his writings: he would not hesitate, as we shall find, to seek legal enforcement of his rights where he felt his work was being travestied in the name of political correctness or in a quest for notoriety (such as with all-women casts in plays written for male actors, performances in the nude or in drag, and generally anything not authorized by his carefully detailed and painstakingly explicit stage directions). He refused steadfastly to don the mantle of the 'great man of letters' that he undoubtedly was and, at least as far as television and the press were concerned, remained a recluse to the end; unlike most prominent people in the arts world, he never went in for the so-called 'rare interview' to promote his latest book or play.

This was not out of disdain – though he *was* a shy person – but because in his view literature was too serious a matter to be trifled with; he felt it grotesque to receive personal attention for giving expression to what he called, in one of his characteristically pithy phrases, 'the issueless predicament of existence'. For as he wondered in his finest poem,

> who may tell the tale
> of the old man?
> weigh absence in a scale?
> mete want with a span?
> the sum assess
> of the world's woes?
> nothingness
> in words enclose?

The answer is that Samuel Beckett did, with a wit, a humility and a compassion that will ensure his immortality.

2

The Literary and Cultural Context: Modernism and Postmodernism

Unlike most other great playwrights, who have usually left a substantial body of work, Beckett's complete dramatic output can be contained in a single volume, and yet he is recognized – on the basis of this surprisingly slight corpus of plays – to be one of the world's foremost practitioners of the art of writing for the theatre. This is something rather new in the history of the medium. By the time of his death Beckett had written some three dozen plays, but a high proportion of them can count only as playlets, or what an earlier generation would have called 'curtain-raisers' – short pieces that might have come in useful to a theatre manager wishing to fill out a particular programme. Of his full-length plays the first and most elaborate, *Eleutheria*, was rejected by its author; in conformity with the wish he clearly expressed before his death it remains unperformed at the present time, and is likely for the foreseeable future to stay so. Of the other plays, normally only *Waiting for Godot* is considered able to stand comfortably on its own in an evening programme.

But slight as some of the 'dramaticules' and occasional pieces that Beckett wrote towards the end of his life undoubtedly are, they do reveal a remarkably restless and fertile talent, albeit one that was by then able to operate only in a small and restricted compass. It was not, however, merely his advanced age that prevented Beckett tackling full-length plays any longer: he had, quite consciously and deliberately, written himself out of the normal form. When it was first produced in 1969, *Breath* – which runs for only a few minutes – seemed like a joke or a spoof, and it was indeed that to some extent (Beckett, despite his reputation as a gloomy pessimist, certainly did not lack a sense of humour), but it was also prophetic of things to come. His plays had been getting inexorably shorter all the time. His first attempt at stage writing was *Human Wishes*; intended as a four-act play based on the life of Dr Johnson, it was begun in 1937 and abandoned after only a few pages were written. *Eleutheria* is in three acts; *Waiting for Godot* is in two, because, as Beckett rather apologetically put it, 'One act would have been too little and three would have been too much': how astute, how sensible that remark now sounds. *Endgame*, as we shall see, began as a two-act play, but Beckett sensibly dropped the interval when it became clear to him that there was no structural justification for it. Since *Krapp's Last Tape*, with the exception of *Happy Days* (1961), which needs an interval for a purely technical reason (the props change required to plant Winnie deeper in the ground), all his plays have been one-act, even single-scene, affairs.

There is no intrinsic reason why plays should take two or three hours to perform, of course; the fact that most do is attributable to sociological factors. Until the advent of motion pictures playing to mass audiences in huge cinemas, and later on the installation of a television set in every living room, the theatre, the opera and the music hall were the standard forms of public entertainment. Since these art forms, unlike cinema and television, came relatively expensive to the individual consumer – and now usually require state subsidy or business sponsorship if they manage to survive at all – the audience expected value for money in the shape of a full evening's entertainment as a return for the outlay on the ticket price. Elaborate evening dress and expensive suppers after the performance all added to the sense of occasion, but also to the cost. Plays, operas and variety shows were therefore created to satisfy the demand for pleasantly distracting ways of filling the time between dinner and supper. Hence the rise of what became known as the 'well-made play' or 'drawing-room comedy': works written by the likes of George Bernard Shaw (1856–1950), J. B. Priestley (1894–1984), Somerset Maugham

(1874–1965) and Noel Coward (1899–1973) that engaged the interest of audiences and entertained them without perplexing them unduly or upsetting them too much. The genre survived just so long as did the leisured classes who had the time to enjoy it and the money to pay for it; when their importance and their influence on the leisure market declined, after a short time lag it fell into desuetude, too, so that by the time Beckett came on the scene in the 1950s the process was well under way.

What makes Beckett a great dramatist, not only of the twentieth century but of all time, is not that he presided over the demise of the 'well-made play' – that was largely a coincidence – but that his contribution is fundamental and original in a way few others' have been. He is not, of course, on a par with the towering geniuses of the medium, Sophocles and Shakespeare, but is certainly comparable with the French playwright Molière and the Norwegian Henrik Ibsen. Like Molière in the seventeenth century and Ibsen in the nineteenth, he perceived instinctively the way things were going and helped them along. Such prescience involves technical innovation, certainly, but is not limited to it. That is why Beckett is greater than other influential twentieth-century dramatists such as the Italian Luigi Pirandello (1867–1936) or the German Bertolt Brecht (1898–1956), both of whom were in some respects more inventive theatrically than he was. His importance is, in fact, more akin to Molière's. Beckett tried to write traditional historical drama in *Human Wishes*, but found that his natural manner of writing dialogue subverted the genre so destructively and comprehensively that he had to abandon the play after a few pages. Molière did write a few traditional plays – in his case, knock-about, vulgar farces – until his own particular genius for the more serious and socially aware type of comedy (which he largely invented) asserted itself. *The Misanthrope* (1666) still retains elements of farce, but they are subordinated to the portrayal of a man who, by obstinately maintaining that total candour is not only desirable but perfectly feasible, finds himself comically at odds with a society that knows only too well that neither is the case: there would be anarchy, murder and worse if everybody spoke their mind with complete frankness. Likewise, *Waiting for Godot* has traditional elements (derived mainly from popular forms such as the music hall and the circus), but these are transcended in a play that stands, fifty years after its first production, as the most apt dramatic image yet created of our situation in a world without God, deprived of the transcendent confidence that belief in the existence of God confers.

Having broken the mould with *Endgame* – after being trapped in it in *Human Wishes* and to a lesser extent in *Eleutheria* – Beckett was freed of the compulsion to write full-length works. His statements could just as effectively – even more effectively – be made in tauter, tighter, more polyphonic dramatic structures. The breakthrough came with *Krapp's Last Tape*, perhaps his most perfect theatre piece. In this play a single character is doubled, then trebled, by the use of a timely mechanical invention, the magnetic tape recorder, thus making possible a dialogue between an old man and his middle-aged earlier self, via pre-recorded tape, and their shared jokes about the young man they both once were. The technical innovation made possible the frame that keeps painful real-life experience at the necessary emotional distance, so that few sensations are more poignant in the modern theatre than the sight of that dirty, drink-sodden old wreck listening forlornly to his earlier self asking rhetorically on the tape, 'What remains of all that misery? A girl in a shabby green coat, on a railway-station platform?', and offering with a bravado that conceals deeply felt regret the opinion that he was 'well out of that, Jesus yes! Hopeless business', and that he was right to break with a lover because 'it was hopeless and no good going on' (*CDW*, pp. 218, 221). Perfect dramatic form, beautifully crafted, and totally convincing in its effortless modernity: that is what strikes us now about *Krapp's Last Tape*.

Few critics and theatre people would therefore be surprised if Beckett is considered by posterity to rank in importance with the masters I mentioned just now, Molière and Ibsen. It is perhaps still too early to say, of course; but it *is* clear that Beckett has done as much as any dramatist in the twentieth century to extend and modify the resources of the stage, to adapt its millennial arts to the expression of the concerns and anxieties of the present age. Just as Shakespeare explored the political and moral dilemmas of the Renaissance, or Molière adjusted the anarchic world of comedy to neoclassical and rationalistic norms, or Ibsen created and transformed patterns of naturalism to give perfect expression to the psychological ghosts that stalked the European bourgeoisie in the overconfident age of imperialism and high capitalism, so Beckett has found the means of setting out the metaphysical doubts that torment us now in forms that, like all radical innovations, surprise at first and then in a short space of time begin to seem natural and inevitable. Brecht and Pirandello in the twentieth century also achieved major theatrical revolutions, as I have acknowledged, but it is arguable that the changes they have brought about have not been as far-reaching, nor are they likely to be as long-lasting, as those Beckett has provoked. It would be difficult to name a single important playwright of the next generation – from Edward Albee (b. 1928) and Athol Fugard (b. 1932) to Tom Stoppard (b. 1937) – be it in the British Isles, France, Germany, the United States or South Africa, who has not been deeply affected by Beckett's example or influenced by his practice. Whatever posterity's verdict about his intrinsic worth and stature as a dramatist, there is no doubt that it will concede, at the very least, that he is one of the most important innovators in the history of the modern stage. This is to some extent because his contribution came at precisely the right moment; as another twentieth-century dramatist, John Spurling (b. 1936) put it, 'Samuel Beckett was waiting for the theatre as the theatre was waiting for Samuel Beckett' (*FS*, p. 15).

That moment – about fifty years ago – was a moment of crisis in Modernism, the great literary and artistic movement that began in the closing years of the nineteenth century, reached its finest flowering in the early decades of the twentieth century with such artists as Proust, Picasso and Stravinsky, and went into decline in the 1930s and 1940s. Economic and political upheaval lasting roughly from Hitler's accession to power in 1933 to the death of Stalin in 1953 forced the movement into abeyance: civilization itself was engaged in a life-and-death struggle with the forces of inhumanity and irrationalism, and so this was no time to pursue art for art's sake. But the end of the Second World War in 1945 and humanity's gradual emergence from a nightmare world of totalitarian oppression, wholesale destruction, and deaths running into many tens of millions, made it possible for Modernism to experience a second and final flowering between the 1950s and the 1970s. In this revival, known as Postmodernism, Beckett played a major role, largely dictating the direction Postmodern literature would take.

Postmodernism's precursor, Modernism, lasted, as I have said, from about 1890 to 1930, and included, among other artistic manifestations, symbolism, surrealism, cubism, expressionism and jazz. Postmodernism, being closer to us, shows less clearly marked temporal and aesthetic contours, but it obviously includes the *nouveau roman* or 'new novel' in France, American abstract expressionism and pop art, electronic music, the films of such directors as Alfred Hitchcock in the United States and Ingmar Bergman in Sweden, and the so-called 'Theatre of the Absurd'. It is this theatrical phenomenon that concerns us here, since it is in the context of the contribution the stage has made to the Postmodern revival that we must view Beckett's significance as a playwright; and that response has been given the convenient if somewhat restrictive label of the 'Theatre of the Absurd'. This has been defined by its leading theorist, Martin Esslin, as tending 'toward a radical devaluation of language, toward a poetry that is to emerge from the concrete and objectified images of the stage itself'; the element of language, Esslin explains, 'still plays an important part in this conception, but what *happens* on the stage transcends, and often contradicts, the *words* spoken by the characters' (*The Theatre of the Absurd*, p. 26). Esslin's point is well illustrated in a fine example of Postmodern drama, Harold Pinter's play *The Homecoming* (1965), in which the banality of north London speech – 'Where's my cheese roll?' is a not-untypical line from the play – masks a complex power struggle between different members of the same family that leads the wife of one of them to desert her husband and accept the role of call girl in their employ. Likewise, the same author's first play, *The Room*, begins with chat about damp in the basement and ends with a murder and blinding of almost Sophoclean proportions; what we see in this work is a characteristically modernist shift, from metaphor in the early scenes (where one of the characters says, 'It's very cold out . . . It's murder.') to realism in the last episode, in which a particularly brutal killing is enacted before our very eyes. The language here, as Martin Esslin would say, is transcended by the action, and the mythic quality of the most everyday utterances brought astonishingly to life.

On the other hand, seldom has language been used more effectively in the theatre, as Dina Sherzer observes:

> Beckett is a great manipulator of, exploiter of, and performer with the manifold resources and possibilities of language. For are not the passages borrowed from other literary texts, the use of banal, everyday conversations mixed with literary language, the slang, puns, and modified clichés, the importance granted to talking (to torment the other or to make time pass), and the careful creation of rhythms and use of repetitions all ways of demonstrating the exuberance of language and Beckett's ability to play with it and to manipulate it, resulting in a new and powerful dramatic expressiveness?
>
> (*French Review*, 1979, pp. 307–8)

In ways like these Modernism raises, for the first time in the history of drama, the issue of *metatheatre* in an acute form. Lionel Abel has defined metatheatre as resting upon two basic postulates: (1) that the world is a stage, and (2) that life is a dream. Neither of these two notions originated at all recently. 'Life is a dream' is the literal translation of the title of a play by the Spanish dramatist Calderón (1600–81), and 'the world's a stage' (or, in Latin, *theatrum mundi*) was a popular phrase long before Shakespeare took it up in *As You Like It*:

> All the world's a stage,
> And all the men and women merely players;
> They have their exits and their entrances;
> And one man in his time plays many parts . . .
>> (Act II, scene vii)

As Elizabeth Burns comments in her book *Theatricality* (1972), 'The *theatrum mundi* metaphor was derived from the idea that God was the sole spectator of man's actions on the stage of life' (p. 143). What happened under Modernism to the venerable life-a-dream and all-the-world-a-stage metaphors was this: they were made to transcend the purely ethical plane that they occupied in the Renaissance synthesis, a sphere and context in which moral observations on the transitoriness of life, the shallowness of human endeavour, and so on, held pride of place, and men and women, as Shakespeare says, were viewed as mere actors in an absurd play, making their entrances and exits upon the stage of life and mouthing their tales 'full of sound and fury', signifying nothing. These basically religious notions were taken over by Modernism and transferred to the realm of aesthetics, where the illusory was opposed to the real, the mask to the face, the stage to the auditorium, and above all the smile was juxtaposed to the tear in that characteristically Modernist phenomenon, the wry grimace of tragicomedy. This mixed genre, which Bernard Shaw defined as being both 'deeper and grimmer' than tragedy, is indeed the Modernist mode *par excellence*. It encapsulates a great deal in the Modernist aesthetic of drama, from Ibsen's *The Wild Duck* (1884) to Beckett's *Waiting for Godot* (which is not subtitled 'a tragicomedy' for nothing).

Tragicomedy is generally considered to be marked by an air of tentativeness, but in fact what really distinguishes it is a confident stance and an assured knowingness, a knowingness shared with and by the spectator, who becomes for the first time genuinely implicated in the construction of a drama, indeed of an entire spectacle. In Ibsen's *The Wild Duck* this spectacle is that of Hjalmar's pretended 'nobility in the presence of death', which we, like one of the other characters, Dr Relling, know to be a sham, because within a year he will be holding forth with maudlin eloquence upon young Hedvig's suicide. It is also the spectacle of those clownish intellectuals in their down-at-heel togs playing histrionically to the gallery as they fill in the empty time waiting for Godot. In both cases the tone is ambiguous: Hjalmar's situation is heartbreaking, and Estragon's is desperate; but the manner in which these situations are presented is enough to make them comical. The end of Beckett's play, which has throughout balanced existential anguish against bowler-hatted slapstick straight out of the films of Laurel and Hardy, offers the ultimate in this mode. The two men have just botched an attempt at suicide: their hanging rope has snapped. Unfortunately the rope that was supposed to put an end to their sufferings also serves as the belt holding up Estragon's trousers. At one of the most sombre moments in the history of drama, at a time when all hope, even of easeful death, has evaporated – at that precise point the victim's trousers concertina around his ankles. 'Pull on your trousers,' Estragon's companion tells him. But even this is not the whole joke, because Estragon, in fine music-hall style, gets it all wrong. 'You want me to pull off my trousers?' he asks with comic oafishness. Astonishingly, we are within minutes only of the final curtain, of the unbearable poignancy of that last silence ('Yes, let's go. [*They do not move.*]' CDW, p. 88) on which the play ends.

Beckett is one of the few dramatists to have adapted popular forms of entertainment, such as the circus (the clownery of the dropped trousers) and the music hall (Morecambe and Wise-type misunderstandings) in this example, to so-called 'serious' drama. His intention throughout is comic: it cannot be emphasized enough that *Waiting for Godot* is, properly performed, a very funny play. As Roger Blin, Beckett's first and greatest director, once said, 'He is unique in his ability to blend derision, humour and comedy with tragedy: his words are simultaneously tragic and comic.' There is no conflict between the circus fun of the dropping of Estragon's trousers and the intense sadness of the end of the play: in a less sophisticated way the circus, and then the masters of the silent film Charlie Chaplin and Buster Keaton, achieved a similar balance between laughter and tears. That is what Nell means in *Endgame* when she says, in words that are cynical only in appearance, 'Nothing is funnier than unhappiness . . . it's the most comical thing in the world' (*CDW*, p. 101). One day, in childhood, we all of us learn to laugh through our tears – 'All that matters', Beckett said once, 'is the laugh and the tear' – and in that moment we experience a great truth: to be able to laugh at our condition is the only way we can set about the necessary business of putting up with it. Beckett's great achievement is to have cast this simple intuition in the form of a witty and moving dramatic symbol: that of two tramp-clowns waiting on a country road for someone who fails to keep the appointment.

Ibsen and Beckett thus represent the poles of Modernism – in time, of course, but also in spirit; Modernism tends to be symbolic, Postmodernism tends to repudiate symbolism. That is the measure of the difficulty. How is one to define an aesthetic of modern drama that needs to embrace two such disparate figures, two giants (in their very different ways) of modern dramaturgy?

There are a few indicators, which the very 'metatheatrical' aspect of Modernism implies. One might, for instance, attach to Modernist dramaturgy the label of 'the aesthetics of silence'. Never before had the fragmentary, the low-key, the inarticulate, even the incoherent and the frankly non-verbal tendencies of theatrical intercourse been so extensively developed. There are, of course, instances in plays dating from earlier periods of characters falling silent, aghast, amazed or terrified; but such moments remain theatrical, within the context of the play; they do not serve as a comment upon it. The silences in Chekhov, in Pinter or in Beckett are equally justified dramatically within the play, but they also serve as a reflection upon it; in Beckett's case, quite explicitly so. 'This is deadly,' comments Hamm to the audience (*CDW*, p. 106) when he (and we) have been exasperated by a particularly tedious piece of 'time-wasting' business from Clov. Or in *Waiting for Godot*, after the dialogue has once again run away into the sand, the characters sigh, waiting for someone to start things off once more. As embarrassed and clumsy as someone invited to a party where few of the guests know each other, Estragon is the first to break the silence through the straightforward device of simply drawing attention to it:

ESTRAGON In the meantime nothing happens.
POZZO You find it tedious?
ESTRAGON Somewhat.
POZZO [*To* VLADIMIR] And you, sir?
VLADIMIR I've been better entertained.
[*Silence.* POZZO *struggles inwardly.*]
    (*CDW*, p. 38)

In spite of this tendency to lapse into wordlessness, Beckett's characters are very literate. The speakers know their classics, and quote from them liberally (Estragon from Shelley's poem 'To the Moon', Winnie of *Happy Days* – with a fine sense of irony – from *Romeo and Juliet*, while Hamm in *Endgame* sardonically distorts Baudelaire's sublime line about the fall of night as the evening of his own life draws in). The inarticulacy, in other words, is in the medium as much as it is part of the message.

The case is not dissimilar with Harold Pinter, who has always countered journalistic clichés about his work with the statement that he is not concerned with the so-called impossibility of communication, but rather with the fear of it; people instinctively take refuge in evasions, he believes, rather than run the risk of having to articulate what is really bothering them. Saying nothing, or talking about something irrelevant, is after all a much safer refuge than making explicit statements. The classic instance of this is the seeming irrelevance of Aston's account (in Pinter's *The Caretaker* [1958]) of his inability to drink Guinness from a thick mug whereas what really troubles him is the haunting dread of another mental breakdown, which would mean undergoing electroconvulsive therapy again. In Eugène Ionesco (1912–94), likewise, language serves rather to mask than to reveal real tensions and conflicts: *The Lesson* (1951) is a perfect exposition of how to project fantasies of rape and murder under a comically parodic form of academic discourse. But the unveiling of erotic tensions through a language to which they bear little apparent relation was certainly not invented by Ionesco: Ibsen does it superbly in *Hedda Gabler* (1890), and so do Chekhov in *Ivanov* (1887) and Strindberg in *Miss Julie* (1888). Likewise Pinter is not the first playwright to show characters evading a realization of their plight: Chekhov's Gayev takes refuge from his embarrassments in *The Cherry Orchard* (1904) by imagining himself playing billiards, 'potting into the corner pocket', as he exclaims, or 'cannoning off the cushions'. The spectacle of language breaking down, the explosion of the hysteria underlying the polite banalities of social intercourse, and violence resulting from quite trivial provocations – all this forms the basis of Chekhov's drama, just as it does of Pinter's. There is a marked difference in setting, of course: the estates of the declining nobility in pre-Revolutionary Russia are a far cry from the seedy bed-and-breakfasts or the trendy modernized farmhouses in which Harold Pinter's characters, from *The Birthday Party* (1957) to *Old Times* (1971), tear each other apart; but both are the authentic locales of their respective periods. Long after the last derelict London mansion has been erased by the developer's JCBs as irrevocably as Madame Ranyevskaia's cherry orchard has been cut down by its new owner's axemen,

Pinter's people, like Chekhov's, will still be probing the resources of speech in order to find loopholes through which to escape from their truths, signalling as they go messages of hostility and repressed antagonism, either by the use of inappropriate discourse (like Mick's assertion to the tramp Davies in *The Caretaker*: 'I understood you were an experienced first-class professional interior and exterior decorator . . . You mean you wouldn't know how to fit teal-blue, copper and parchment linoleum squares and have those colours re-echoed in the walls? . . . You're a bloody imposter, mate!'), or by non-verbal means, as when in the same play the Buddha statue is smashed against the gas stove.

In pursuing further this theme of metatheatre as the one possible unifying characteristic of Modernist drama, one cannot fail to note the 'life is a dream' motif that runs through so much of it. Central to the theatre of Pirandello is the ambiguous interaction of the 'fictive' and the 'real', but this derives in its turn from Strindberg's *Dream Play* (1901), a work of profound and revolutionary originality, and leads on afterwards to one of the most perfect works thrown up in the post-1950 rebirth of Modernism, *Professor Taranne* (1951) by Arthur Adamov, in which an eminent academic finds himself accused of a list of offences of ever-increasing gravity, ranging from lack of courtesy towards colleagues and students, to plagiarizing the work of another scholar, and finally to indecent exposure. It is impossible to be sure, within the terms set by the play itself, whether or not the professor is the victim of a concerted campaign of defamation and distortion, or genuinely guilty of the offences alleged against him. When, on being told the contents of the Belgian vice-chancellor's letter explaining why his invitation to come and give lectures is not being renewed, Professor Taranne slowly starts taking his clothes off as the curtain falls, the audience is unsure if he is merely conforming to the nightmare, or confirming its truth. The success of this play lies in the fact that its ambiguity remains entire: is Taranne's professorial demeanour a mask for paranoia and deviant behaviour? What is the reality, and what the illusion? These are questions that Modernism is adept at posing, undermining our categories and destroying our confidence in familiar things and places – such as a middle-class flat, a safe enough place, one would have thought, until Eugène Ionesco in *Amédée* (1954) peopled it with an expanding corpse and covered its carpets with mushrooms; or until Harold Pinter in *The Room* made it the scene of the Sophoclean ritual murder and blinding I referred to earlier. Life is here implicated with art, and art with life: when tragedies are enacted in the drawing room, when – as in Pinter's *The Homecoming* – Iphigenia is sacrificed in North London, or when Shakespeare's *The Taming of the Shrew* is sardonically rewritten by Edward Albee as *Who's Afraid of Virginia Woolf?* (1962), we return by another route to that essential tragicomedy which, as we have seen, is so inseparable from Modernism.

Equally characteristic is an attitude to the theatrical space that either divides it somewhere across the middle, or throws the barrier around the playhouse altogether. Drama before Modernism sought to foster the illusion that the audience was eavesdropping, that a 'fourth wall' had fallen away unbeknown to the characters and that the spectators were looking straight in. Ibsen does not disdain this trick, since trick is what it is: *The Wild Duck* begins in the most conventional manner imaginable, with the family servant explaining to the hired waiter the situation from which the drama is to spring (similar to what, in classical theatre, was known as the exposition, a function normally carried out in the prologue). It is a rather obvious device, since Ibsen has arranged, by this simple artifice, for the audience to be 'put in the picture' and the action started. This awkward but essential phase once past, the play is performed just as if an audience were not watching; indeed, it needs to be so performed if dramatic tension is going to be effectively created. The actors have to concentrate hard on the situation; any hint of a gesture to the gallery would destroy the illusion.

Yet it is precisely this illusion – the illusion of realist drama, epitomized by the juxtaposition of a darkened, hushed auditorium and a brightly lit, busy stage – that Bertolt Brecht sought to abolish. This did not entail removing the footlights and making the stage and auditorium continuous. On the contrary: to do that would have been to create another illusion, just as totalitarian, that the world *within* the theatre walls is a real world, the only genuine one – an illusion theorists like Antonin Artaud (1896–1948) and playwrights like Jean Genet (1910–86) strove to promulgate in their work. As a Marxist, Brecht was the exact opposite of mystics like Artaud and visionaries like Genet: his rejection of realistic illusion had a didactic and political purpose, but his innovations have opened the way to much else that is vital in contemporary theatre, not least the works of Samuel Beckett, which self-consciously play 'across' the footlights. In *Waiting for Godot* the emptiness of the auditorium is humorously commented upon by the actor/characters; in *Endgame*, Hamm – like the 'ham' actor (meaning an actor of indifferent talent) that he is – plays to the gallery, and when Clov asks what it is that keeps them there, replies, truthfully enough, 'The dialogue' (*CDW*, p. 121); and in *Happy Days* Winnie begins her day (*CDW*, p. 138) like an old trouper, aroused by the peremptory bell summoning her like a stagehand rapping on her dressing-room door, limbering up for another run through the familiar material. Likewise, Ionesco never tires of reminding the audience that they are sitting in a playhouse, watching a game the rules of which may be modified but which still need to be respected. In such stage discussions Ionesco is not above puckishly referring to himself by name; on the other hand, neither he nor Beckett would have approved of the lengths to which some producers will go in such playing 'across' the footlights. In 1988, for instance, Mike Nichols (better known as the director of such films as *The Graduate* and *Catch-22*) put on a production of *Waiting for Godot* in New York in which he not only encouraged the actors to ad-lib, but even got Vladimir to ask someone in the audience the time, and directed Estragon to borrow a programme during Lucky's speech, as if to check the actor's name.

It is clear that these and other features can, in default of a single and consistent aesthetic, be seen as helping to make up the Modernist synthesis. Some of the other features (ritual and fairy tale, mask and dance, stylization and formalization, relativity and flux), though equally important, need not detain us: they all derive essentially from the major traits that I have identified. Many of these aspects can, naturally enough, be observed operating in parallel in other performing arts in this century, such as the ballet, the cinema or, more recently, television.

To summarize, the principal characteristics of drama since Ibsen and Chekhov can be enumerated as follows:

1 A tone of 'serious levity' towards drama, and particularly towards the classics of the medium, as we saw in Edward Albee's reworking of Shakespeare's *The Taming of the Shrew* in his play *Who's Afraid of Virginia Woolf?*, and which can also be found in Tom Stoppard's Postmodern revision of *Hamlet*, first performed in 1967, *Rosencrantz and Guildenstern Are Dead*.

2 The exploration of antagonism and violence, particularly of a psychological kind, in the shadow of what Stoppard has called 'the great homicidal classics' (chief among which of course is *Hamlet*; as Stoppard points out, it is 'a slaughterhouse', accounting for 'eight corpses all told' by the end).

3 'Metatheatre' (founded, as we saw, on two basic postulates: one, that the world is a stage, and two, that life is a dream), signifying a medium totally aware of itself and involving the spectator in an equally searching act of self-awareness.

4 A preference for the mixed genre of tragicomedy rather than the 'purer' forms favoured by classical theatre, tragedy or comedy.

5 A movement – sponsored particularly by Brecht – away from the 'picture-frame' stage towards a tendency to play 'across' the footlights.

If all this seems confusing, it is because modern drama since the turn of the twentieth century has been one of the most bewilderingly lively and inventive of European art forms. There is no simple pattern, but rather a tension, a continual dialectic. The twin forces pulling in different directions in Beckett's theatre – those of rigour on the one hand, and of feeling on the other – are a case in point. It is such interaction, not only within modern drama, but also between contemporary plays and the classics of the past, that makes the theatre of the latter half of the twentieth century in general, and its leading exponent Beckett in particular, such a fascinating object of study. This book aims at giving you every possible assistance in that investigation.

3

Beckett's Development as a Dramatist

In a writing career spanning six decades, from the early 1930s to the late 1980s, it is not surprising that Beckett developed considerably as a dramatist. His evolution can be traced in six broad phases (see also the Chronology, pp. xi–xii). The first represents the apprentice years during the 1930s, in which he wrote with Georges Pelorson a college sketch (*Le Kid*, a parody of Corneille's drama of 1636, *Le Cid*) and began the ambitious four-act play *Human Wishes*, about the relationship between the great English writer Dr Johnson and his benefactress Mrs Thrale, of which only part of one scene was ever completed. Then came the forced interruption of the war years (1939–45), immediately after which Beckett wrote two full-length plays, *Eleutheria* (still unperformed) and *Waiting for Godot*. These represent his second phase, in which he was finding his own distinctive voice as a playwright; neither work is, however, fully mature as first written. *Eleutheria* Beckett was content to abandon once it became clear that *Godot*, with only five characters as opposed to over three times that number, would be cheaper and easier to put on than the first play. *Waiting for Godot* then developed considerably in production. The differences between the first published text in French (1952), and the version Beckett used in productions in which he himself later became involved, are considerable; as James Knowlson's monumental edition of the theatrical notebooks – see chapter 5 (p. 98), and Select Bibliography, p. 218 – makes clear, the current text is both shorter and tauter, much more an acting script, than the often rather self-indulgently literary version that a less experienced playwright handed to his publisher shortly after it was written. The remarkable thing is the originality of the basic conception, which Beckett needed only to refine and sharpen over the years; even if he was not always sure about details, and allowed the circumstances of individual productions to dictate minor variations from the basic scheme he laid down in the notebooks, he never had any doubts or hesitations about the essential shape and thrust of the play.

For several years after completing *Waiting for Godot* he abandoned writing for the stage and spent much time instead translating his French works into English; but the notoriety of that play put pressure on him to write another. The BBC suggested that he try his hand at radio drama, then a flourishing medium (this was the period immediately following the 1954 broadcast of Dylan Thomas's verse masterpiece for radio, *Under Milk Wood*), and *All That Fall* (1957) was the result. At the same time Beckett was struggling with another stage play, and finally produced *Endgame*. These two works, plus the *Acts Without Words*, the 'roughs' (or fragments) for theatre, and *Krapp's Last Tape*, constitute, in the late 1950s, a third phase.

All That Fall was, for Beckett, a new departure, in that he moved into a different medium: radio; but in itself it is a relatively traditional work with a naturalistic setting and everyday characters. *Endgame*, on the other hand, was a radically experimental work by any standard. The claustrophobic set, the terminal situation and the characters without identifiable origins that all characterize *Endgame* made *Waiting for Godot* seem a work almost of social realism in comparison (it tells us something, after all, about tramps' preferences where root vegetables are concerned, not to mention the problems they have with footwear). The harsh and unremitting nature of *Endgame*, its refusal to make any concessions to the audience's hunger for progression or development of the situation onstage, link it with the remorseless monologues in the novel *The Unnamable* (1953) and in the *Texts for Nothing* (1955), whereas, as Beckett himself suggested, the tone of *Waiting for Godot* is closer to that of the pre-war novel *Murphy* (1938). *Krapp's Last Tape* is equally radical, a monodrama in which the characters are reduced to one, an old man communing with an earlier self via the tape recorder that brings back voices from his past. Although at first sight the dramatic situation appears dangerously compressed, the play succeeds brilliantly in conveying the agonizing poignancy of Krapp's loss. No spectator who has seen a competent production (and the play, as we shall see, is technically quite difficult to stage) can ever forget the intense emotion felt when decrepit old Krapp listens helplessly to his middle-aged predecessor waxing lyrical about 'the fire in me now' (CDW, p. 223), a fire that, all too obviously, was long ago extinguished in the decayed geriatric we see before us.

A fourth phase opens in 1959 with Embers, a radio play as radical in conception as All That Fall is traditional. This time Beckett seizes on the fact that the origin of a sound on the radio is essentially ambiguous and uncertain: is it meant to be live, recorded, or merely imaginary? Is it inside the protagonist's head or has it some independent source? In the other radio plays of this period Beckett exploited this discovery to the full, and indeed worked it through so that, after Cascando (1963), he found no further challenge in this medium. He was already moving into film (with Film, 1965) and television (with Eh Joe, 1966). Indeed, he quickly discovered a particular affinity with the intimate, small-scale possibilities of television, the reduced décors, the limited number of actors, the concentration and informality of the small screen, and above all the feasibility of using the camera as a character in its own right. He was encouraged in this new interest by Süddeutscher Rundfunk (SDR), the television service in Stuttgart in southern Germany, which invited him to direct Eh Joe himself, in German translation; the resulting production was in fact transmitted by SDR before the BBC, for whom it was written, got the English-language version on the air. Beckett returned several times to Stuttgart after that to direct works for television that he had written with this enlightened patron specifically in mind.

This phase was equally rich in stage plays of great originality. From Happy Days (1961), through Play (1963) and Come *and Go* (1966) to *Breath* (1969), Beckett continually invented new ways of using the theatrical space. In *Happy Days* the protagonist is imprisoned in the earth surrounded by her meagre possessions, and is forced to act, to play, by the peremptory ringing of a harsh bell. 'Begin your day, Winnie,' she tells herself (*CDW*, p.138), and – as we saw – gallantly takes up the challenge like the seasoned old pro that she is. In *Play* three individuals, barely recognizable as human beings, retell at the behest of an inquisitorial beam of light as domineering as Winnie's bell a sadly comic tale of adultery. The innovation here is to have them repeat the play they have just run through so that two acts, as it were, are squeezed out of one. *Come and Go* and *Breath* reduced drama to the briefest statement possible; *Breath*, in particular, is just that, an inhalation and an exhalation heard as an amplified recording on a stage empty of everything except rubbish.

Many thought that Beckett had written his last play in *Breath*, seen in 1969 as the culmination of his entire development as a dramatist to that date. They were wrong. He did not write another play for some years, admittedly, spending much time in the late 1960s directing his own plays in Paris and Berlin; but a fifth phase began in 1972 with *Not I*, a punishingly difficult work for an actress to perform, since her delivery must be carefully articulated but so rapid as to be barely comprehensible. Then followed two further explorations of extreme theatre: *That Time* (1976), with nothing but a lit face and three monologues pre-recorded by the same actor; and *Footfalls* (1976), with low, slow voices conducting a ghostly dialogue as an old woman shuffles to and fro. Two further and even more reduced experiments in television, *Ghost Trio* and *... but the clouds ...*, belong to this phase of the mid-1970s.

The sixth phase began in 1979 after another busy interval of self-direction with theatre companies in London, Paris and Berlin. All the dramatic works of the last period of Beckett's life are short, even 'occasional', in the sense of having been written for a specific event, such as a benefit night for a persecuted fellow playwright, or conceived for a particular actor whose work had impressed Beckett. Thus *Catastrophe* was written in 1982 to support the Czech dissident Vaclav Havel, and *A Piece of Monologue* (1979) for David Warrilow to perform. Slight as some of these late works written more or less to order are, they have their moments of dramatic intensity, and they all show that, even in old age, Beckett remained theatrically as inventive and unpredictable as ever. In his last play *What Where* (1984), the penultimate sentence: 'Make sense who may,' provoked many spectators to sigh, 'Yes, indeed,' which was perhaps what had all along been the intention of our frequently jocular, sometimes teasing, author.

Performance and response

It all began, not (as one might expect) with *Waiting for Godot*'s crucial opening on 5 January 1953, but with a piece of juvenilia I have already mentioned. This was a college parody staged anonymously long before *Waiting for Godot*: between 19 and 21 February 1931, in fact, when the Peacock Theatre in Dublin saw the first (and last) performances of Beckett's earliest dramatic work, *Le Kid*, written in collaboration with a lifelong friend, Georges Pelorson, at that time French exchange lector at Trinity College, Dublin. Apart from giving rise to a laconic review in the student newspaper, this début made few ripples, although the less than ecstatic reaction to the unveiling of a new work by a novice playwright does not differ markedly from others I shall be discussing. As the next play, *Human Wishes*, never got beyond the first scene, and the one after that, *Eleutheria*, remains unperformed, we jump more than twenty years to the saga of the staging of *Waiting for Godot*.

Beckett wrote *Waiting for Godot* rapidly, in the winter of 1948 to 1949, between the novels *Malone Dies* and *The Unnamable*, and on this occasion he naturally aimed at something more professional than a college production. It happened (the way these things often do, more or less by chance) that at the time Roger Blin, who had been a friend of the great theorist I have already mentioned, Antonin Artaud, and had acted in one of his experimental works before the war, was putting on Strindberg's *Ghost Sonata* at a small left-bank theatre in Paris, and Beckett went to see it. Thinking that Blin was the ideal person to stage his own play, he sent him the typescript. When he had overcome Beckett's shyness sufficiently to allow them to meet, Blin was curious to know why he had been chosen. Because he was faithful to Strindberg, both to the letter and the spirit, and because the theatre was nearly empty, was the reply. Beckett felt sure – Blin was later to relate – that his own text would therefore be respected and that the theatre would be empty, which seemed to the novice playwright the ideal conditions for a good performance.

Undeterred by the eccentricity of this view, Blin was won over by the play, but it took him another three years to put it on. A small government grant enabled him, early in 1953, to stage the play at another small Paris theatre, the Théâtre Babylone; and the rest, as they say, is history. Press reaction was predictably mixed, but what counted was the reactions of fellow-writers, which were uniformly enthusiastic. The great French playwright Jean Anouilh (1910–87) did not beat about the bush: the opening of *Waiting for Godot*, he asserted, was as significant as the first staging, in Paris forty years earlier, of a Pirandello play, and he was telling the simple truth – Pirandello's impact on the dramaturgy of the inter-war years was on much the same scale as Beckett's has been in the last few decades. The influential avant-garde novelist Alain Robbe-Grillet (b. 1922) perceptively credited Roger Blin with emphasizing the 'circus aspects' of the play and thus contributing materially to its success. Blin was, in fact, one of the few directors to have influenced Beckett: it was at Blin's instigation that he cut several passages that seemed too long or literary, or that broke the tension in some way. This explains why the second French edition, which appeared after the Babylone première, differs from the first of 1952, and why the English translation, carried out by

Beckett himself and published in 1954, shows extensive deletions. A measure of his gratitude to Blin for giving him confidence as a playwright is shown by the dedication of *Endgame* to his first director, whose basic approach to *Waiting for Godot* has broadly been accepted as definitive. The play on which Blin so indelibly left his mark has established itself as an uncontested classic of the French stage: almost like Racine's tragedies, one critic half-jokingly remarked, it has become one of the pillars of the nation's theatre, a remarkable feat for an author who was not even born in France.

The fortunes of *Waiting for Godot* elsewhere in the world have been, if anything, still more brilliant. It was seen in Warsaw, the capital of Poland, then part of the Soviet empire, even before it was staged in London, where it ran, first at the Arts Theatre, then at the Criterion, from August 1955 to the following May. Despite this success, the London production was preceded by the same rather sordid material difficulties as the Paris creation had been, and the New York staging was, too. The Earl of Harewood wished to put it on, but had to give up the project through lack of funds. The next idea was for Peter Glenville to direct the world-famous actors Ralph Richardson in the role of Estragon and Alec Guinness in that of Vladimir, but Richardson's initial enthusiasm for the part was dampened by the failure of Beckett (who took an instant dislike to him) to offer any elucidation as to what Pozzo represents; so, on finding that the author could not (or would not) 'explain' the play to him, he let the part go, only to regret his decision later. In this he was quite unlike the even more famous British actor John Gielgud, who, when later approached about *Endgame*, turned it down because he 'couldn't stand it or understand it' (*Sunday Times*, 24 September 1961). In fact, apart from Bert Lahr, America's first Estragon, and Madeleine Renaud, the first French Winnie in *Happy Days*, few prominent stars or famous performers have managed to accommodate their style to Beckett's plays; these have, on the whole, been much better served by initially less well known but more flexible actors, such as Jack MacGowran or Billie Whitelaw. Such performers, in common with the directors for whom they worked, were able to accept that a play may have a poetic meaning that cannot be summarized in a few sentences and which, in any case, only emerges in a performance that seeks as faithfully as possible to follow the author's instructions and leave the overtones to take care of themselves. It was probably better for the play, in fact, that Richardson did not in the end take the part of Estragon: he would undoubtedly have given a fine performance, but it would have been very much a *performance*, not unlike that offered by Madeleine Renaud as Winnie in *Happy Days*, rather than the more effective playing of, say, Alfred Lynch, who was all the more eloquent in the role of Estragon in a new staging of the play in 1964 because he was less famous, more self-effacing, and allowed the character to come alive through him.

Waiting for Godot eventually fell in the way of a little-known young man, Peter Hall (now the much better-known Sir Peter Hall), who became its first British director. His Pozzo, Peter Bull (1912–84), suffered acute discomfort from the bald wig he was required by the part to wear and, since he found so many of the cues identical, tended to leave out whole chunks of the play. In other ways, too, Hall's production was far from perfect: it overstressed the tramps aspect, going beyond Beckett's spare stage directions by adding a dustbin and miscellaneous rubbish to the required tree, and gave correspondingly less weight to the clownish elements that later productions, not least Beckett's own, have tended to highlight instead. Perhaps not surprisingly, the London daily papers treated the first night with bafflement and derision, but the following Sunday the influential drama critic Harold Hobson published one of the most moving and perceptive notices of his entire distinguished career in the play's defence. This turned the tide, and *Waiting for Godot* has never failed to attract British audiences since.

Early in 1956 Faber and Faber, who had managed to secure the British rights despite some initial hesitations, published

Beckett's English translation of the play. This was reviewed in the cultural establishment's weekly broadsheet, the *Times Literary Supplement*, by a leading critic, G. S. Fraser, who claimed that the play 'extracts from the *idea* of boredom the most genuine pathos and enchanting comedy'. He went on to remark that it is 'essentially a prolonged and sustained metaphor about the nature of human life', and this unassuming exegesis triggered off a correspondence with the editor about the 'meaning' of the play that continued for several weeks and in which the great critic and poet William Empson (1906–84), among others, took part. After publishing six of his readers' letters the editor closed this very British exchange by singling out for special praise a correspondent who had suggested that Vladimir represents the soul, Estragon the body, and Pozzo and Lucky damnation; and he expressed the hope that the author himself would write to the paper and clear up the mystery. Needless to say, Beckett did no such thing, which is perhaps not so surprising in view of the discovery (made by one of his fictional characters, Molloy) that the *Times Literary Supplement* serves admirably as a makeshift blanket, since 'even farts made no impression on its never-failing toughness and impermeability' (*Three Novels*, p. 30).

London's next major production of *Waiting for Godot* – Alan Simpson's with an Irish cast from Dublin – prompted the great socio-literary critic Raymond Williams (1921–88), in his review in the *New Statesman* (19 May 1961), to stress Beckett's 'very powerful dramatic imagery, of a virtually universal kind'. With characteristic perceptiveness, Williams took the opportunity to draw attention to the play's basic, 'quite formal' structure, and to the fact that 'because of its flexibility and subtlety, even its deep ambiguity of tone, it is a play that requires an emotionally educated audience'. The BBC, which had already done something to educate that audience with *All That Fall* in 1957, continued the good work by broadcasting *Waiting for Godot* on television in 1961 and on sound radio as part of a series 'From the Fifties' in 1962. When the play was revived at the Royal

Court Theatre late in 1964, there was little difficulty about the audience, which 'clapped and clapped and went on clapping', according to the *Daily Telegraph* reviewer. The production (by Anthony Page, supervised by Beckett himself) had the kind of authoritativeness shown in the Paris Odéon staging of 1961. The press this time was uniformly favourable. 'I admit it,' confessed Bernard Levin in the *Daily Mail*, 'Mr Hobson was right'; not all the tucking into humble pie was as forthright as this, but the general tenor was the same. Reviewers even wondered what all the fuss had been about nine years previously: the play, they roundly asserted, was not in the least obscure, but had the limpid simplicity of a great classic. On the eve of opening, the *Daily Mail* indulged in a facetious Christmassy note: 'a stone's throw from the citadels of panto, Lucky makes his bow, but it's a far cry from *Jack and the Beanstalk*,' because now nobody was afraid of the big bad wolf any more. With characteristic modesty Harold Hobson refrained from crowing 'I told you so', but he did just allow himself this aside: '*Waiting for Godot* – we all know it now – is a very great play' (*Sunday Times*, 17 January 1965). For the rest of his notice he bestowed glowing (and fully merited) praise on Nicol Williamson's performance as Vladimir and 'his jaunty Scots accent, his sudden bursts of gaiety, his agilely shambling half-run, half-walk, his confident assertions followed immediately by doubts and qualification, his innumerable suggestions for games and diversions, his brief but total collapses'. In such moments Williamson stood 'absolutely forlorn in broken bowler and ragged trousers, nothing moving except his sad, distressed eyes . . .' There was equal praise for Jack MacGowran in the part of Lucky ('he has acted himself so far into Beckett's mind he almost seems part of its imagery', wrote the *New Statesman*'s critic), and so well did he, like Paul Curran as Pozzo and Alfred Lynch as Estragon, serve their roles that a newcomer to the play might have been forgiven for assuming it had been written specially for them. They were given credit by reviewers for achieving the far from easy feat of establishing clear differences between the characters:

Estragon came over suitably 'morose', Pozzo 'hectoring', Lucky 'doleful' and Vladimir 'restless'.

By this time the battle over Beckett's status as a dramatist had moved from newspaper offices to university campuses, where student directors and actors took him up enthusiastically, and professors like myself began turning the spotlight of their critical scholarship on the most obscure corners of his collected writings, with, as one might expect, unequal results. Some academics, such as the American Hugh Kenner and the Frenchman Jean-Jacques Mayoux, have left an indelible mark on Beckett studies (as they soon came to be called: by 1976 there was even a *Journal of Beckett Studies* gracing library shelves, a fact that gave wry amusement to its much-studied subject); but other learned responses were less felicitous. In his review of one scholarly tome the leading playwright John Mortimer (b. 1923) singled out for scornful rebuttal a claim that what Vladimir and Estragon do is of no importance: on the contrary, replied Mortimer, 'what Vladimir and Estragon do is of supreme importance, demonstrated by the minute and beautiful care with which the play is contrived'. The professor's well-meant but misguided attempts to 'disregard the actual incidents of a play and apprehend instead the general theme of the author' fell foul, Mortimer argued, of the reality that in the work of an 'undoubted genius' like Beckett there is 'total lack of a general theme', merely 'an intense and painful individual expression'. Playwrights in general have, perhaps not surprisingly, been far more perceptive than most academics in discerning the precise nature of Beckett's theatrical achievement: the American dramatist Thornton Wilder (1897–1975) considered *Waiting for Godot* one of the greatest modern plays, and the Spanish playwright Alfonso Sastre (b. 1926) maintained that, 'while we are left cold by many dramas of intrigue in which a great deal happens, this "nothing happens" of *Waiting for Godot* keeps us in suspense'. As for writers of the following generation, we have seen that Harold Pinter and Tom Stoppard, to name but two, owe him a great debt.

The all-pervading influence of Beckett's language and imagery is nowhere more tellingly revealed than in the uses newspaper cartoonists and television impressionists have put them to. During the last days of the Conservative government in 1964 the great left-wing satirist Vicky (Victor Weisz, 1913–66) was inspired to depict Prime Minister Harold Macmillan as Vladimir and one of his cabinet colleagues as Estragon ruefully contemplating newspaper headlines about 'Budget Hopes' and declaring: 'We'll hang ourselves tomorrow . . . Unless Godot comes.' More recently, in May 2001, Alistair McGowan included in his television show an impression of Terry Wogan as Vladimir in a pastiche of *Waiting for Godot*, and he confidently expected the audience to pick up the allusion (McGowan's 'Vladimir' spoke, of course, in an Irish accent modelled on Wogan's). Truly, as the critic Ronald Bryden saw in 1965, Beckett had 'become a climate of opinion'; his clowns had not only tramped all over the globe; they had become part of twentieth-century mythology.

After such an apotheosis, it was perhaps only to be expected that the creation of *Endgame* (the work that gave rise to such critical clichés of the time as 'dustbin philosophy' and 'ashcan drama') would turn out to be something of an anticlimax. As we shall see, Beckett had begun thinking about writing a new play in 1954, but only started work on it in December 1955. At first it consisted of two acts, but since it soon became clear to Beckett that there was no aesthetic justification for a binary structure, as there had been in *Waiting for Godot*, in revising his first typescript he removed the interval and cut out other unsatisfactory material to leave the longish one-act play we are familiar with. It gave him far more trouble than *Waiting for Godot*: not until October 1956 was Roger Blin able to begin rehearsals, once again without immediate hope of finding a theatre in which to put it on.

In the end, since no Paris house could be persuaded to risk it, Blin accepted the Royal Court Theatre's invitation to première *Endgame* in London on 3 April 1957. Though I was a hard-up student at the time, I was determined to be there, and was privileged to watch Roger Blin create the role of Hamm and Jean Martin that of Clov, but I have to admit, nearly half a century later, that the well-intentioned compromise of performing a new and difficult French play in London was not a success; Beckett described the occasion to another theatre person soon afterwards as 'rather grim, like playing to mahogany, or rather teak'. The fault cannot, however, be said to lie entirely with an audience that of necessity did not fully understand the language the actors were speaking; the production itself must bear part of the responsibility for the semi-fiasco, being rather monotonous, shrill and disjointed. Jacques Noel's décor consisted of an over-literal grey-green cave-like interior, which added to the oppressive effect. Clearly the actors were not at ease at the Royal Court, nor in their roles: a kind of sullen resentment seemed to flow back and forth across the footlights, and even a sympathetic reviewer such as Georges Belmont (Pelorson) regretted a certain slowness and forced quality in Blin's delivery. When the production transferred to the pocket Studio des Champs-Elysées, on 26 April, the Paris critics received the play with respect on the whole, but with little enthusiasm, and Beckett's old friend of Trinity days, A. J. Leventhal, had to concede in the *Dublin Magazine* that '*Endgame* cannot hope for the same success that attended *Waiting for Godot* . . . an audience, faced with uttermost pain on the stage, is likely to wilt at the experience, though it may well be a catharsis for such who have hitherto refused in their euphoria to look beyond the end of their optimistic noses.'

In Beckett's English translation this time, *Endgame* returned to London and to the Royal Court on 28 October 1958 in a double bill with *Krapp's Last Tape*. The director was an old friend of Beckett's, George Devine, and he played Hamm; Jack MacGowran took the part of Clov, and made it one of his greatest roles. Critics reacted with distaste or with facetiousness, but Roy Walker sprang to the play's defence, arguing in *The Twentieth Century* that Beckett cannot be written off as a 'unique pathological oddity'; his 'scathing satires on the sin and instability of man' must be seen as ranking 'among the greatest plays yet to appear upon the modern stage', for 'he has found in the depths of despair 'the right kind of pity' for the individual and universal condition of our time'. Walker drew attention to Shakespearean overtones in *Endgame* (Hamm being, in his view, a cross between Prospero and Richard III), but the most thoroughgoing exploration of this particular theme was a controversial essay entitled '*King Lear*, or Endgame' by the influential Polish critic Jan Kott: 'in both Shakespearean and Beckettian Endgames it is the modern world that fell; the Renaissance world, and ours'. Modish as Kott's views tended to be, they had the merit, in treating Shakespeare's plays as savage parables for our own age, of illuminating several parallels of mood and theme between them and Beckett's, suggesting incidentally that the latter may, of all twentieth-century playwrights, be the one who approached nearest to Shakespearean universality and poetic directness.

Endgame was next seen in a major production in London in July 1964. Starring Patrick Magee (for whom, as we shall see, *Krapp's Last Tape* was written) in the role of Hamm, and Jack MacGowran once again as Clov, it had already enjoyed a successful run in Paris (in English). Once again, too, Beckett took a hand in the direction, and reviewers were not slow to notice that in contrast to Blin's rather frigid, even humourless version, it revealed a bawdy, coarse robustness that made the whole livelier and and more interesting dramatically. Critics were unanimous in their praise for the Magee–MacGowran duo, whose interpretation, they declared, was as near to definitive as those in the 1964 audience were likely to see. *Endgame*, as Beckett himself recognized, is a difficult play to get right. So perhaps the initial critical resistance to the work was due in part to production teething troubles; or perhaps it is quite simply easier for us to take the play now. 'A masterpiece of ambiguity', in the view of the Australian academic Ross Chambers, deliberately less rich and more spare than *Waiting for Godot*,

Endgame is arguably a greater achievement, with its Shakespearean and Strindbergian dimensions (there could well be, in the choice of setting, a conscious reminiscence of the fortress in Strindberg's *Dance of Death*).

Beckett's next stage play, *Krapp's Last Tape*, was, unlike *Endgame*, recognized straightaway as a dramatic masterpiece. Beckett had been impressed by Patrick Magee reading (in a truly unforgettable gravelly voice) extracts from his novels on BBC radio in the late 1950s, and wrote the play, and designed the part of Krapp, with him specifically in mind. The Irish actor duly created the role under Donald McWhinnie's direction as the curtain-raiser in the 1958 double bill with *Endgame* mentioned earlier. In the review already cited, Roy Walker confidently predicted that 'future histories of the drama' would 'have something to say' about *Krapp's Last Tape*, a play in which a character engages in dialogue with a person present onstage, though not in the flesh, but rather recorded on tape. 'Flawless', 'economical', 'haunting' and 'harrowing' were some of the laudatory epithets heaped on the production by critics, one of whom went so far as to call it a 'lyrical poem of solitude'; but as with other works – notably *Happy Days*, *Play* and *Not I* – audiences had to wait for something close to a definitive interpretation until the author was able to become more closely involved. This occurred in 1969 at Berlin's Schiller Theater, with Martin Held starring as Krapp, directed by Beckett himself, in a production that has come to represent a sort of benchmark for later actors to take into consideration as they prepare their own performance in the role.

Problems of interpretation

As we saw, when *Waiting for Godot* was first put on in London, a flurry of articles and letters to editors attempted to answer the question: 'What does the play mean?' It is now quite clear, after the passage of nearly half a century, that the answer is simply, as Beckett said at the time, 'It means what it says.' There are two main reasons for this. Firstly, none of the 'interpretations' offered, Christian or otherwise, fitted all the facts, and most were obliged, in order to put forward a coherent view, to ignore passages that did not square with that reading. Secondly, Beckett's other works have become more widely known since 1955, and they show clearly that he is not a didactic author concerned to put across a 'message' in literary form. Such 'truths' as he does enunciate are simple observations about the human condition that have been common coin since Job and Sophocles. It is an undeniable fact, for instance, that, as a life-assurance tycoon put it recently with unusual candour, we are all, sooner or later, going to die, and many people today are doubtful whether anything lies beyond death. Beckett's works are not, however, *statements* of this theme, but *meditations* upon it, and early critics mistook the latter for the former. They were, it is true, misled to some extent by the Christian echoes that abound in *Waiting for Godot*. For example, when Vladimir asks, 'We are not saints, but we have kept our appointment. How many people can boast as much?' (*CDW*, p. 74), spectators who know their Bible can answer, 'the Wise Virgins' (see Matthew 25). Some writers, such as William Golding (1911–93), might incorporate an allusion like that into a complex, but coherent, religious statement. Not so Beckett. The reason for the presence of Christian elements in his works is simple: 'Christianity', he once said to an enquirer, 'is a mythology with which I am familiar, so I naturally use it.' In other words, he is interested in mythologies for their own sake, without any commitment to them whatsoever. As he put it to another interviewer, 'I'm not interested in any system. I can't see any trace of any system anywhere.'

Beckett is, in truth, the complete agnostic: he is simply not interested in whether the Christian church is telling fairy stories or not. Even were God to exist, the fact of his existence would not, according to Beckett, make any difference: he would be as lonely, and as enslaved, as the voice in *The Unnamable*, and as isolated and ridiculous as humankind is, in a cold, silent, indifferent universe. If *Waiting for Godot* can be called religious at all, it is a poem about a world without any divinity but a kind of malignant fate, a world in which human beings wait and hope for something, anything, to give meaning to their lives and relieve them of the absurdity of a death which, as far as they are concerned, puts an irrevocable end to everything they have ever felt and experienced. But they wait in vain, and so our life is as meaningless as our death. Between a human being's life and a mayfly's there is, in the last analysis, little to choose; hence Pozzo's remark, 'the light gleams an instant' (CDW, p. 83) – an instant only. It is, after all, a monstrous paradox that, for the individual, life is an eternity while it lasts, but that it is less than an instant with regard to cosmic time, just as a person's five or six feet in height is nothing compared with the immense distances separating the galaxies. Human consciousness, of course, is all; but the consciousness by which people are aware of their individual existence is continually at risk from bodily failure or mental breakdown.

Humankind is in any case held in a two-dimensional prison: time. In this prison, only forward motion is possible, but humanity deludes itself that it is progressing of its own free will to some sort of goal. As Beckett put it in *Proust* (1931), 'we are rather in the position of Tantalus, with this difference, that we allow ourselves to be tantalized'; little wonder, then, that 'we are disappointed at the nullity of what we are pleased to call attainment' (p. 3). In Beckett's best-known play, that nullity is called 'Godot'. Birth is a 'calamity' because it launches us on our one-dimensional way (see the discussion about repentance for 'being born', CDW, p. 13), and the only release from that is death. *Waiting for Godot* is therefore, put simply, a portrayal of the antics of humankind as it tries to distract itself until 'Godot' comes. But Godot is only death. He is not, however, seen as death, because we flatter ourselves with groundless hopes; thus Godot becomes anything the expectation of which helps us to bear our existence. Or as Estragon puts it: 'We always find something, eh Didi, to give us the impression we exist?' (CDW, p. 64).

It is therefore evident that a Christian interpretation, which would see some hope of salvation, in spite of all, in the arrival of Pozzo or the boy messenger, is as unhelpful as a Marxist reading, which would see the play as an indictment of the alienation of man under capitalism. Both these and other exegeses – even those that see it as a manifesto for atheism – make the mistake of assuming that a work of the imagination must have a *positive* meaning, whereas this one avoids the positive and the definite like the plague. It operates exclusively by hint and understatement; it has, in fact, been most aptly termed 'drama of the non-specific' (Alec Reid). To look for a 'specific' meaning in such drama is like searching for the magnetic pole in the Antarctic. Beckett's art avoids definition because he believed passionately that 'art has nothing to do with clarity, does not dabble in the clear and does not make clear'. The writer is no 'magus' possessing privileged insight or knowledge not revealed to other mortals; all he or she can do is distil in words, however imperfect, a vision or experience of the misery and desperateness of life. That, for Beckett, was 'poetry' broadly defined, and it was for him the only thing that ultimately had any value.

He had, of course, a 'philosophy of life' like anyone else, but it was an intuition rather than a systematic set of beliefs. Like the German thinker Schopenhauer (1788–1860), whom he greatly admired, he felt that Will is evil, and that desire is the source of our misery: such happiness as there is, therefore, can only be obtained by the 'ablation' or removal of all desire. This, he said in *Proust*, is 'the wisdom of all the sages, from Brahma to Leopardi' (p. 18), the nineteenth-century Italian poet whose lines he quoted frequently.

Beckett felt a deep kinship with writers like Schopenhauer and Leopardi, and shared their repudiation of cheerful optimism, but it did not lead him to quietist renunciation. Like one of the characters in *Murphy* (1938), no doubt, he heard 'Pilate's hands rustling in his mind' (p. 170), but he did not give up on that account. He wrote novels that tell of humanity's derisory, but heroic, attempts to conquer the 'silence of which the universe is made', and plays that portray its doomed efforts to master time. The two things were closely related in his mind. In *Waiting for Godot*, he told me, 'Silence is pouring into the play like water into a sinking ship': the characters are terrified of silence because silence threatens cessation. The multiple fall in Act Two symbolizes this.

In directing his own plays later in life Beckett maintained, as we shall see, an emphasis on the symmetries of speech and on action punctuated by stylized gesture; tempo and manner alike made few concessions to verisimilitude. In his 1979 London production of *Happy Days* with Billie Whitelaw at the Royal Court Theatre, for instance, he safeguarded, over the intentions of Winnie's husband Willie at the end of the play, the carefully structured ambiguities of the text; is Willie wearily struggling uphill to touch Winnie, or the revolver? and if the weapon, for what? one wondered: to keep it from Winnie, or to use it on her? Or on himself? The curtain fell on Willie reaching out still. (I shall be returning to the topic of Beckett's own productions of his plays in chapter 5.)

In view of what has been said, this work – or indeed *Waiting for Godot*, *Endgame* and *Krapp's Last Tape* – should present few difficulties of interpretation, despite the many scholarly analyses and attempts at critical elucidation that serve merely to bewilder theatre-goers; they experience onstage a clear and intelligible, if admittedly complex, metaphor about the nature of existence. As David Warrilow, the great Beckett actor, put it:

> I know that if a performer gets up on stage and starts to play the 'meaning' of the thing it dies, it just dies.
> 'Meaning' is whatever happens in the viewer's experience of it. I don't feel that there really is 'intrinsic meaning'. I also think that ideas are value-less; everything happens in action, and the action in performing a Beckett play is making the instrument resonate.
>
> (*BiP*, p. 229)

We may know that the tree (like the dance) is a common image for the isolation and majesty of the artist, and in *Waiting for Godot* Beckett's tree, no exception, shares in the aura of the archetype; but at the same time we should bear in mind that the changes in the tree, like the sudden rising of the moon, 'are stage facts, important only in the way in which the protagonists react to them. Of themselves they have no other meaning or significance and Beckett has no other interest in them' (Alec Reid). In brief, this play can no more easily be reduced to a formula than can any other work of art worthy of the name. Some may declare that it means: 'Where there's life, there's hope'; others may retort that it says rather: 'Life is hope, and hope is life.' Both assertions have some truth in them – Beckett's characters certainly indulge in a kind of existential Micawberism – but neither does more than touch the surface of this extraordinary work. I look at it, and the other major plays, in more detail in the following chapters.

4

Survey of Interviews Given by Beckett

In reply to the editor of *The Times*, who in late December 1983 had asked a number of leading personalities what hopes and resolutions they had for the new year, Beckett sent a telegram. Its message, the newspaper noted, was characteristically short, sharp and to the point:

RESOLUTIONS COLON ZERO STOP PERIOD HOPES COLON ZERO STOP • BECKETT

or, translated into non-telegraphese: 'Resolutions: zero. Hopes: zero.'

Beckett maintained that he never talked to the papers and never gave interviews. As we can see, this was not strictly true. He could perfectly well have thrown the editor's enquiry in the waste-paper basket, but he chose instead to send a witty reply, one that was moreover totally in character. No wonder *The Times* published it prominently on page one of the Saturday Review dated 31 December 1983 to 6 January 1984. It stood in sharp contrast to the almost uniformly pompous and high-minded new-year resolutions printed on the rest of the page.

It is the case, however, that Beckett gave few interviews in the last four decades of his life when he was famous (and of course none before that, when hardly anyone had heard of him), and on the rare occasions when he did, he was unwilling for them to be referred to as interviews when they *were* published. Some so-called profiles (like the one that appeared in the *Observer* on 9 November 1958 under the forbidding title 'Messenger of Gloom', written by the novelist and critic Rayner Heppenstall), were clearly based on a face-to-face conversation. In Heppenstall's case the information that Beckett 'is a little in doubt whether he should be described as a married man but is certain there are no children' could only have come from the playwright himself (because he did not marry his long-term childless partner Suzanne Deschevaux-Dusmesnil until two and a half years later, on 25 March 1961).

The earliest recorded interview that did not pass itself off as a 'profile' referring to him in the third person, was as jokey as the *Times* telegram. It was unsigned and appeared in 1948 in *Transition*, an English-language avant-garde magazine published in Paris:

> Samuel Beckett is a Dublin poet and novelist who, after long years of residence in France, has adopted the French language as his working medium . . . He informed us that he did not know why he wrote in French, nor indeed why he wrote at all. Some considerable time later, as we chanced to encounter him emerging in unusual good humour from the 'Multicolor' in Avenue Wagram, we begged him to make a further effort, in his own interest and in that of literature as a whole. Drawing us then aside into the little-frequented rue de Tilsitt, and having first looked in every conceivable direction to make sure no doubt that we were not observed, he confided at last, in a strong or, if you prefer, weak Dublin accent: 'pour faire remarquer moi!'
>
> (*Transition Forty-Eight*, June 1948, pp. 146–7)

If Beckett really uttered these words, he was making an undergraduate kind of joke. *Pour faire remarquer moi* (literally 'to get myself noticed') is ungrammatical French, and not at all the kind of statement a fluent French speaker like this playwright would dream of making unless he wished to be facetious. (The correct French would be: *Pour me faire remarquer*.)

As I have already pointed out, what Beckett certainly never went in for – unlike many prominent people in the arts world – was the so-called 'rare interview' to promote his latest book or play. Not once was his face seen on the front cover of a glossy magazine below a banner headline announcing: 'The publicity-shy dramatist talks to us exclusively about the star-studded production of X, opening this week at the Y Theatre on Z Avenue.' Likewise, he never appeared on *Parkinson* or any other television chat show. He could have made a great deal of money if he had been willing to participate in enterprises of that sort; but Beckett was, quite genuinely, not interested in amassing wealth, and he found fame 'horrible' (Bernold, 1992, p. 84).

Provided he could be sure that they would not misuse the material by selling it to the newspapers, Beckett was always willing to talk to students and university teachers, even if he thought privately that much of what was written about him by academics was 'madness' (Juliet, 1995, p. 147). I myself had the good fortune to meet him when I was a graduate student in France in the early 1960s writing a thesis on his work. It happened like this (I later heard from other academics that they got to know him in a not dissimilar manner): I had been to see the Sorbonne professor, Jean-Jacques Mayoux, with a query I had arising out of an essay that he had written on Beckett. He advised me to look up Geneviève Serreau, wife of the director and theatre manager Jean-Marie Serreau, because she had kept a collection of press clippings relating to the 1953 première of *Godot* at the Babylone Theatre, which her husband had once run. I called on her at the office of the literary periodical where she worked, and she let me see the cuttings file and take notes. She also asked me if I would review Beckett's most recent novel, the French version of *How It Is*, for her journal, and this led to my first academic publication.

She then enquired whether I had met Beckett, and offered to write to him to introduce me. Not long afterwards I received a brief typewritten letter from him in which he said that he could not discuss his work and never did, but that he would be happy to try his best to answer any questions I had relating to his life and the publication history of his writings. Very little was known about either at the time. Since the help I wanted from him was, fortunately, exclusively biographical and bibliographical, I readily accepted his conditions, and on the mutually agreed day – 26 May 1961 – I called to see him in his Montparnasse flat overlooking the Santé Prison, for whose inmates he told me he felt an instinctive sympathy. I was, of course, intensely nervous when he came to the door but, despite the rather curt tone of his letter, he was kindness itself. He gave full answers to the questions I put to him, and offered me several valuable bibliographical leads, which I followed up fruitfully in the next few months. Then he suddenly produced a typescript, which he told me I was welcome to borrow; he had found it, he said, while going through some old papers. It was his first novel, *Dream of Fair to Middling Women*, written in 1932 but unpublished – indeed quite unknown, at the time. (Little did I realise that it was the only copy; I now shudder to think of the agonies of remorse I would have gone through if I had lost it in the Métro on the way home.) Before I left, he asked me if I liked Irish whiskey. I had to admit that I had never come across it, but would like to try some, so we had a drink to seal our new friendship. As a result, I have felt great affection for Jameson's ever since, just as I once did for a French brand of cigar called 'Voltigeurs' after he informed me that his idol James Joyce used to smoke them.

I next met him three years later. I had sent him a draft list of his works, the forerunner of the bibliography that was published in 1970, and we went through it together in the bar of the Closerie des Lilas, a favourite Montparnasse haunt of his. Several glasses of champagne later we put the list to one side and talked of ordinary things. Beckett knew that I was due to take up a post in French at Durham University, and asked me if I liked teaching. I said I did, and he told me that when he had been lecturer at Trinity College, Dublin in the early 1930s he had hated it. I got great pleasure from listening to his soft Dublin accent and watching him laugh. He had a wonderful laugh, and the most remarkable eyes that riveted your attention to his lined, well-constructed features.

I am far from alone in thinking that Beckett is the only person of genius I have ever met, or am likely to meet. It is often said that geniuses are different from the rest of us, and for once it was true. Although at first I found his writings, especially his prose works, very baffling, there was of course no question of asking him to explain them. I had to work it out for myself. On a rare occasion when I was rash enough to enquire where a character named Yerk came from, he replied curtly, 'Don't know'; on the other hand, he did drop a hint that the Saposcats in *Malone Dies* (1951) were modelled on his own parents, and that their son Sapo was an *alter ego* ('He got a bit out of hand,' was his uncharacteristically frank comment about that). I did, gradually, find a theme emerging that helped me understand the fiction. Thinking it might similarly assist others, I wrote my first book, *The Novels of Samuel Beckett*, in which I traced the steady decomposition of the Beckettian hero from Belacqua in *Dream of Fair to Middling Women* – how grateful I was to have been lent that typsecript! – to the man in the mud of *How It Is*, a breakdown that reflects, and is reflected in, the way the fictional medium itself implodes.

I went on seeing Beckett at intervals for a long time, and we continued writing to each other until a few years before his death. Towards the end, however, I felt – as did others who, like me, could not lay claim to a particular intimacy with him – that he was getting so frail that it was unfair to inflict on him the strain of visits that were not strictly necessary.

While he was still fit enough to see people, numerous academics arranged appointments with him at the Closerie des Lilas, which had been made famous by the fact that Hemingway among other well-known writers had once drunk there (plaques on the tables indicated where they used to sit). 'In old age', recalls John Pilling, Professor of English at the University of Reading and author of several studies of his work, 'Beckett was likely to warm to conversation about Dante, Dr Johnson or Schubert's piano sonatas,' and always preferred to talk about James Joyce and the Joyce circle rather than about himself. If the conversation did stray into areas that he did not like, Pilling records – and I too remember this clearly –

he registered discomfort by hanging his head or wringing his hands – such economy marked his every move. He had the skull of a mathematics professor and the frame of a 400-metre runner. Talking to him privately, one could feel Beckett belonged to a different order and relish this aware-ness of the presence of genius – though any such suggestion would have struck him as ridiculous.

(*Fortnight*, 283, p. 1)

Another Reading professor, James Knowlson, got to know Beckett so well that he was given permission to write an autho-rized biography, published in 1996 under the title *Damned to Fame*; the many letters they exchanged, and the numerous interviews conducted by Knowlson until shortly before the end, are distilled in this indispensable work of reference, which no serious student of Beckett can afford to ignore.

Academics came from all over the world to consult the writer whom they admired above all others. One such fan was Kitts Mbeboh, then a young university teacher of English literature at the University of Yaoundé, Cameroon, West Africa, and now a diplomat holding the post of Cultural Counsellor in his coun-try's High Commission in London. The record of his interview is typical of many, and since it is not readily accessible, it is worth transcribing the bulk of it. To obviate the need for foot-notes, I insert my own comments in square brackets:

Paris on 18 November 1981 is warm for this period of the year. The 9.30 flight, on which I came from London, leaves me no time to organize my thoughts. I am taken straight from Charles de Gaulle airport to the Hotel PLM-Saint-Jacques, 17 boulevard Saint-Jacques, arriving one minute later than the 11 am of my appointment. [Beckett was, famously, always punctual; as for this hotel, he would have chosen it because it was very close to his flat.] As I leave the taxi and fly into the hotel lobby with anxiety written all over me, a thought crosses my mind as to whether if I meet him I will recognise him.

But there he is! Samuel Beckett! Unmistakably him. The straight hair, the sharp piercing eyes, and an almost cautious look on the face (conspicuous on all his photographs) are all there. He looks fitter than I had anticipated as he rises agilely from his lobby seat to meet me and actually twenty years younger than his late age [75], and though a little frail on the arms, his face retains a fresh look later to be confirmed by his keen presence of mind.

We occupy a table at the far end of the coffee room and sit facing each other and he orders two double coffees for both of us. I cannot hide from him how delighted I am to meet him and how much more reassuring it is that he looks fitter and different from the eternally suffering human scrap that literary adventurers tend to make of him.

I ask him about his recent holiday in Tangiers at the time when most of his plays are being revived at the Paris Autumn Festival, attracting, as always, all sorts of people, including old American friends. A slight hint that the holiday enabled him to escape from the horde of interviewers and literary fortune seekers occasioned by the mini-festival underlies it all.

I talk about my recent visit to Northern Ireland. 'I spent a night in Coleraine in a seaside hotel', I say. 'Coleraine' he muses, emphasising the middle 'e' the way it should. He was educated in Northern Ireland (Portora), where his school used to play cricket with a famous public school there. I know the school. I had been told of his being a very good cricketer and this brings a smile and slight protest to his face.

He enquires about theatre in Cameroon. A lot of theatrical activities, mostly amateur, a good number of promising writers, but little of the professional theatre, I explain.

I take him back to the festival in Paris which I regret to have missed having come so close to seeing it. This brings unqualified praise for Madeleine Renaud. (She is preparing to stage some plays of Beckett again between the end of November and December.) We order two small coffees.

This musician, I forget his name [Marcel Mihalovici], who created an opera out of the French translation of *Krapp's Last Tape*. Is he still living? Yes. Here in Paris. They used to see each other quite often but they have not seen each other for some time now. The opera was presented in Berlin. His wife saw it and didn't like it. It was not successful. Why? Beckett pauses a while. The work does not lend itself to opera. 'Krapp does not sing, you know', he adds.

At first he engaged a young English writer, Patrick Bowles, to carry out all his translations. But every time he felt bad having to change what someone else had translated, he says. In the end, in fairness to Bowles, he decided to do it himself.

People, I tell him, have often asked me the question, 'a Cameroonian such as you are, what do you hope to gain from a study of Samuel Beckett? Isn't he odd,' they tend to go on, 'and isn't his writing difficult and depressing and so forth?' Such people, it is understandable, could not possibly relate to *Waiting for Godot* when it first came to London in 1955, having been conditioned by the plays of Eliot and Fry. Beckett agrees, and adds, 'Eliot hated my work. I guess hated is not the word but he disliked my work and made no secret of it.'

I tell him, without any exaggeration, how truly universal I find him as a writer, a fact confirmed by the number of my students who over the years have related easily to texts of his plays. At this he adds, 'yes, and children like my work'. But his indifference to fame and praise is genuine.

And in talking about Ireland he shows great attachment to family back there to whom he pays occasional visits, and his cousin John Beckett [the musician] clearly occupies the warmest place in his heart. He will not accept that his work is without its Irish trademarks. 'There is a lot of local colour in my work', he says. 'There are lots of scenes taken directly from the Irish countryside in my books.' The road in *All That Fall*, he reveals, is the road of his childhood.

[This is the road along which Maddy Rooney walks to the station at the beginning of the play and along which she and her husband Dan return home at the end.] He remembers every single house on that road including the house from which the music of Schubert's *Death and the Maiden* is made to come in the play. 'Why *Death and the Maiden*?' I ask. 'The music is beautiful,' he says, 'the music is lovely.' He remembers the preacher whose name is mentioned in the play, a certain Hardy. 'A clergyman,' he says, 'a very special type of clergyman', who wrote a book, *How to be Happy though Married*, he reveals. 'It must have been a scandal in his day', I cut in. 'Yes', he replies, 'they tried to unseat him, but couldn't. He never preached.' Whereupon I ask, 'why then does he preach in *All That Fall*?' 'No particular reason,' he says, 'there had to be a preacher.' [There has to be a preacher so that the Rooneys can '*join in wild laughter*' (*CDW*, p. 198) when Maddy informs Dan that the text for the sermon that Sunday, taken from Psalm 145, is 'The Lord upholdeth all that fall.'] It was his first play for radio, he recalls.

I bring him back to his life before the recognition that came with *Waiting for Godot*, and enquire how he managed to keep on writing in the face of such public neglect as attended *Murphy* [1938], for example. Writing was a 'last ditch', he says. He had no choice. He had abandoned teaching at Trinity College, Dublin, in 1931 because it just wasn't possible, and then tried literary journalism, but that too had failed. All he could do was carry on writing. It was indeed 'the last ditch'.

Do we expect anything from him soon? Yes. Something in prose. I am really delighted at this. At his age still so busy. He is at the same time working on the English translation [*Ill Seen Ill Said*] of his latest work in French, *Mal vu mal dit*. Why this highly suggestive title? I ask. Has it anything to do with a judgement of his life's work so far? He hesitates. Then protests, 'You know I do not really like to

59

talk about my work'. I apologise sincerely, and although determined from the beginning not to violate this golden rule when talking to Beckett, I guess I cannot really let go the point. After a brief silence, he says 'Yes'.

(*African Theatre Review*, 2, 1986, pp. 92–6)

Another young academic who befriended Beckett was André Bernold, a Frenchman who now teaches in the United States. He was born in 1958, so was Beckett's junior by more than half a century. Despite the age gap – or perhaps because of it – the two got on extremely well, and their friendship lasted for a decade, from 1979 to the author's death in 1989. This is how another Beckett biographer, Anthony Cronin, describes the way the relationship began not long after Bernold wrote from his home town of Colmar in Alsace to the great man:

His letter had posed a query which could be replied to with a yes or a no, and he had asked only for this. Beckett took him at his word and replied, 'Yes'. When Bernold came to Paris to study at the École Normale Supérieure [where Beckett himself had taught in the late 1920s], he was too shy to make direct contact, but began to haunt the 14th arrondissement [where the author lived] hoping to see Beckett in the street.

(Cronin, 1996, pp. 568–9)

When their paths did by accident finally cross, it was outside the École, where Beckett seems to have been making a rare visit to his old haunts. Bernold was struck by the fact that he spoke French with an Irish accent. He invited the young man to keep in touch, and eventually a meeting was arranged in a café. 'An hour was allotted to this first interview,' Cronin writes, 'but it passed almost entirely in silence' (p. 569). In fact the two communicated, Quaker-like, for the most part non-verbally. This seemed perfectly natural to Bernold, who, unlike other academics, had no questions he wanted to ask about the work, and who looked upon Beckett's silences as those of a man who had little to add to what he had expressed in his books. When they did converse, it was mainly about ordinary, everyday matters; in fact, Beckett 'seemed to take a "tireless interest" in the elementary things of existence, in sleep, comings and goings, what form of heating Bernold had in his room, and in birds – for instance in an owl which Beckett had heard, saying that he found the cry of the owl very moving' (Cronin, pp. 569–70; in his greatest novel, *Molloy*, the hero's emotions are stirred by the 'terrible battle-cry' of the eagle-owl, to which the cries of other owls, sounding more 'like the whistle of a locomotive', are unfavourably compared). They spoke, too, of dreams, Beckett confiding that in his own 'there were no words, only images and forests', and of hands, 'to which he seemed to devote great attention: he would like to have given an entire play to them, he said' (Cronin, p. 570). (In fact, to some extent he had already done so, in the 1966 playlet *Come and Go*.) Beckett recalled with particular admiration the beautiful hands of Buster Keaton, the great comedian of the silent cinema who had starred in his only movie, *Film* (1965), and whom he admired, sadly, far more than Keaton admired him (*FC*, pp. 182–3).

Bernold's account of the friendship, *L'Amitié de Beckett* (1992), is one of the most valuable sources of information about the writer's last years, and especially about the genesis and production of his late dramatic works (though he did occasionally comment on earlier plays, describing Krapp for instance as a '*pauvre type*', a 'poor sod', p. 32n). He was conscious that his greatest achievements were behind him, and that he was in danger of repeating himself: 'All my life', he told his young friend, 'I've been hitting the same nail on the head' (p. 46). His ultimate aim in the theatre, he confided, had been to give expression to the flat, toneless human voice (p. 108) – on one occasion he even recited in Bernold's presence Clov's exit speech in *Endgame* 'very slowly' to demonstrate how it ought to be delivered on stage (pp. 61–2) – and he revealed that he had always written for a particular voice, either that of living actors such as Patrick Magee and David Warrilow (the inspirers

of *Krapp's Last Tape* and *A Piece of Monologue* respectively),
or for a voice heard in his head (p. 107). Furthermore, he
explained the significance of the title of *Catastrophe* (1982) as
deriving from the original meaning, in Greek drama, of plot
reversal, the overturning in the play of the protagonist's fortunes (p. 106).

On the subject of *What Where*, his last dramatic work, Beckett
told Bernold (pp. 35–6) that although it was a story he had been
'carrying around' within himself for a long time, he did not
understand it and was not satisfied with the way the text had
turned out. 'I wondered what was meant by "where",' he said;
'perhaps it was "where is the way out?" That old chestnut, the
way out.' He was undoubtedly thinking here of *Text for Nothing
IX*, written about 1950 (some years before Bernold was born),
which has this magnificently Dantesque coda:

> And I have no doubts, I'd get there somehow, to the way
> out, sooner or later, if I could say, There's a way out there,
> there's a way out somewhere, the rest would come, the
> other words, sooner or later, and the power to get there,
> and the way to get there, and pass out, and see the beauties
> of the skies, and see the stars again.

This is how, in conversation with Bernold on 19 July 1985 –
the younger man is always commendably specific about the
dates of their meetings – Beckett described the way the 'grim
business' turned out (originally written for the stage, *What
Where* was adapted for television in his presence at the studios
of the South German Broadcasting Corporation between 18
and 28 June 1985; the explanatory comment in square brackets is Bernold's):

> It all went very well. I was pleased with what we'd
> achieved. It was very difficult to pull off. I'd gone to
> Stuttgart with my head full of silly ideas that had to be
> abandoned, like drumbeats and the business of colours
> based on the vowel scheme devised by the poet Rimbaud

[Bam, Bem and so on were seen as vowels; each character was to sport his Rimbaldian colour and, like the hooded figures in *Quad*, to enter to the sound of percussion]. All these embellishments were dropped. As the days passed everything was simplified; as the work progressed we got to see what we could do away with. So no headgear, no hair either. Just the face. It was technically very difficult. There was one camera per actor. The chief problem was how to represent visually Voice of Bam (V), and it was solved magnificently by Jim Lewis. He came up with the answer, a very special image, that of Bam reflected in a slightly distorting mirror. Whoever happens to be on stage at any given time, this image is present throughout the play. It was very difficult for the actors: they had to remain motionless for hours. I don't like inflicting that sort of thing on people, but it was necessary. Standing, without moving. They had headrests. The four actors were fairly different physically speaking, but were made to look alike thanks to excellent make-up. They never complained. They remained motionless for fifty minutes or so, with nothing to do, to allow adjustments to be made. Fifty minutes' preparation for a few moments of filming. The whole thing only lasts twelve minutes. It's the result of ten days' work, at the rate of about seven hours a day, from 9 to 5, with a break in the middle. All the interruptions, all the corrections made by V were dropped. V's face, the face of Bam reflected in the mirror and lit throughout, is motionless, and his eyes are closed. He makes only one gesture: alone at the end, he bows his head. V – Bam's voice – was pre-recorded, which raised the problem of differentiating between V and the voice of Bam himself. In the question-and-answer sequences, the two voices had a slight intonation [Beckett gave some examples]. V is a toneless voice, very hard to find.

At this point Bernold enquired, 'When, during the first question-and-answer session, Bam asks Bom "He didn't say anything?"

[*CDW*, p. 472], who is "he"?' Beckett's reply was: 'He is the one who does not appear. He is dead, *erledigt* [finished]. He's the fifth vowel, Bum. It's a grim business,' and he quoted (in German translation) the lines '*Es ist Winter. / Ohne Reise*' ['It is winter. / Without journey', *CDW*, p. 476]. He then added, somewhat inconsequentially, 'There is a large, magnificent park in Stuttgart, with squirrels that come and eat out of your hand. I went for a great many walks there' (pp. 35–8).

Not the least interesting parts of Bernold's book are the graphic descriptions he gives of characteristic aspects of the man: firstly, of Beckett's capacity for remaining silent for long intervals without embarrassment, expressing a kind of 'mute exclamation' (p. 70; I remember that when I was with him I talked too much because the pauses made me feel distinctly uncomfortable, and others have said the same thing); next, of his marked reluctance to show anger ('he rarely expressed annoyance in words: instead his whole body became tense and he pursed his lips in disapproval; then he would turn aside, and he had a unique gift of disappearing before actually leaving the room', pp. 39–40); and, finally, of his characteristic way of walking, 'at once circumspect and majestic, possessing both an indefinable aerial aspect and an almost sardonic element, as if dancing a jig' (p. 102).

One of the earliest and most revealing interviews given to an academic – it has been much quoted and reprinted since – was published when André Bernold was a mere toddler. Tom F. Driver (b. 1925) was Professor of Literature and Theology at the Union Theological Seminary in New York when he made an appointment to meet the great writer near the church of La Madeleine in Paris. Let him take up the story (the interview first appeared in *Columbia University Forum* in summer 1961):

> Nothing like Godot, he arrived before the hour. His letter had suggested we meet at my hotel at noon on Sunday, and I came into the lobby as the clock struck twelve. He was waiting.

My wish to meet Samuel Beckett had been prompted by simple curiosity and interest in his work. American reviewers like to call his work nihilistic. They find deep pessimism in them, even despair. But to me Beckett's writing had seemed permeated with love for human beings and with a kind of humour that I could reconcile neither with despair nor nihilism. Could it be that my own eyes and ears had deceived me? Is his a literature of defeat, irrelevant to the social crises we face? Or is it relevant because it teaches us something useful to know about ourselves?

My curiosity was sharpened a day or two before the interview by a conversation I had with a colleague, a well-informed teacher of literature, who assured me that Beckett 'hates life'. That, I thought, is at least one thing I can find out when we meet.

Professor Driver then gives a graphic description of Beckett's appearance: 'His rough-hewn Irish features look as if they had been sculptured with an unsharpened chisel; the light-blue eyes, set deep within the face, are actively and continually looking, as if leaving communication to the rest of the face, particularly the mouth, which frequently breaks into a disarming smile.'

Drawing attention to the fact that in the ensuing conversation Beckett's accent was noticeably Irish, 'combined with slight inflections from the French', Driver goes on:

His talk turns to what he calls 'the mess', or sometimes 'this buzzing confusion'. 'The confusion is not my invention. We cannot listen to a conversation for five minutes without being acutely aware of the confusion. It is all around us and our only chance now is to let it in. The only chance of renovation is to open our eyes and see the mess. It is not a mess you can make sense of.'

I suggested that one must let it in because it is the truth, but Beckett did not take to the word 'truth'.

'What is more true than anything else? To swim is true, and to sink is true. One is not more true than the other.

65

One cannot speak any more of being, one must speak only of the mess. When Heidegger and Sartre speak of a contrast between being and existence, they may be right, I don't know, but their language is too philosophical for me. I am not a philosopher. One can only speak of what is in front of one, and that now is simply the mess.'

Then he began to speak about the tension in art between the mess and form. Until recently, art has withstood the pressure of chaotic things. It has held them at bay. It realised that to admit them was to jeopardise form. 'How could the mess be admitted, because it appears to be the very opposite of form and therefore destructive of the very thing that art holds itself to be?' But now we can keep it out no longer, because we have come into a time when it invades our experience at every moment. It is there and it must be allowed in.'

I granted this might be so, but found the result to be even more attention to form than was the case previously: if we look at recent art we find it preoccupied with form. Beckett's own work is a prime example: plays more for-malised than *Waiting for Godot*, *Endgame* and *Krapp's Last Tape* would be hard to find.

This observation provoked Beckett into making one of the most explicit statements he ever formulated about the aesthetic project he had been engaged in since the famous 'vision at the end of the jetty' recalled in *Krapp's Last Tape* (CDW, p. 220). This is how he put it:

'What I am saying does not mean that there will henceforth be no form in art. It only means that there will be new form, and that this form will be of such a type that it admits the chaos and does not try to say that the chaos is really something else. The form and the chaos remain sepa-rate. The latter is not reduced to the former. That is why the form itself becomes a preoccupation, because it exists as a problem separate from the material it accommodates.

To find a form that accommodates the mess, that is the task of the artist now.'

All his writing life Beckett wrestled with the problem of 'finding a form to accommodate the mess', and Professor Driver is to be congratulated for eliciting this uncharacteristically explicit pronouncement from him. He disliked making personal statements of any kind, and particularly about anything relating to life, art, religion or politics. When asked in 1937 to sign a manifesto in support of the anti-fascists in Spain – a cause in which he wholeheartedly believed – he eschewed the verbose declarations of most of his fellow-signatories and opted for a one-word declaration that cleverly drew a parallel between the republican cause in the Iberian peninsula and his own country's recent independence struggle: '¡UPTHEREPUBLIC!' (Brian Coffey recalls, in an article that I discuss below, that when Beckett received his copy of the pamphlet, its cover proclaiming that it contained the views of 148 authors in 10,000 words, he looked quickly at his own contribution, briefly scanned the rest, and smiled.) He must therefore have felt particularly at ease with Tom Driver to have spoken so clearly and eloquently, and at such length, about his theory of art, without getting embarrassed.

The interview then turned to the question of meaning in his plays. Because 'where you have both dark and light you have also the inexplicable', the key word in all his work, he suggested, was 'perhaps'. Asked if a religious significance was to be found in his drama, he was quite emphatic:

'None at all. I have no religious feeling. Once I had a religious emotion. It was at my confirmation. No more. My mother was deeply religious. So was my brother. He knelt down at his bed as long as he could kneel. My father had none. The family was Protestant, but for me it was only irksome and I let it go. My brother and mother got no value from their religion when they died. At the moment of crisis it had no more depth than an old school tie. Irish Catholicism is not

attractive, but it is deeper. When you pass a church on an
Irish bus, all the hands flurry in the sign of the cross. One day
the dogs of Ireland will do that too, and perhaps also the
pigs.'

This sardonic humour – the reverse of 'politically correct', to
use a term that was not invented until much later – is vintage
Beckett: one can almost see the play on his features of that 'disarming smile' as the words are uttered. He did concede, however, that his works 'deal with distress' and that 'some people
people object to this in my writing'; but that, he implied, was
their problem.

In addition to PhD students and academics, journalists were,
of course, always keen to make contact with Beckett. They
were rarely successful; but, *pace* John Calder, a few did manage
to penetrate the author's defences. Calder assured Hans Hiebel
that Beckett 'ran away' from newspaper people because 'they
distorted everything he said'; nevertheless, there were still
reporters 'stupid enough' to think that they could gain access
to him (Hiebel, 1991, pp. 80, 94). The earliest of these was an
(evidently far from stupid) American, Israel Shenker, who managed to secure an interview for the *New York Times* (5 May
1956, section 2, pp. 1 and 3) to coincide with the Broadway
production of *Waiting for Godot*, which opened shortly before
the article appeared. From internal evidence it would appear
that the playwright agreed to talk to Shenker only on condition
that his words were not quoted directly. If so, he was betrayed.

Beckett speaks precisely like his characters – with a pained
hesitation, but also with brilliance, afraid to commit himself to words, aware that talk is just another way to stir
dust. If he would relax his rule on interviews, this is what
he would say (he has said it all, in precisely this phrasing)
[Then follows, in Beckett's own words, an outline of his
early career, which concludes]:
  'I didn't like living in Ireland. You know the kind of thing
– theocracy, censorship of books – that kind of thing. I pre-

ferred to live abroad. In 1936 I came back to Paris and lived in a hotel for a time and then decided to settle down to make my life here. I was in Ireland when the war broke out in 1939 and I then returned to France. I preferred France in war to Ireland in peace. I just made it in time.'

[Immediately after the end of the war Beckett began writing in French.]

'I just felt like it. It was a different experience from writing in English. It was more exciting for me – writing in French. I wrote all my work very fast – between 1946 and 1950. Since then I haven't written anything. Or at least nothing that has seemed to me valid. The French work brought me to the point where I felt I was saying the same thing over and over again. For some authors writing gets easier the more they write. For me it gets more and more difficult. For me the area of possibilities gets smaller and smaller.'

[Then follows a rebuttal of the frequently alleged influence of the great Czech writer Franz Kafka (1883–1924). Of Kafka's major works the only book he has read in German is *The Castle*.]

'I must say it was difficult to get to the end. The Kafka hero has a coherence of purpose. He's lost but he's not spiritually precarious, he's not falling to bits. My people seem to be falling to bits. Another difference: you notice how Kafka's form is classic, it goes on like a steamroller – almost serene. It *seems* to be threatened the whole time – but the consternation is in the form. In my work there is consternation behind the form, not in the form. At the end of my work there's nothing but dust – the namable. In my last book, *L'Innommable* [*The Unnamable*], there's complete disintegration, there's no way to go on.

'With James Joyce [1882–1941], the difference is that Joyce was a superb manipulator of material – perhaps the greatest. He was making words do the absolute maximum of work. There isn't a syllable that's superfluous. The kind of work I do is one in which I'm not master of my material. The more Joyce knew the more he could. He's tending towards omniscience and omnipotence as an artist. I'm working with impotence, ignorance. I don't think impotence has been exploited in the past. There seems to be a kind of aesthetic axiom that expression is achievement – must be an achievement. My little exploration is that whole zone of being that has always been set aside by artists as somehow unusable – as something by definition incompatible with art. I think anyone nowadays who pays the slightest attention to his own experience finds it the experience of a non-knower, of a no-can-er [someone who cannot].'

On being asked if his system was the absence of system, Beckett replied, 'I can't see any trace of any system anywhere,' and when taxed with the objection voiced by some critics that *Waiting for Godot* had no discernible structure, he pointed out – rightly – that 'one act would have been too little and three acts would have been too much'. So once again we hear in this interview the note struck of Beckett's preoccupation with the theme of the eternal dichotomy between 'form' and 'the mess'; and on the impasse he found himself in after *The Unnamable*, he accepted – he said much the same thing later to André Bernold, of course – that he was obliged, as a writer, to just keep on going in an attempt to find the way out. Suicide was out of the question for him, even though for others, like the painter Nicolas de Staël (1914–55), the only solution had been to 'throw themselves out of a window – after years of struggling'.

A few years later, in 1961, a French journalist, Gabriel d'Aubarède, managed to get an audience with Beckett, presumably at the instigation of his publisher, since the interview took place while Beckett signed copies of the French version of *How It Is*. D'Aubarède obviously found getting the author to talk at all quite heavy going, perhaps because his questions revealed only a superficial acquaintance with the man and the work; but he did glean a few nuggets of information. Like

Shenker, he was told that *The Unnamable* represented an impasse from which the novelist had tried to break loose with the *Texts for Nothing*. When he asked if the problem of being (which at the time lay at the heart of much contemporary French philosophy) afforded a key to the work, he at first received a reply similar to the one that Driver got, but then he was fortunate to have it elaborated in an interesting and revealing way:

> I never read the philosophers. I understand nothing of what they write. There is no key, there is no problem. If the subject of my novels could be expressed in philosophical terms, I wouldn't have had any reason to write them. I am not an intellectual. All I am is feeling. I conceived *Molloy* and the rest the day I became aware of my stupidity. Then I began to write the things I feel.
>
> (*Nouvelles Littéraires*, 16 February 1961, pp. 1 and 7)

While some of this much-quoted declaration is disingenuous (Beckett was nothing if not an intellectual, and as a young man he read widely in philosophy), it rings true on the main point: that there is no key, metaphysical or religious, to his work, which he himself does not fully understand because it springs from a source in the unconscious that is not accessible to rational thought.

One of the reasons why there are so few press interviews compared with other authors – Iris Murdoch, for instance, gave nearly two hundred – is that it was difficult for journalists to get an appointment to see Beckett. It was, however, made a lot easier if they were permitted to eavesdrop on rehearsals where, either because he was advising the director or because he was directing the play himself, he happened to be present. Then, if he took to the reporter, he would let his guard drop and say things that he would never allow himself to utter in a less privileged situation, and he even turned a blind eye to the fact that his words were being written down. One of the lucky ones to benefit from this dispensation was the *Guardian*'s

Hugh Hebert, who with a photographer attended preparations for the staging of *Endgame* and *Krapp's Last Tape* by Rick Cluchey in London in 1980:

> After two hours of rehearsal they took a rest, and Samuel Beckett turned round and stretched his arms high to get the cricks out of his skinny frame, looked at us directly and broke into a huge, relaxing grin. All morning, though he knew we were there and had accepted that we should be there, the pretence was that we were not (Beckett's reluctance to speak to journalists is legendary). And here he was, a stiffly upright figure, angular as a clothes-horse, now smiling and approaching.
>
> After my second question, he said, very mild, 'Is this an interview, or a friendly chat?' Since he never gives interviews the answer made itself, and he said, 'Good,' to which I added swiftly the hope that he would not mind if I used some of it in my article. A question he did not answer then, knowing that I should know, but at the end of our friendly chat he suddenly said: 'Use it sparingly.'
>
> And when he doesn't want to continue a particular line of conversation, the look in the very pale eyes drifts off, and his polite murmured 'Oh I don't know . . .' disappears in ambiguous dots.

Beckett – who was seventy-four at the time – spoke of giving up directing plays, though not of giving up writing. Rehearsals, he told Hebert, were 'too tiring',

> 'there's too much preparation', and the way he does it, he still wears out actors before himself: demonstrating, or standing ramrod, bending a little only as he points to this one or that as the conductor of an orchestra will bring in the woodwind or the brass.
>
> Part of his preparation for this production of *Endgame* has been to learn the text by heart. He wrote the play originally in French, and aspects of his own translation

into English now seem unsatisfactory to him. So will he change it?

He looks as though I have suggested something definitely improper. 'I won't change the printed text, no. I make little cuts in the production, small changes there.' But the text is the text. When he corrects an actor, from his rote-knowledge, Beckett still looks to the man holding the prompt copy, just to check. And if he is wrong about what the text says, then the text wins. Only very occasionally does he override what he himself wrote twenty-odd years ago, and is now enshrined in print.

We talk about the work he has on the stocks, *Quad*, a four-hander with percussion (but no words) for German television. He is not, at the moment, writing a stage play, but that, he says, 'does not mean that I will *never* write another play'. He would rather like to see *Waiting for Godot* staged again by Peter Hall, only this time at the National Theatre, which has an option on the work. But each conversational sally is brief, and ends in the dying fall of Beckett's 'Oh I don't know . . .'

He is working with the San Quentin group, led by Rick Cluchey. 'I always prefer to see *Endgame* played by itself. But it's a bit short. For Rick to do *Endgame* and *Krapp* in the same evening – it's inhuman.'

Hebert's article is particularly interesting for the light it sheds on Beckett's way of working with actors, especially on the answers he gives to their questions:

'I've never quite got this straightened out, Sam. Why is it that when he gives me the dog, I throw it away, and say, "Dirty brute!" [*CDW*, p. 120]. What's my motivation?' Beckett: 'You don't like the feel of the dog.'

But most of the time, you cannot hear what Beckett is saying to his actors, even from a distance of maybe a dozen feet. It's like a parliament of moths. All you can hear is that soft, fluttering sound of the muted voices as Beckett conducts

them, and they seem not to hear but to read their instructions in that extraordinary face, or the brief flickering
movements of those bony fingers.

When Beckett denied that he ever heard a particular voice or a
special sound in his head, Hebert took leave to doubt it, and
sure enough, a couple of the actors had an interesting story to
tell:

> While he was directing Cluchey in *Krapp's Last Tape*
> Beckett found it impossible to get exactly the right sound of
> shuffling footsteps as Krapp paces up and down the regula-
> tion, text-sanctified number of paces. Nothing sounded
> right to him, shoes, slippers, nothing. Then one morning he
> came in and said to Cluchey, 'What size shoes do you take?'
> Cluchey told him. Beckett threw down an ancient pair of
> black leather slippers. 'There you are. I've worn them for
> twenty-five years.' And they made the right sound.

Early in 1984 Beckett was back in London, rehearsing
Waiting for Godot (again with Rick Cluchey), when *The
Times*'s Brian Appleyard caught up with him. They were work-
ing on the famous 'all the dead voices' passage (*CDW*, p. 58):

> 'Like *leaves*.' Samuel Beckett demonstrates how to speak the
> line – with a suggestion of argumentative insistence. He
> almost whispers in a soft, surprisingly light Irish accent. The
> actor tries gain. 'Like *leaves*.' Beckett nods his approval. The
> atmosphere in the theatre is one of intensity with no prospect
> of relief. Beckett's very presence imposes a powerful aura of
> concentration which engulfs the entire auditorium.
> The figure that is the focus of all attention is skeletally
> thin. His lined, haunted, aquiline face is familiar from a thou-
> sand photographs, but the light voice, the depth of the Irish
> accent and his shy warmth come as a series of mild shocks.
> 'You're not interviewing me, are you?' he asks and fixes
> me with a pale, unwavering stare through his thick glasses.
> 'I don't give interviews.' But once the distinction between

interview and chat is established his conversation becomes surprisingly frank. He is genuinely unhappy to be talking about himself, preferring to direct attention to the actors and director. He never makes the usual vain assumptions of the famous that his interlocutor knows all about his career.

At 77 his age is beginning to tell. His posture, always described as 'athletic' or 'ramrod straight', has acquired a stoop around shoulder level, and he betrays a slight impatience with his lapses of memory. In rehearsal he stands by the stage, his unwavering gaze fixed on the action. Occasionally he murmurs directions, waving his hands like a conductor to catch the rhythms of the language. Every so often he walks up to the actors, whispers in a voice inaudible to the rest of us, and demonstrates how to move, walking slowly with a curious stiff gait.

Everything he does reinforces the symmetries of the play, tightens it, makes points more explicit and action more precise. No variation from his instructions goes unnoticed by him. Nobody kids themselves that perfection is possible.

At lunch the obligatory Beckett fanatic pops up. A man elbows his way into the conversation. 'Excuse me, Mr Beckett, you don't mind do you? I've been a fan of yours all my life. I've been reading your stuff for forty years.' 'You must be very tired,' responds Beckett, and breaks out into a startling gale of laughter. For the duration of lunch Beckett indulges the fanatic, clearly happy to be engaged in slightly mindless banter.

But the rest of the time the overwhelming impression is of a winter of painful and shocking sensitivity. The deaths among his few loyal freinds – especially Patrick Magee and Roger Blin – have evidently cut him deeply. The austere and profoundly moving course of his work has always suggested an approaching cul-de-sac, but invariably in the past he seems to have found new ways ahead. Whether he can do so again remains to be seen.

(*The Times*, 25 February 1984, p. 8)

75

Beckett's eightieth birthday, in 1986, was marked by extensive press coverage, including (quite exceptionally, we must
assume) an interview with John Barber of the *Daily Telegraph*,
conducted at the Closerie des Lilas which, as we saw earlier,
was the place where many appointments were arranged: 'After
ordering for us from the menu – his French has the Dublin lilt
of his English – he lit a cigarette, threw his granny specs on the
table, and I faced those disconcerting pale blue eyes. His features are tanned, craggy and noble – like a sculpture of himself.' Barber's interview proves curiously unenlightening,
consisting mostly of a biographical summary (not all of it accurate) based on the sort of information that could have been –
and perhaps was – gleaned from a good cuttings file. It ends
well, though:

> Beckett's gentleness has grown with old age. His tenderness
> for others has always attracted friends, and today they
> attend to his few wants. He enjoys chess. He eats little. He
> brushes off questions about his war ('boy scout stuff') and
> everything personal. He will probably do a little writing till
> the day he dies. Without it, he says, he could not have gone
> through the wretched mess of the daily round. He had to
> leave 'a stain upon the silence', and remind men of the eter-
> nal truths of life and death.
>
> (*Daily Telegraph*, 5 April 1986, p. 12)

The only journalist to have got to know Beckett well and to
write about him with real insight is Peter Lennon of the
Guardian, but in accordance with the pact they made at the
outset, nothing of their conversations was published during
the author's lifetime. The book he eventually wrote, *Foreign
Correspondent: Paris in the Sixties* (1994), is journalism of the
best kind, full of insider gossip, some of it refreshingly irrever-
ent, not only about Beckett, but also about Peter O'Toole,
Jack MacGowran and others whom I will be discussing in
chapter 6.

When Lennon (who was born in 1935) approached Beckett

for the first time in 1961, he was undoubtedly helped by the fact that he was himself Irish:

> We met at the Closerie des Lilas. He had said that he did not give interviews but would be prepared to meet a Dublinman, friend of whoever it was had given me his address, I forget now who. The understanding was that while I was free as a journalist to write about his professional activities I would not reveal anything of our private encounters, an agreement I kept throughout his lifetime.
>
> When Beckett came in the door of the Closerie, a lean, alert man, upright carriage, graceful in a very masculine way, I knew instantly that this was no McDaid's Irish pub scribbler. The lined face was that of a frontiersman and his piercingly clear blue-green eyes gave me an appraising stare. I put on my Sunday morning behaviour. It was the right approach. Although not socially a fastidious man Beckett was repelled by bad manners which he saw as a fundamental lack of consideration for others.
>
> What first surprised me was that this scholarly man had a recognisable Dublin accent, the suburban middle-class version, and a good command of idiomatic Dublinese. (He told me later that one reason he didn't like London was that taxi drivers called him 'Paddy'.) We recalled places in Ireland, especially around the Dublin and Wicklow mountains, and Killiney, of course, where the remnants of his family still lived within strolling distance of the bay. We drank Irish whiskey, no more than three glasses.
>
> (FC, 1994, pp. 68–70)

These meetings became a ritual indulged in at protracted intervals. As Lennon got to know better not only Beckett, but the Paris cultural scene generally, 'it was thrilling never to be disappointed in people's reaction to him. In the rancorous world of the theatre, at the mention of his name all ungenerous or vindictive considerations evaporated. Everyone spoke with unforced respect and without a trace of envy of a man whose

77

reputation had, in the previous ten years only, assumed unassailable proportions.' And so they should have done. Lennon firmly puts paid to malicious stories about Beckett's misbehaviour when drunk, for instance. 'Drink never made him boisterous. If anything it made him more remote. He was a physically reticent man and mentally always under some constraint or control. But he was not morose.' At the end of a long evening spent with friends at the pub, 'he would say goodnight with a stretched handshake, leaning shyly back, his head at a slant, a grimace of regret' (*FC*, pp. 104 and 109).

Lennon quotes him as confiding to Patrick Magee, 'I have never had a single untroubled moment in my entire life', but adds as a corrective:

> If Beckett was a tormented man it never led you to regard
> him as an invalid or to treat him like one of the confused,
> neurotic creatures of which Montparnasse had plenty. What
> you sensed in him was an inability, or more likely a refusal,
> to turn from an unblinking confrontation with life. Not
> only in his work, but in his daily life, Beckett seemed to
> stand and stare it out.
>
> (*FC*, p. 216)

Theatre people were of course in close contact with Beckett over the years, and I shall be discussing several of them in chapter 6. Few interviewed him, however. An exception was Charles Marowitz (b. 1934), who met him at the Closerie des Lilas early in 1962 to discuss a new production of the mime play *Act Without Words II* scheduled to be staged later that year:

> The man has the look of a nearsighted hawk; his hair
> appears to be trying to escape from his scalp. I find myself
> frightened in his presence as I might be in the presence of a
> man who had come within a hair's-breadth of death and
> survived. There is no prefatory blather; no ice-breaking
> civilities. My contrived lead-in about having difficulty in
> finding the place sounds as phoney as it is. He gives no

quarter. He will not collaborate in any warm-ups. [In this, as we have seen, Marowitz's experience is untypical; perhaps the interviewee felt as intimidated as the interviewer did.] When Beckett is not speaking he is entirely turned off. His accent is an odd mixture of Dublin and indistinguishable continental influences. He appears to be wholly at ease in Paris, speaks ruefully of his two years in London, and even more ruefully of the one week that recent business compelled him to spend in Dublin.

So, there being little scope for pleasantries, Marowitz 'whipped out the script' and they 'immediately talked shop'. In the conversation that followed Beckett laid down certain principles of stage performance – relating in particular to stylized movement – which he would put into practice later when working with actors on his own productions, especially the ground-breaking *Waiting for Godot* at the Schiller Theater, Berlin. It is these remarks that give the often-quoted Marowitz interview its value and significance:

For Beckett, mime is not sufficient unto itself. And the term itself does not apply to either of his mime plays, for they are merely, as named, acts without words. 'With Marcel Marceau [the famous French mime artist, born in 1923]', says Beckett, 'I always feel the absence of words; the need for them.' In his own mime works, actions are a self-sufficient substitute for language. As for mime proper, he thinks the art form is being stretched beyond its bounds – being asked to do things it cannot do by itself and which language does better. (I disagree of course, but am trapped in a sort of elongated Beckettian pause as he speaks.) His interest is not so much in mime but in the stratum of movement which underlies the written word. 'Directors don't seem to have any sense of form in movement. The kind of form one finds in music, for instance, where themes keep recurring. When, in a text, actions are repeated, they ought to be made unusual the first time, so that when they happen again – in exactly the same way – an audience will recognise them from before. In the revival of *Godot* [Paris, 1961] I tried to get at something of that stylised movement that's in the play.' He believes there is an inevitable sort of correspondence between words and movement; certain lines simply cannot be delivered from certain positions and without compatible actions. 'Isn't this a matter of each director's interpretation?' I ask. 'Yes, and within the limits of a specified text the director has plenty of scope for interpretation. But in a lot of cases producers go directly contrary to what is intended.'

(*The Village Voice*, 1 March 1962, pp. 1 and 13)

An interesting sort of interview was included in a tribute volume to the great stage designer Jocelyn Herbert. This interview was a compilation, drawn from various sources, and so was anonymous (presumably were it to be signed, the editor of the book, Cathy Courtney, ought to be credited with it):

I had trouble finding a theatre in France for the first production of *Endgame*, so I came to the Royal Court in London to do it. The atmosphere there in the 1950s and 1960s was very good and everyone was extremely keen. George Devine [Jocelyn Herbert's partner] was omnipresent, the whole heart of the theatre. He and Jocelyn were so deeply involved with the theatre that they carried their involvement into their home. When George directed and acted in the first English production of *Endgame*, I remember going to discuss the set with Jocelyn in the Royal Court's workshops in Chelsea and finding her very striking, but I only got to know her well after George's death. She was deeply shattered when he died but was tremendously brave and very stoical about not showing her grief. I remember going with her to a big Bonnard exhibition at that time, and that we admired the same things. She became my closest friend in England, and she designed all the productions I did at the Royal Court.

Theatre began for me as relaxation. I was writing the *Trilogy* and got blocked and, at the end of *Malone Dies*, I had to have a break from it. I turned to the theatre as one turns to light, needing to write something with a limited shape and space instead of the blackness of a novel. *Waiting for Godot* was written between *Malone Dies* and *The Unnamable*, and was finished in 1948. To me, it is an allegro which breaks, pauses, and then the allegro starts again [this is presumably a reference to the two-act structure of the play]. It was turned down by everyone until 1953 when Roger Blin did a very good production in which I was involved. Giacometti designed the tree for a later Paris production and that worked very well. I think Peter Hall now realises that the set for the first London production was overburdened – I had asked for an empty space with a tree and a stone and he had it cluttered with a complicated labyrinth.

I wrote *Krapp's Last Tape* for Patrick Magee. I hadn't met him, but I'd heard his voice reading texts for the BBC Third Programme and was so impressed that I wanted to write a monologue for him. That's how *Krapp* began. Magee was tremendous, a very good actor, and I liked working with him. I was fairly involved in George Devine's Royal Court production of the play, hanging around most of the time, adjusting parts of it and saying what I thought.

Directing for me is months and months of preparation and it is that, rather than the actual stagework, which is terrible; you have to know every detail in your head and have the text by heart. I was always very happy when I was working with Jocelyn and I don't remember any reserve on her part; she was wholeheartedly in harmony and I thought I was lucky to have her. I remember the trouble she took over the costume for *Footfalls*. It seemed all right to me, but she still found details that were wrong. She took endless pains to get it right. She has a great feeling for the work and is very sensitive and doesn't want to bang the nail on the head. Generally speaking, there is a tendency on the part of designers to overstate, but this has never been the case with Jocelyn.

(*JH*, p. 219)

Where they could not speak to Beckett personally, theatre people would write to him with their queries. In 1952, for instance, Michel Polac, a Paris radio producer, got a straight answer to a question asked by many: 'I do not know who Godot is. I do not even know if he exists. I do not know in what spirit I wrote the play. As for wanting to find in all this a broader and loftier meaning to take home after the performance, I cannot see the point in doing so.' The subsidiary characters of Pozzo and his manservant Lucky were added, he said, merely to 'break the monotony'. And in reply to Desmond Smith, a Canadian stage director, he insisted that a certain ambiguity was a vital ingredient in any production: 'Confusion of mind and of identity is an indispensable element of the play and the effort to clear up the ensuing obscurities, which seems to have exercised most critics to the point of blinding them to the central simplicity, strikes me as quite nugatory [i.e. footling, trifling]' (*The Times*, 17 June 1996, p. 12).

Apart from academics, journalists and the occasional theatre person like Marowitz, various other people who are or were famous authors in their own right have recorded their conversations with Beckett. Brian Coffey (1905–95), for instance, was a friend from Dublin days. He was accorded in the 1930s the rare privilege of reading *Murphy* in manuscript. A not inconsiderable poet himself, some thirty years later he wrote an interesting article entitled 'Memory's Murphy Maker: Some Notes on Samuel Beckett', consisting, he said, 'of memories of a time when friends were together and of reflections on that friend's writings':

When we used to meet in Paris, Beckett and I ate nearly always in an Italian restaurant where we could order the same kind of meal each time: plain omelette with spinach, and a glass of pale rosé wine. And so we could drink our wine, far from Ireland, with on our plates a close approximation to the Irish flag. This kind of ritual is not unknown to Beckett's characters, like Murphy (the fourpenny lunch), or like Belacqua (the charred toast). I believe they interest Beckett because he sees them as habits in men, and because his strong universalising tendency seeks to know what there is in man. When, in 1938, there was, for a while, a proposal that Beckett should translate a novel by the Marquis de Sade, I remarked, in addition to noting how deeply he appeared to have been affected by Sade's text, how he took special notice of the almost geometrical character assumed by ritual in Sade.

This last point throws light on the very last plays, especially *Quad*. Coffey's reminiscences continue:

He was a walker and a swimmer. Once when we were taking the walk to Liffey mouth and round back towards Ballsbridge, with reference to a Baudelaire poem which may symbolise a decaying civilisation, perhaps European, Beckett said: 'It will take a long time, centuries.' He seemed to me to see the dreadful prospect.

The speed of his typing, using two fingers only, is arresting. He has an excellent eye for such games as cricket and golf. I liked the fact that he could play good golf, without losing the thread of the much more important activity involved in thoughtful conversation and without missing any of the lovely features of the daytime among the rising and falling reaches of the course at Carrickmines.

Someone said of him once: 'When he is looking at a picture, it is lovely . . . he becomes filled with the picture.' I would have said, he becomes the picture (or if it is music, he becomes the music), so intensely does the cognitive process seem to have taken place in Beckett. He unites the object he knows, and the word he proffers to us in return for his knowing is the object made anew out of Beckett's vision of it and his multiform experience and desire.

Coffey has some interesting recollections about the circumstances of Beckett's adoption of French:

It was, I believe, when he did not find an English publisher for *Watt* [completed in 1945] that he finally accepted the necessity of writing in French. It was, I know, very much earlier, in 1937, that his work on a commissioned article in French [perhaps 'Les Deux Besoins', *D*, pp. 55–7] stopped when I remember him to have said, 'I don't know where I am going.' The final word of a sentence led directly into a geometrical diagram. I noticed that he was keeping close to known French sentences selected from, for example, [Descartes's *Discours de*] *La Méthode*, or from traditional proverbs and wisecracks such as '*Paris vaut bien une messe*' [the cynical observation made by the future king Henri IV, who was a Protestant, that he was prepared to attend mass if that is what it took to gain Paris and succeed to the French throne], which he altered slightly to suit his purposes. When, a year later, he showed me another piece of writing in French, this time a poem of the *conversation galante* type [probably *FF* 253A], he was clearly enjoying a much greater liberty in using the second language, relatively speaking, for he had used French excellently from years before; but now he was well started on the road of toil, which led to his achievement of prose style, the distinguishing touch, in the French language.

(*Threshold*, 17, 1962, pp. 28–35)

At the opposite end of Europe from Brian Coffey's Ireland is Romania, the birthplace of the philosopher, critic and essayist E. M. Cioran (1911–95). By coincidence he settled in Paris the same year as Beckett, 1937, and they later became friends. This is his highly individual account of their relationship; it contains numerous valuable insights into the kind of person Beckett was, especially into the psychology of a remarkable human being:

To perceive the sort of *separate* man that Beckett is, one would have to ponder the expression 'to stand apart' – his tacit motto of every moment – its implication of solitude and subterranean obstinacy, the essence of a being on the outside, pursuing an implacable and endless task. Beckett, or the incomparable art of being oneself. Yet with this, no apparent pride, none of the stigmata inherent in the awareness of being unique: if the word amenity did not exist, one would have to invent it for him. Hardly to be believed, almost unnatural: he never disparages anyone, he is ignorant of the hygienic function of spite – its salutary virtues, its usefulness as an outlet. I have never heard him belittle friends or enemies. And although he feels completely at home in France, he has no affinity whatever with a certain hardness, a trait that is eminently French, Parisian to be precise.

Even if he were like his heroes, even if he had never known success, he would still have been exactly the same. He gives the impression of never wanting to assert himself at all, of being equally estranged from notions of success and failure. 'How hard it is to figure him out! And what class he has!' That's what I say to myself every time I think of him.

I come from a corner of Europe where effusiveness, lack of inhibition, immediate unsolicited shameless avowals are the rule, where one knows everything about everybody, where living with other people is almost equivalent to a public confessional, where secrets in fact are inconceivable and where volubility borders on delirium. This alone would suffice to explain why I was to be subjected to the fascination of a man who is uncannily discreet.

Amenity does not exclude exasperation. At dinner with some friends, while they showered him with futilely erudite questions about himself and his work, he took refuge in complete silence. The dinner was not yet over when he rose and left, preoccupied and gloomy.

About five years ago, we bumped into each other by chance, and since he asked if I were working, I told him I had lost my taste for work, that I didn't see the necessity of bestirring myself, of 'producing', that writing was an ordeal for me. He seemed astonished by this, and I was even more astonished when, precisely with reference to writing, he spoke of *joy*. At the same moment I recalled that at our first meeting, some ten years earlier at the Closerie des Lilas, he had confessed to me his great weariness, the feeling he had that nothing could be squeezed out of words any more.

Words – will anyone love them as much as he has? They are his companions, and his sole support. This man who takes no certitude for granted – one feels how firm and secure he is among them. His fits of discouragement undoubtedly coincide with the moments when he ceases to believe in them, when he feels they are failing him, evading him. Without them, he is left dispossessed, he is nowhere.

With writers who have nothing to say, who do not possess a world of their own, one speaks only of literature. With him, very rarely, in fact almost never. Any everyday topic (material difficulties, annoyances of all kinds) interests him more – in a conversation, of course. What he cannot tolerate, at any rate, are questions like: do you think this or that work is destined to last? That this or that one deserves its reputation? Of X and Y, which one will survive, which is the greater? All evaluations of this sort tax his patience and depress him. 'What's the point of all that?' he said to me after a particularly unpleasant evening, when the discussion at dinner had resembled a grotesque version of the Last Judgement. He himself avoids expressing opinions about his books and plays: what's important to him are not obstacles that have been overcome, but obstacles yet to be faced. He merges totally with whatever he is working on. If one asks him about a play, he will not linger over the content or the meaning, but over the acting, whose most insignificant details he visualises minute by minute – I was about to say second by second. I will not soon forget his spirited explanation of the requirements to be satisfied by an actress wishing to play *Not I*. How his eyes gleamed as he *saw* that mouth, insignificant and yet invading, omnipresent!

(*Partisan Review*, 43, 2, 1976, pp. 280–85)

The relevance of this last observation by Cioran will become more apparent in chapter 6 when I discuss the work that Beckett did with the British actress Billie Whitelaw on *Not I*.

Women writers were understandably drawn to Beckett – I say understandably, because they found him very handsome. When she arranged my meeting with him, Geneviève Serreau told me that he was '*très beau*', and Susan Sontag, the American novelist and essayist (b. 1933), herself blessed with striking good looks, claimed that he was the 'sexiest man she had ever met', being particularly moved by his 'beautiful Irish musical voice' (*OB*, pp. 410 and 413). Partly in homage to him and partly to bring comfort to the suffering people of Bosnia, she directed an eccentric, if well-intentioned, production of *Waiting for Godot* in Sarajevo in 1993, arguing that 'the poverty of their theatrical means put all the participants in closer touch with Beckett and helped the healing spirits to flow' (Worth, 1999, p. 7) .The Irish novelist Edna O'Brien (b. 1936) recorded her impressions of her fellow-countryman in an article published on the occasion of his eightieth birthday:

Not a day passes but I think of Samuel Beckett – he embodies a particularly Irish sensibility that is both scalding and ecstatic. On he goes, private, elusive, crochety at the thought of intrusion, wishing to be left alone, fretful at the fact that so many hound him, and by now such a figure that the thought of meeting him has, for some, the talismanic sanctity of touching the robe of Christ.

That is certainly true of Susan Sontag, who said, 'Beckett is probably the only person I have ever really *wanted* to meet. I was very pleased to be in his presence. I felt and feel a great reverence for him' (*OB*, p. 409). Edna O'Brien goes on:

> Fiercely discerning, he is oddly enough extremely approachable. I don't know of any Irish person who asked for a meeting being turned down. It is not that he is a nationalistic writer – he is far too great, far too subtle, and far too fastidious for that – but he does have the fibulations of his country in him, while at the same time doing everything to disown and ridicule the unctuous, gombeen, crubeen twilightitis mistakenly thought to be Celtic. Whether he writes in English or in French his voice is indisputably Irish, and his mental landscape recalls those bare exigent and endless acres of limestone that are to be found in the Burren in County Clare. That he is revered so widely is almost despite himself, because never has writer compromised less. His communications – almost always on a postcard – are eerily cryptic and his handwriting a study in fugitiveness. In his books the jokes are excruciating as if in laughter he wishes on the reader some kind of fit.
>
> He has the reputation of being austere and hermetic, but those who have met him always attest to the mildness and courtesy of the man. On his face, though, you see evidence of a psyche that must have wrestled for every second of its waking life with the cruelty, crassness and barbarity of mankind. His body by comparison is young, lithe, as if by some happy chance it was freed from the torments of the upstairs department. He is as straight and unassuming as an ash plant and the blue eyes have the particular gaze of an eagle in that they convey both hurt and fury. His searching disposition unwittingly cautions you not to talk cant, not to humiliate him or yourself with intemperate drivel, in fact not to talk at all unless you have something of import to say. But he could not be called austere, having that particular charm and receptivity that makes you recognise that here at last is a born listener.

The first time I met him was at a reception given by his publisher in London. I found him remote and daunting and became too nervous to utter a word. As often happens I ran into him the next day coming out of the underground and he invited me to have a cup of coffee. Barely a dozen words were exchanged. The comedy as well as the pointlessness of it must have struck him but we muddled through, shook hands and even expressed the mutual wish that we might meet again. Time and the years changed things, and when we met in Paris, or in London, the strain seemed to have miraculously lifted.

My son, Carlo, who was going through a 'palm-reading' phase, asked to read his palm and wrung a glorious smile when he said, in all seriousness, 'You have a very thin artistic line.' Carlo's next divination was that the palm's owner would have a serious break in his love life, and I remember Beckett looking at me ruefully and saying, 'Only one?' There was no shortage of talk – mothers, motherhood, Ireland, psychoanalysis and the writer's haunted fear of being found or trapped. The perils of fame and the clamorousness with which people pursue him can make him sick. Like most great artists he is something of a recluse; he knows that the only route for the writer is to go further and further back into the unconscious, to the terror zone. However to describe him as being too serious would be a travesty. Remembering that I had a penchant for Irish dirges, he said, as he came through the door, 'No wailing, Edna,' and then proceeded to sit at the piano and play and wail Schubert to me.

When we talked on the telephone for the purpose of this piece he was kindness and solicitude itself, but he declined to say anything for publication; I recognised the old pattern of evasion and beguilement. It was not that he resented the questions I put to him as much as that his belief in his own pronouncements remains questionable. As ego-less as you can get.

(*Sunday Times Magazine*, 6 April 1986, pp. 51–3)

In the early 1950s the French playwright and novelist Robert Pinget (1919–97) had just started work at the Editions de Minuit, Beckett's publisher in Paris, when he met the Irish author. This was how he describes the way they got to know each other:

> I was short of money and decided to dust off my English so as to earn something as a translator. For this I had to spend time in Britain. But I knew no one there. What to do for some addresses? The answer was simple. Get them from that fellow Beckett whom I'd not so much as seen. I was thirty years old but acting like a schoolboy.
>
> My letter to Mr Beckett. I don't recall exactly what I wrote but the answer came straight away. Beckett informed me that he had no addresses in England but quite a few in Ireland. Pushing my tactlessness to the infantile, I wrote again to ask if Ireland was really the place to learn good English. In his reply he told me 'not to worry – they speak the King's English there'. And so we got to know each other.
>
> He offered me a modest sum to help pay for my journey and so I was off. I went on writing to Beckett though I didn't call him Sam and kept strictly to the formal '*vous*' form. But by the time I came back our friendship had grown enough for him to insist on the informal '*tu*'. The years that followed were marvellous. We often met in Montparnasse and he would ask my advice about points of detail that to me seemed unimportant; how to motivate Winnie's rejection of her parasol, for instance. He finally came up with that burst of sunlight which floods the stage, setting the thing alight. This heightened awareness of the seemingly most insignificant details was an invaluable lesson to me. He would explain that everything in the theatre should arise from the context, that is from the scene itself. How many other practical counsels he gave me, important for his work and mine!

He did me the honour of wanting to translate my little play *La Manivelle*. The feel of it pleased him so much that he asked permission to change the setting to Ireland where two old Irish gentlemen could speak the King's English with those archaic turns of phrase. It was called *The Old Tune* and for reasons of professional honesty he indicated as subtitle not 'English translation' but 'English text' by Samuel Beckett.

I shall be returning in chapter 6 to Barbara Bray's radio production of *The Old Tune*, which was a BBC commission. Meanwhile, this is how Robert Pinget's reminiscences conclude:

Beckett then suggested that *I* do the French version of *All That Fall*. But Mrs Rooney is another practitioner of the King's English, and I did not know the language well enough to capture her tone. He had to rework the text. The manuscript is full of his corrections. In spite of this he still gave out that I was the author.

Generosity, humour, intelligence, superb erudition. It didn't matter what came up, he knew it all. An elephant's memory, he said of himself. I should stress too his horror of lies. As for his generosity, he shared the Nobel prize money out among his needy friends. With the cheque to Roger Blin [as mentioned earlier], he tucked in this note: 'Neither thanks nor "no".'

He pursued his work right up to the end, trying to remove all trace of rhetoric, until he reached the threshold of silence with *Stirrings Still*. As for his despair, it was the very spring of his art. 'Hold tight to your despair and make it sing for us,' he wrote to me when we were just getting to be friends. His despair hid something which he wanted to keep for ever quiet and which had to do with his great compassion for human suffering. He expressed it in such a way that everyone can interpret it as he sees fit. Open revolt or humble submission. That paradox was and remains his noblest concern and best-kept secret.

(*Eonta*, 1, 1991, pp. 9–10)

Charles Juliet (b. 1934) is a French writer and art critic. He got to know, first, the artist Bram van Velde (1895–1981), who since 1937 had been a close friend of Beckett, a lifelong passionate advocate of his work (when I visited Beckett in his flat, he was keen to show me his collection of paintings by van Velde). Because Juliet was trusted by van Velde, he secured an introduction to Beckett without difficulty. His conversations with the writer were published in French in 1986 and in English translation nine years later. When he called at the flat in 1968 he was, like so many others, completely tongue-tied at first, and the conversation only really got going when he asked politely after his host's state of health, which led naturally to the topic of old age: 'I have always hoped [Beckett said] to have an alert, active old age. The spirit not ceasing to burn even though the body packs up. I've often thought of W. B. Yeats. He wrote his best poems when he was over sixty.' This was, of course, Beckett's own age at the time; it is significant that he who had written so much about death revealed to his young visitor that he was in no hurry to embrace it himself. He was equally forthcoming about the genesis of his most famous works: 'I had to find the right language. When I wrote the first sentence of *Molloy*, I had no idea where I was heading. And when I finished the first part, I didn't know how I was going to go on. It all just came out like that. Without any changes. I hadn't planned it, or thought it out at all. As for *Waiting for Godot*, it all came together between hand and page.' But now, he said,

the previous work forbids any further progress in that direction. Of course, I could write texts like the ones in *No's Knife* [1967], but I don't want to. I have just thrown away a little piece for the theatre. Each piece has to represent some sort of advance. (Long pause.) Writing has led me to silence. (Another long pause.) However, I have to go on. I am up against a cliff wall, yet I have to go forward. It's impossible, isn't it? All the same, you can go forward.

Advance a few more miserable millimetres. I am like a mole in a molehill.

This is how Juliet recalls the way their first meeting ended:

While he stands up to reach for one of his books and seats himself at his desk to sign it for me, I let my gaze linger on him. His grave good looks. His concentration. His surprising timidity. The density of his silences. The intensity with which he brings the invisible to life. I reflect that the strong impression he makes is due in particular to his absolute simplicity of manner, thought and speech. A person who is essentially different. A superior human being. Someone who chooses to dwell in the very depths, engaged in a continuous and intimate enquiry into the fundamental issues of life. Beckett, the inconsolable. Out on the landing, we are still deep in conversation. He is anxious to know how I am going to spend my time in Paris. I tell him I have no plans, and that I came there simply to meet him. 'Oh no, really. You shouldn't have come all the way from Lyon just to see me.'

They did not meet again for another five years. By the time they did, Beckett had directed several stage productions, particularly in Germany, which he said he found 'interesting', but 'yet another distraction'. Of those he did not direct, 'he deplored the fact that the Cologne production of *Endgame* ignored his stage directions and set the play in a home for the elderly, turning it, he complained, into something of a caricature'. Interestingly, he told Juliet that he disagreed with the idea of the Theatre of the Absurd, with which, as we saw in chapter 2, he has often been associated by the critics, especially by Martin Esslin. These were his reasons for dissenting from the theory of the Absurd: 'Because that implies making value judgements. You can't even talk about truth. That is part of the general distress. Paradoxically, it's through form that the artist can find a kind of solution – by giving form to what has none. It is perhaps only at that level that there may be an underlying affirmation.' These last remarks, made in 1973, hark back interestingly to what Tom Driver was told in 1961 about the need for the artist now to find a form to accommodate the mess. Likewise, he 'smiled and nodded' when Juliet reminded him of the words (quoted above) that he had spoken to Gabriel d'Aubarède in the same year, 'I conceived *Molloy* and the rest the day I became aware of my stupidity; then I began to write the things I feel.' Beckett was nothing if not consistent in his pronouncements to academics, journalists and fellow-writers alike.

Another interesting point to emerge from Beckett's conversations with those who were engaged in the same craft as he was is that he felt quite uncomplexed about discussing what the British playwright John Spurling (b. 1936) called 'the ones that got away' (*FS*, p. 47) – that is, the plays that were abandoned. Robert Pinget was told about an 'unfinished play where two characters were having it out: "On the right hand side, way back in the back, I heard a canary sing three notes"; that was a signal for the dialogue to move ahead' (*Eonta*, p. 9). Beckett went into even more detail with Juliet about another idea he had had:

'And what are you working on these days?'

'Last night, I couldn't get off to sleep for a long time and I thought of a play. It would last exactly one minute.'

Suddenly, he comes to life, brings his chair round to face me and sweeps aside our glasses, his lighter and the metal box containing his small cigars, so that he can demonstrate stage placings on the table-top.

'A solitary figure is standing silent and unmoving, rather off to one side, not far from the wings.' (He indicates the position on the table-top.) 'Everything takes place in the half-dark. A second character appears. He advances slowly. Suddenly he catches sight of the person standing there motionless. He stops, startled.

'"Are you waiting for someone?"
'The figure shakes its head.
'"Something?"
'Same response. After a few seconds, he continues on his way. Then the other character says:
'"Where are you going?"
'"I don't know."'
    After a moment, Beckett concludes, smiling: 'It might be a possibility.'

(Juliet, 1995, pp. 137–63)

For such information alone, the record of Beckett's conversations with fellow-writers would be invaluable; but they also, like all the others I have been discussing in this section, shed a revealing light on the kind of man, and artist, that he was. He may have dreaded being questioned, but we must be grateful to those who did manage to interview him, in spite of himself, and who then wrote down for posterity what he said.

5

Beckett as Director

Beckett's own productions of his plays and his published *Theatrical Notebooks*

Beckett did not become a director of his own plays overnight. The reason why he did do so has been well put by his friend and publisher John Calder:

> He would come to London quite frequently during the late 1950s and 1960s, mainly to oversee productions of his plays that were usually being directed in a way totally against his particular wishes. So I would hear in the evenings his misery over the rehearsals he had been through during the day as, little by little, he tried to get the actors to do things his way and to persuade the particular producer to follow his directions, even the printed directions in the text itself. Little by little he did manage to build around himself a devoted core of actors who knew exactly how he wanted things done, and the Beckett actor came into being because of his insistence, usually against the desires of the theatre management, on imposing his own particular will on the plays and the ways he wanted them done. Every time he went to rehearsals of his own plays, he memorised the entire text. He never had to look at the page. He had every rhythm in his head. He watched the actors, followed them, stopped them, and could give them the lines exactly the way he wanted them to do them. At BBC rehearsals of his radio plays, he would read the text for actors to follow his voice.
>
> (*BD*, p. 113)

In other words, Beckett became a director because he felt that no one else – with the possible exceptions of Roger Blin and Alan Schneider – could or would put his plays on in exactly the way he envisaged when he wrote them. As with the translation of his works into English, in order to get things right, he had to do the job himself.

John Calder makes another important point: that Beckett always ensured that he had mastered the script before expecting actors to do so. The only record we have of his actually treading the boards himself is when he played the part of Don Diègue in *Le Kid*, the parody of a French neoclassical play, *Le Cid* (1636), which was written, as we have seen, in collaboration with Georges Pelorson when the two of them were junior lecturers at Trinity College, Dublin, in 1931. Pelorson remembered many years later 'the intensity Beckett put into his acting, the way he evidently relished playing: his every action was that of someone who was clearly a man of the theatre' (*BD*, pp. 125–6).

There are two principal sources of information about Beckett's work as stage director. One is an excellent book by Dougald McMillan and Martha Fehsenfeld, *Beckett in the Theatre* (1988, here abbreviated as *BTh*). The intention was that this should appear in several volumes, but in the event only the first was published, covering the plays from *Le Kid* (1931) to *Krapp's Last Tape* (1958), with an appendix on the staging of *L'Hypothèse* (1966); this play was written by his friend Robert Pinget, and it was the only time Beckett directed a work by another dramatist. McMillan and Fehsenfeld drew extensively on Beckett's notebooks, which the author had donated to the Reading University Library and which at the time were unpublished. The notebooks have since been prepared for publication by James Knowlson and others under Professor Knowlson's general editorship and issued as *The Theatrical Notebooks of Samuel Beckett* (for details, see Select Bibliography, p. 218) which, together with Knowlson's own writings on the subject and those of the American scolar Ruby

Cohn, constitute the other major source of information on Beckett's work as director.

Knowlson has published two important essays on this topic. The first, written while Beckett was still alive, offers an insight into some of the ways in which the directorial notes can assist or confirm critical interpretation, and begins by explaining what the notebooks consist of:

They are notes prepared by Beckett when he is about to direct his own plays: they are consulted by him prior to, but not normally in the course of, actual rehearsals, and they are sometimes corrected by him subsequently in the light of rehearsal changes. The notebooks are numerous, very detailed and extremely meticulous; they are, first and foremost, practical working documents, dealing frequently with precise, immediate problems of staging, such as the various positions of Estragon and Vladimir in *Waiting for Godot* vis-à-vis each other, the tree and the stone; how Pozzo and Lucky should lie when they fall from the vertical; how many paces Clov should take in *Endgame* when he is 'having an idea' or May when she is 'revolving it all' in her 'poor mind' in *Footfalls*; and so on. They also raise specific questions which Beckett usually, though not always, manages to answer for his own benefit as director, or for that of the actors, the lighting engineer and the stage manager; questions like: should Clov's response to Hamm's whistle be instantaneous or ought there to be a time lag? (answer: instantaneous), or how will the cuts that need to be made in the parasol sequence of *Happy Days* synchronise with the slow consuming of the canopy? (answer: try it and see).

Knowlson quotes Beckett as saying that when he came to direct his own work in the theatre, he studied the text as if it had been written by someone else, adding that in a way it did come from someone else, since it had been written so long ago. (On another occasion – to Charles Juliet, p. 148 – he made a similar point after re-reading *Molloy* for a new edition – namely, that the text seemed not to have come from himself.) Moreover, Knowlson goes on, current work seems to have influenced the interpretation of earlier plays, and vice versa: 'There are several examples where Beckett's experience in directing one play seems materially to have affected his work on another,' such as the fact that the sound and rhythm of Krapp's or Clov's pacing to and fro in San Quentin Drama Workshop productions in the late 1970s 'almost certainly arose out of his work at the Royal Court on *Footfalls*' in 1976, and such as the fact, also, that the use of different lighting levels in *That Time* and *Footfalls* harked back to early experiments with the spot in *Play* in the mid-1960s. In a number of cases, too,

it seems clear that Beckett's own attitude towards one of his plays itself evolved: it is difficult to believe, for example, that the Beckett of 1979, who when directing Billie Whitelaw in *Happy Days* insisted on the lack of awareness, unheroic nature and almost manic quality of Winnie, would have admired as much as he did at the time the courage and lyricism displayed in Madeleine Renaud's performance in the same role in 1963. But as anyone who has directed in the theatre will appreciate, there is a major factor that has always to be taken into account, namely the voice, the physical appearance, the personality and the degree of technical expertise of the actors who are cast in a particular production. *Happy Days*, for instance, could never be the same with Billie Whitelaw playing the part of Winnie as with Madeleine Renaud, and *Krapp's Last Tape* would always be different with Patrick Magee, Pierre Chabert or Rick Cluchey in the role of Krapp. Then there are the constraints imposed by the size of the stage itself, and by the availability of technical resources such as lighting; Beckett found himself spending much time confronting, often with flexibility and considerable ingenuity, the inescapable choices and compromises that the theatre obliges the director to make, even going so far for instance as crawling himself over the mound on the *Happy Days* set at the Royal Court in order to see if it could be done by the actor chosen for the part. In his rethinking of the dramatic text he would sometimes propose changes, such as in the 1980 San Quentin production of *Endgame*, where he decided to add further deliberate deceitfulness to Clov's relations with the blind Hamm. Clov suffers constant pain in his joints, and so tries to move as little as possible; this obliges him to pretend to carry out Hamm's orders, such as doing a brief tramp-tramp on the spot (two steps loud, two less loud) in a simulation of walking, or knocking on the steps of the ladder to give Hamm the impression that he is climbing it as ordered. 'Why do you lie to me?' asks Hamm when he gets wise to this [*CDW*, p. 104], but the more he bullies Clov, the more Clov deceives him. Beckett's direction clarifies the cruelly symbiotic relationship which lies at the hub of this play.

As in so much of his drama (Beckett told his Schiller Theater cast in Berlin), 'everything in *Endgame* is built on analogy and repetition'. Between his two productions in 1967 and 1980 the only significant difference in his attitude to parallelism was an even more meticulous attention to acting detail of the kind that Knowlson here draws attention to. Much the same is true of *Krapp's Last Tape*:

> Looking at the play from the outside in order to direct it brought Beckett to focus much more clearly than any critic had previously done on themes [such as the opposition of light and dark, of immobility and sudden movement] that widened the resonance of the play, and to incorporate details into his direction that both removed what was inessential and highlighted the central theme of separation and reconciliation. As a result the post-1969 production version of the play [which Beckett devised] functions dramatically far more successfully than did that of 1958 [directed by George Devine and Donald McWhinnie].

In the case of *Waiting for Godot*, it would be rather surprising if, after all this time, Beckett's notebooks were to throw much light on this most studied of plays. Yet they do provide striking evidence of how the author regarded some of the play's most fundamental themes a quarter of a century after its composition:

> They show, for instance, how important crucifixion images are to Beckett's Berlin production. There are cruciform patterns formed by moves across stage on the upstage horizontal line and back down the vertical central line on a raked stage; after their fall to the ground the bodies of Pozzo and Lucky lie in the shape of yet another cross; and in the context of a long drawn-out martyrdom Estragon in particular stretches out his arms in the form of a cross. The notebooks show, too, Beckett's concern to stress that all the characters, and not just Lucky, are 'entangled in a net' [*CDW*, p. 39], the theme of incarceration being one that pervades the whole of his theatre. When Vladimir and Estragon go off stage, they are merely beating their wings like birds trapped by the strands of the net, bouncing back as if on elastic into the stage space to which they are inextricably tied.
>
> (*Modern Drama*, 30, 1987, pp. 451–65)

Knowlson's other major essay, published after the author's death, focuses less on the theatrical notebooks and more on Beckett's role as stage director, and begins with a revealing piece of reminiscence:

> Beckett once complained to me of the failure of a famous English actor [Albert Finney] to capture the poetry of his lines: 'You hear it a certain way in your head, and he just can't do it,' he said. And 'He's doing it ahl whrang,' he famously whispered to Alan Schneider of another actor's performance as they attended the British première of *Waiting for Godot*; through the director Peter Hall, he went on to proffer words of advice to the actors after the

performance. He listened to his wife's or his friend's accounts of various productions, read reviews, or simply looked at photographs or listened to sound recordings of his plays, and found that often they simply did not work, sometimes for the most obvious, practical reasons, sometimes for more complex, sophisticated ones: the urns were too far apart in *Play*; the chair was not the right height in *Endgame* or the windows were wrongly placed; the tempo was quite wrong in parts of *Godot* and there was not enough silence; and so on.

It is not, contrary to what many people persist in believing, that Beckett thought that there was only *one* way of doing his plays. Indeed, the differences in his own productions of the same play disprove this allegation totally. But he did have a vision to which certain elements of certain productions were clearly not being faithful, or against which they were actively working. I also think that he felt that the words of the text, taken along with the stage directions (however precise these may be – and, in Beckett's case, they are remarkably precise), still only partially conveyed the way that he saw his own plays. For what was *not* written down counted almost as much for him as what was set out on the printed page.

By what was not written down, I mean, among other things, the echoing and contrasting tones of balancing or differing voices, the pace and the rhythms of the dialogue, the frequency and the duration of the pauses, the quality of the voices and the looks, the variety of the gestures, the volume and the quality of the lighting. To take one example, that of pace: when George Devine was directing *Play* with the author in attendance, Beckett kept saying 'faster, faster', while Laurence Olivier wanted them to go for intelligibility by slowing it down; Devine agreed with Beckett and in the end the play went at an enormous speed. It was for these, among other, reasons that Beckett chose to direct his own plays. But he had in fact been closely involved with the actual staging of his works from the very beginning of his career as a dramatist. He started by attending rehearsals of *Waiting for Godot* late in 1952, discreetly advising Roger Blin, and he did the same, only with much more self-assurance, with *Endgame* in 1957. Then, for a further period of ten years, he went to rehearsals of first productions of his plays in London, Paris and Berlin, learning from, as well as advising, experienced directors like Blin, Devine, Donald McWhinnie, Jean-Marie Serreau and, later, Anthony Page.

I myself can confirm this. Beckett told me in May 1961 that he helped with the Paris revival of *Waiting for Godot*, which I had just been to see. Roger Blin had had to go to London on other business, and during his absence Beckett attended all the rehearsals, paying particular attention to the need to adapt the production to the wider stage of the Odéon theatre (the Babylone was a small venue), and altering the timings to suit his preferences rather than Blin's original ideas about pacing. 'But', Knowlson continues,

> although he had a due sense of all that he could learn from these talented directors, he also retained a very clear perception of what, as author, he wanted from a theatrical realisation of his work. So, from the mid 1960s onwards, until he was nearly eighty years old, he directed many productions of his own plays, mostly at the Schiller Theater in Berlin but also at three theatres in Paris and at the Royal Court Theatre and the Riverside Studios in London.

After explaining the background in this way, Professor Knowlson goes on to analyse Beckett's special characteristics as a director:

> First, he pays scrupulous attention to every minute detail of the production in order to make it part of an overall conception of the play. His rigour and absolute meticulousness as a director are legendary. A glance at his notebook for the Berlin production of *Waiting for Godot* shows how inten-

sively he worked on the text prior to rehearsal; it contains detailed lists of repetitions, of repetitions with variation, of what he calls *Wartestellen* (waiting points), of sketches of moves, of arrows to indicate the direction of these moves and their shape, of changes of voice and tone, of synchronisations of text with moves, and of parallels and echoes between different moments of the play. The meticulousness reveals an enormous effort of concentration and a very precise, obsessive, almost pedantic visualisation of every instant of the work.

An example of what some might consider pedantry is one of the first notes he passed to Billie Whitelaw: 'Billie, would you make those three dots, two dots.' It is difficult to see how any performer, even one as talented as Ms Whitelaw, could make clear to an audience the difference between three dots on the printed page and two dots, but the anecdote shows how far Beckett was prepared to go in his planning and close attention to detail. And as we have already seen (in the interview with Hugh Hebert quoted above), in rehearsals for *Krapp's Last Tape* with Rick Cluchey

> he spent an enormous amount of time and trouble trying to establish exactly *what* noise the boots worn by Krapp should make as Krapp shuffles slowly across the stage. One pair of boots was rejected, because the sound was wrong. They next tried attaching sandpaper or a piece of metal to the soles of the boots, but this did not work either.

Finally, as we saw, Cluchey ended up wearing Beckett's own black leather slippers; and in the 1979 Royal Court Theatre production of *Happy Days* Beckett plotted every move made by Willie on the other side of the mound even though the actor is totally invisible from the auditorium:

> Clearly the purpose of this is so that his partner, Winnie, may know precisely where he is supposed to be at every moment of her own text so that she can speak with absolute

conviction, gesturing, for example, like a policeman in a market-place: '. . . now . . . back in' [*CDW*, p. 147].

At the beginning of each act of *Happy Days*, Winnie is wakened from her sleep by a bell. But what kind of bell, one needs to know when directing the play. How loud should it be? How long should it last? In his production notebook Beckett writes that bell is the wrong word and knife or gouge are more appropriate, and at rehearsal he said, 'I'm after a searing, cutting quality; the bell should be brief and cut off suddenly, like a blow, or a knife on metal.'

But if the bell is as loud and cutting as that, it cannot be made to last for the ten seconds of the English printed text or even the five seconds of the French translation. This is too long for the audience's ears to bear, so there were lengthy experiments with different kinds of bells at the Royal Court Threatre. Beckett finally settled for the theatre fire-bell and used it for much shorter bursts, solving the problem, as he did with Krapp's footwear in *Krapp's Last Tape*, in a thoroughly pragmatic manner. This leads Knowlson to make an important point:

> For there is one myth that ought to be dispelled about Beckett and theatre practice. He emphatically did not belong to the improvisational school of directors, those who create virtually spontaneously on the rehearsal studio floor. He liked to have the text fully by heart himself and his *mise en scène* blocked out in intricate detail before he ever began to rehearse. But he was not inflexible or impractical as a director, insisting on doing things exactly as he had first envisaged, disregarding the practical difficulties involved, or at the expense of the feelings or wishes of the performer. Indeed, the notebooks have numerous erasures with, on one occasion, in his notebook on *Godot*, 'unrealisable' written across the page. He would abandon ideas as being too intellectual in conception and unlikely to register with an audience: the suggestion, for instance, that Krapp should turn only in one direction when he moves, and never

to the left. Several actors have explained how patiently he worked with them on stage actions that would more satisfactorily replace something that they felt was not working.

Sometimes, of course, the writer and the director in Beckett did clash. He was visibly pained by mistakes made in the text by one British actress (Brenda Bruce) because of corrections he had introduced only after she had already learnt the script by heart. Earlier in his career as a dramatist there were disagreements with actors who found it hard to accept that rhythm counted for more than expression where he was concerned, and who felt that he was trying suppress all individuality in them (this was particularly true of Brenda Bruce and Peggy Ashcroft, as we shall see in chapter 6). Others, however, such as Patrick Magee, Jack MacGowran, Billie Whitelaw and David Warrilow, found that there was a great freedom to be found in working within strictly defined limits; it enabled them to produce performances in which emotion was restrained but was still able to be expressed.

As Knowlson goes on to point out, music played an important part in Beckett's life; he was married to an accomplished pianist, and was himself no mean performer on the instrument, especially of the works of his beloved Schubert. In rehearsing *Footfalls* with the equally musical Rose Hill in 1976, he told her: 'We are not doing this play realistically or psychologically; we are doing it musically.' In discussing Mother's monologue with her,

he quite naturally employed terms like *scherzo*, *andante* or *piano*, just as in the *Krapp's Last Tape* production notebook he described the vocal principle as constituting a slide from the major key, which expresses an initial tone of assurance, into the minor key which betrays its artificiality whenever the themes of 'solitude', 'light and darkness' and 'Woman' surface to disrupt this initial tone. It is not just that Beckett used musical terminology in his notebooks or at rehearsals with those actors who understood his vocabulary. His own work as director followed musical principles very closely; they provided often-repeated echoes of gestures and movements, and of rhythms and intonations, that correspond to repetitions and to repetitions-with-variation within the printed text.

Repetition, contrast and balance, Knowlson goes on, were indeed among Beckett's principal concerns as a director, a prime example being his many productions of *Krapp's Last Tape*, in which numerous small actions and looks were picked up and repeated, sometimes in very different contexts:

At the Schiller Theater, for instance, when Krapp, after looking up the word 'viduity', closed the dictionary on the term 'vidua-bird', he lapsed into exactly the same stare that he had adopted earlier to accompany the ledger entry 'Farewell to love' [*CDW*, pp. 219, 217]. Indeed, every time he went into a daydream at the mention of a woman (and particularly the recollection of the beauty of her eyes), he took up the same position of the head and the same look. Many of the repetitions of postures, actions, looks and ways of saying certain phrases in *Krapp's Last Tape* function in terms of balanced opposites. 'The play,' wrote Beckett in his Schiller production notebook, 'is composed therefore of two fairly equal parts – listening and non-listening': the listening was equated with immobility and the non-listening with movement. And so in sections headed 'Motionless listening' and 'Listening actions', Beckett worked out the many contrasts in Krapp's acting between listening and non-listening, movement and stillness, daydream and feverish activity, and he elaborated in the most intricate detail the physical expression of these opposites in terms of opening and closing the eyes, raising and lowering the head, and so on.

Yet, while acknowledging the dramatic value of repeated actions, particularly in as short and concentrated a play as

Krapp's Last Tape, Beckett also recognized the dangers of excessive stylization. 'So Krapp's gestures, looks, grunts, curses and sounds of impatience were all carefully varied and timed to avoid that particular pitfall,' Knowlson explains, and goes on:

In his writing as a whole Beckett pays, of course, great attention to echo and analogy, to rhythm and balance, and as a director he worked just as hard as he had as a writer to establish verbal echoes and parallels. On occasion he was quite prepared to change the words of his text or his stage directions to establish verbal or visual patterns to echo from one section of the play to another. For example in *Happy Days*, when Winnie takes a strand of her hair from under her hat, by changing the text Beckett creates one of the simplest and yet most moving moments of the play. In the revised text she now does not let the strand of hair fall – as she did in the original printed text [*CDW*, p. 146] – but holds it in her left hand, as she says nostalgically, raising an imaginary glass in her other hand, 'Golden you called it that day, the last guest gone,' so that when in the second act we hear: 'The pink fizz. The flute glasses. The last guest gone' [*CDW*, p. 166], we recall with remembered emotion the earlier gestures and words that echo movingly over a long stretch of the play.

In *Waiting for Godot* Beckett changed the text in several important respects to reinforce such internal echoes, the most significant alteration here being Estragon's responses to Vladimir's often-repeated statement that they cannot leave because they are 'waiting for Godot'. In the printed text his replies vary, but in Beckett's production they were all made the same – 'Ah yes' – a phrase, Knowlson says, that 'picks up an additional burden of lassitude every time it is spoken', and so

at the end of the play, when Vladimir tells Estragon to pull on his trousers, instead of saying as in the printed text 'True', he replies 'Ah yes', finishing then with the laugh that

Beckett wanted, but a laugh which, by its enhanced association with the 'We're waiting for Godot' that it has so often
followed, is replete with melancholy resonance. Not only
does Beckett the director work to get the echoes of words,
rhythms, sounds and even gestures exactly right, he also
establishes counterpoints, often ironic ones, between one
part of the play and another. In *Endgame*, said Beckett to
his Berlin cast in 1967, 'the play is full of echoes; they all
answer each other'. His productions show that the arrange-
ment of forms in space, or the movements of living actors
orchestrated into a very precise choreography of repeated
actions, can provide something which, akin to ballet, provides a form of visual poetry that creates (to use his own
phrase) its own 'subliminal imagery'.

But Beckett does not use repetition, balance and contrast
merely as structural devices. They are also closely related to
the fundamental themes of his plays. Repetition lies for
instance at the very heart of *Krapp's Last Tape*. With both
his 'listening to an old year' [*CDW*, p. 218] and his birthday recording, Krapp repeats a ceremony that he has been
performing for the past forty-five years. The many repetitions and echoes link Krapp with his former self, and yet
allow us to perceive discontinuity as well – to hear some of
the same ideas and phrases, and yet to note the change of
voice and tone and see his decline from assurance to slightly
bitter resignation mixed with nostalgic yearning. It is repetition that makes this complex, ambivalent response possible.

For Beckett uses every element of theatrical space cre-
atively to set up striking visual imagery that exercises its
impact and its resonance. Perhaps ultimately, as well as for
being a great prose stylist, it will be for his success in creating these striking, resonant, scenic images – stage pictures
which (like the frozen tableau at the end of *Waiting for
Godot*) stay engraved in the mind's eye – that Beckett will
be best remembered. The silences that figure prominently in
his plays are filled by the spectator measuring what is being

seen against what has just been said, or following, within specific constraints, the multiple associations aroused by preceding statements or patterns of statements. For, in a very real sense, Beckett's verbal and visual imagery echoes not on the boards alone but in the mind of the spectator.

(*BD*, pp. 9–23)

Covering the whole field and using, as we have seen, the complete set of working manuscripts that Beckett donated to Reading University Library, James Knowlson has produced invaluable studies of the theatre notebooks that reveal how Beckett conceptualized and realized his own writings for the stage. The work of other critics has been more piecemeal, but no less enlightening for that. The earliest detailed account of Beckett's involvement in production was published in the *Sunday Times* in 1964 by the American novelist Clancy Sigal (b. 1926). He spent eleven days in the author's company during rehearsals in London for a production of *Endgame* that was shortly to be staged in English at the Studio des Champs-Élysées in Paris before returning to London for a successful run at the Aldwych Theatre. His day-by-day account reveals a simultaneous close-up of a great writer and of the creative process itself. The rehearsals were put on in various locations according to a plan agreed between the author and his young producer, Michael Blake, who soon faded into the background. The work atmosphere, Sigal records, was 'always quiet, curiously formal, even delicate, often intense'. What he does not mention, though James Knowlson does, is the heavy drinking that the two leading actors and their author indulged in, both at lunchtime and in the evenings after rehearsals; fortunately, it does not seem to have affected the playwright's concentration or impaired the actors' performances (*DF*, p. 514). Here is Sigal's account:

First day
Beckett is not due until tomorrow. Blake, the producer, is fond of using words like ambiguity and paradox. Jack

MacGowran (Clov) and Patrick Magee (Hamm) are politely sceptical. 'Death,' explains Blake, 'has no finality.' 'Yeah,'
scowls Magee, 'but how do you treat it?'

Second day
Beckett has arrived. The actors are more hesitant, much less
sure of themselves in his presence. He positions himself in
front of them, a few feet away. Michael Blake, his eyes
bright and loving on the action, hunches over elaborate
graphs, marks and notes at a nearby table. As the players
run through their lines Beckett pores over the text as if
hearing it for the first time. He glares sharply, neutrally, at
the action, infrequently prompting. 'A little more pause
there.' A grainy, almost silent voice, a courteous Iris lilt and
lisp, with a repressed, lean bark. Leanness is the chief, the
central characteristic of this astonishingly handsome man.
All morning he stands, leaning lightly against a wooden
rail, hands in pockets, fascinated as Hamm and Clov
wrench out their splendid, racking arguments ('If I could
kill him I'd die happy,' says Clov [*CDW*, p. 105]). He flow-
ers, tightly smiles, under the anguished raillery. Clearly, he
admires the actors, none of whom is however quite sure
what the play is about. Beckett affects complete ignorance
of the larger implications. 'I only know what's on the page,'
he says with a friendly gesture. 'Do it your way.' Later, he
advises: 'You should be horrified by Hamm, and also sorry
for him. Hamm is not assured. Feverish. His assurance is
always put on. He is afraid.' Magee and MacGowran busy
themselves with the first movements of the play. Beckett
leans forward. He is crucially interested in the problem of
the actual stage space in which the players manipulate
themselves. He is critically attentive of Nagg (Sidney
Bromley) and Nell (Nancy Cole), with whom he is never
quite happy. He tells Sidney and Nancy to delete the emotion from their faces. 'Murmur,' he tells them. 'No smile at
all, completely impassive.' His eyes fly up from the text to

the actors, his dry hands pushing his steel-rimmed spectacles up onto his forehead. His interruptions are directed wholly to the centre of the action. He is both decisive and terribly afraid of giving offence to the actors.

Third day
A gloomy, slow morning. Nancy's Nell is still over-emphatic. In the moments when he isn't 'on', MacGowran broods or stares into space. Magee, with less of Beckett in his nature, strolls about, talks, tells stories. My respect for him increases hourly. MacGowran has been 'plugged in' from the start, but he is worrying. His Clov is lack-lustre today. Nobody is much good. Yet, for no apparent reason, the author is beginning to 'swing' with his play. He smiles with rather grim satisfaction over Hamm and Clov. He consults the text greedily, pressing his nose to the printed page because of his poor eyesight. His interventions are almost always not on the side of greater subtlety but of increased simplicity. The actors tend to want to make the play abstract and 'existential'; gently and firmly he guides them to concrete, exact and simple actions. He mouths the words, again and again, of the opening exchange between Hamm and Clov, his eyes with a kind of piercing stillness on the actors, nodding sharply when he is satisfied that the point has been driven home.

Fourth day
Beckett alone with MacGowran and Magee, working out the 'business' of Clov placing the ladder under the two windows at the start of the play. This is obviously central to Beckett, that the audience immediately be told something is wrong on the day the action begins. And as Beckett decides on numerous changes of detail, something emerges: his closest attention and affection are reserved for Clov, the 'creative intelligence', the tense individual who serves as the eyes of the blind and crippled Hamm, towards whom, the 'brute will', he displays a cruel but respectful distance, as

befits someone whom Beckett, when pressed, characterises as 'a bit of a monster'.

Fifth day
Beckett's face is utterly transformed watching the play unfold. It screws up, particularly during the Hamm–Clov exchanges, in an unselfconscious, mask-like grin. Asked if he ever sees anything new in the English text of this play which he originally wrote in French, he replies: 'Yes. Mistakes. The more I go on the more I think things are untranslatable.'

Sixth day
'Bottle him', Hamm orders his servant. MacGowran slams the imaginary lid on the dying father, Nagg, with that same terrible swishing movement he has used since the first day: a quick, chilling movement. A visitor asks Beckett if, just conceivably, Hamm believes Clov's seeds might sprout [CDW, p. 98], thus implying some hope for the future. Beckett is instantly on guard. 'I don't know what's in Hamm's head,' he politely replies, moving off aloofly, not unkindly, even a little regretfully. He doesn't like questions like that.

Seventh day
Beckett watches intently as Magee launches into Hamm's long, halting chronicle-narrative of how he refused aid to a dying survivor and his son, who might have been Clov. An expression of repressed glee passes over Beckett's face.

Eighth day
As Sidney expels his speech of paternal spite against Hamm [CDW, pp. 119–20], Beckett urges more venom: 'It's a *malediction*.' Likewise he smiles intently on Hamm and Clov shouting hatred at each other. Later the whole company is transfixed by Magee's rendering of the 'If I could drag myself down to the sea' speech [CDW, p. 122].

Ninth day
Beckett is perkier: everyone is. A much more rousing run-through today.

Tenth day
The author is off at an appointment somewhere, and Blake works alone with Magee and MacGowran. Afterwards, the two actors grumble to themselves. Their interest is in how to do it, and they dislike the young man's ardent commentaries. When Beckett returns he is consummately attentive to Hamm's opening speech from the wheel-chair, and at the end of the day's rehearsal, the venom re-emerges and the play abruptly comes alive with a shattering rendering of Hamm's 'Old stancher' speech by Magee [*CDW*, p. 134], the final stoical act of Hamm meeting his death. Beckett, having ridden it out to the last echo, turns away; that is over. But the tension, the high-veined pitch which I think comes from his near knowledge of nothingness, never goes out of him. A solitary writer passed beyond hope to a man's singularity.

Eleventh day
A slow start. Beckett alone with his two chief actors. He wants Hamm to loosen up a bit. He knows exactly how he wants the lines read. He drives hard on plausibility, on Hamm and Clov being possessed of a markedly human relationship. 'Let's get as many laughs as we can out of this horrible mess,' he says, meaning the play.
   Magee and MacGowran work out a quick movement with the wheel-chair seven times before it is right. Magee begins to speak, whipping up Hamm's brief exclamation of anxiety over his geographic position ('Put me right in the centre!', *CDW*, p. 105) to a terrible, bowel-shaking crescendo.

Last day
This is the last run-through with all present. Magee is slouched, waiting, in the wheel-chair, his eyes concealed

behind a blind man's pasted-up spectacles. It starts.
Beckett's face takes on that fantastic drawn grin, his features stretched tight and working along with the staccato
recriminations between Hamm and Clov. The timing is
good, intensities and voice levels locked high. Magee deliv-
ers a fine reading of the long 'chronicle' speech [CDW, p.
121]. It is intact and completely convincing. Now it is
Hamm–Magee who commands. The play takes its course.
Clov–MacGowran's burst of hoarse, put-on laughter breaks
up Beckett, who laughs louder than I have ever heard him.
The thing has taken flight.

(*Sunday Times Magazine*, 1 March 1964, pp. 17–22)

The value of Clancy Sigal's own 'chronicle' lies in its immedia-
cy. We really can see Beckett at work, almost for the first time,
directing one of his own plays. The *Endgame* rehearsals in
London gave him useful experience as well as the confidence to
continue in the same vein. A couple of years later he was working on *Play* and *Come and Go* in Paris, but before that he had
been involved in his first, and indeed only, work for the cinema,
Film (1965).

This is a minor work, and certainly not a movie masterpiece.
Its chief interest lies in the fact that it features the great silent-
screen comedian Buster Keaton (1895–1966), in one of his very
last roles. It is, the *Radio Times Guide to Films* (2000) tells us,
'notable not only for its ambiguity, but also for bringing
Keaton back from semi-retirement; paring cinema down to its
visual essentials, it's a parable of an old man fending off the
futility of existence and his own obscurity' (p. 487). But it is
also interesting in the present context for having given rise to
the most extended discussion in existence by Beckett of the
issues involved in the realization of one of his works. A series
of preparatory conversations took place in New York in the
summer of 1964 and were recorded on sound tape; the participants included (in addition to Beckett himself) the director
Alan Schneider, the cinematographer Boris Kaufman and the

producer Barney Rosset. An edited transcript was published by S. E. Gontarski in 1985. It reveals both Beckett's intense interest in the technicalities of film-making ('How would you realise that cinematographically?' he asks at one point) and his diffidence about imposing a particular way of doing things ('All that can be changed', he says at another point; 'it can be done otherwise'); but, as in his involvement in the production of his stage works, he was quite settled in his view of the basic way he saw things, and firmly, though always courteously, did not hesitate to make clear what he had in mind:

> 'What's important is the gesture of unveiling. He perceives the window from the door, some distance away. His behaviour when he draws the curtain across the window is similar to his behaviour when he veils the mirror. He is careful not to see himself in the mirror when he veils it, and he is careful also not to expose himself before the window when he veils it, so that there is no profile of the window in his vision at all. He sees the window from the door and the various things, and he decides then that he will be rid of it.'
>
> (Gontarski, 1985, p. 190)

It was soon after these remarks were recorded that Beckett was drawn irrevocably into what Gontarski, in another context, calls 'self-collaboration' – that is, 'taking full charge of directing his own works for the stage'. The roots of this self-collaboration, however, lay further back – in the 1964 French production of *Play* – as Gontarski explains:

> Working uneasily in Paris with Jean-Marie Serreau on staging the French text before the London rehearsals, Beckett wrote to George Devine that he had decided on some fundamental changes. In addition to altering the *da capo* ending ['The repeat may be an exact replica of first statement or it may present an element of variation' (*CDW*, p. 320), rather than 'Repeat play exactly,' as in the first edition],

he also revised the fundamental relationship between the inquisitorial light and its urn-imprisoned victims: the enquirer (light) began to emerge as no less a victim of his enquiry than they, and as needing to be free, within narrow limits, to act the part, that is to vary if only slightly his speeds and what Beckett called his 'intensities'.

His involvement with productions not only in England, but also in Germany and France, led him, in a gradual and natural progression, to be

prepared to change and even at times substantially rewrite the published versions of his texts based on the practicalities, the realities and the insights that working in stage space brought to light, at a time when he was rethinking the staging of all his work. Roger Blin, for example, was directing *Happy Days* in French with Beckett in October 1963. Beckett was heavily involved with Anthony Page's staging of *Waiting for Godot* at the Royal Court in December 1964. And [as we have seen] he was also, in early 1964, preparing a new production of *Endgame* with Jack MacGowran with only nominal assistance from Michael Blake. Such close and frequent theatrical work began to suggest various insufficiencies or clumsiness in his texts, so that the changes he made to *Play* would soon become the pattern with every piece he subsequently directed.

Two years after the French première of *Play*, the work was revived, and Beckett now found that there was 'no escape' from assuming total direction of the staging himself. Serreau was still nominally in charge, and featured as the director of record, but he had other commitments that kept him away from Paris.

So it was Beckett's productions of *Play*, *Come and Go* and Robert Pinget's *L'Hypothèse* which opened at the Petite Salle of the Odéon-Théâtre de France on 28 February 1966.

That production of *Play* began a long period of Beckett working through Beckett, this time as author/director in collaboration with himself. Directing became a crucial part of his creative process, and turning a directorial eye on his earlier works gave him the opportunity to 'correct' (his word, not mine) the theatrical insufficiencies he found there and to reshape the works with an aesthetics which coalesced with the writing and staging of *Play*. The shift in aesthetics was towards a radical simplification, a disencumberment, a further de-theatricalisation of theatre. It tended to substitute extended monologues, often delivered in a flat tone, for dialogue, and to feature renewed emphasis on the static stage image, still point, *tableau vivant*, which bears more resemblance to sculpture than to traditional theatre.

This Paris production lauched Beckett on a career of self-direction in earnest, beginning the following year with *Endgame* in German at the Schiller Theater Werkstatt in September 1967. Gontarski calculates that, in all, between the Odéon *Come and Go* in 1966 and the valedictory television version of *What Where* broadcast by Süddeutsche Rundfunk twenty years later on his eightieth birthday, Beckett directed some sixteen stage productions of his work and some seven works for German television, 'each time making at least adjustments to his texts, each time creating the final text in rehearsals'. And as we have seen, he drew up detailed notes on staging that have since been published and in which, as well as methodically working out moves, gestures and timings, he meticulously revised his texts, whether in German, French or English.

On the other hand, Gontarski goes on, he 'never incorporated into any published text, even subsequent German editions', the cuts and changes he started making from 1966 onwards, although before his death he did authorize the inclusion in the Faber and Faber *Theatrical Notebooks* of 'acting texts' that did take account of his revisions. Some critics have condemned what they view as a contradiction here, but, in common with Professor Gontarski, I see none. While understandably not wishing to order the withdrawal of the standard printed editions, which by then existed in millions of copies around the world, Beckett preferred actors and producers to use where possible the scripts he had arrived at after years of trial and error. This seems to me entirely reasonable. After all, there are no single, universally accepted texts for Shakespeare's plays – or for the books of the Bible, for that matter – and we have managed perfectly well without them all this time. So, while Beckett considered his final revised *Godot* the best version for stage use, he also believed, Gontarski tells us, that 'no single production – not even his own – was the definitive one, if by that we mean the single accepable performance'. When asked in 1967 if he had come to Berlin 'to give the authentic version' of *Endgame*, his reply was unambiguous: 'No, I don't claim my interpretation is the only correct one.' On the contrary,

as he developed as a theatrical artist (as opposed to playwright), Beckett relied more and more on revisions made in the heat and turmoil of rehearsals. The decision in the midst of the 1982 taping to add a second part to the mime for television, *Quad*, a monochrome repeat at slower speed with less percussion, was made after the original recording was completed. He chanced to observe the replay on a black and white monitor and decided that he wanted that image (tantamount to the creation of a second act to a ballet) as well. The broadcast version was then called *Quadrat* 1+ 2, but that single revision was crucial. With the taping of Beckett's last work, his complete rewrite of the stage play *What Where* for German television, his cameraman, Jim Lewis, observed, 'He was not sure what he wanted until the very last day. That's when it all came together.' To date no version of Beckett's revised *What Where* exists in print, although it will appear in the fourth volume of the *Theatrical Notebooks of Samuel Beckett* series.

Thus, Gontarski continues, Beckett began his career as a theatrical producer late in life, in 1967, when he was sixty-one, after a fourteen-year apprenticeship beginning in 1953 with his presence at the rehearsals of Roger Blin's *Godot*. Thereafter, as a director of his own plays, he continued almost up to his death to surprise audiences and critics alike. This is not a sign, Gontarski argues, of an author in his dotage tinkering clumsily with his earlier and greatest works, but evidence of continuing and sustained creative vitality. That is a judgement with which it is hard to disagree.

It is also difficult to dissent from Gontarski's next point: that there is a fundamental realism in Beckett's work that was recognized as early as 1957 by the inmates (one of whom was Rich Cluchey, to whom I shall be returning in the next chapter) of San Quentin, a maximum-security prison in California, when the San Francisco Actors' Workshop was invited to perform *Waiting for Godot* for their benefit. The play was chosen – despite its awesome reputation as the intellectual's happy hunting ground – because it had no female roles, a necessary precaution in a jail built to hold men convicted of serious offences, chiefly crimes of violence:

> While the rest of the world puzzled over the meaning of Godot – was it God? Happiness? Eternal Life? Christian Salvation? Any sort of salvation? The future? – those life prisoners understood the play immediately, on a primary, visceral level. For them *Waiting for Godot* was straight realism. They knew well the waiting game, waiting for change in their condition, waiting for letters, for appeals, for pardons, waiting and having nothing to do, waiting and having nothing happen, and so having to fill in the time. As the reviewer in the prison newspaper put it, 'We're still waiting for Godot, and shall continue to wait. When the scenery gets too drab and the action too slow, we'll call each other names and swear to part for ever – but then there's no place to go.'

Or as Beckett himself put it, more pithily but no less movingly, 'There is no escape from the hours and the days' (*Proust*, 1931, p. 2). During the period of martial law in Poland in the early 1980s the catchphrase 'We're waiting for Godot' became a subversive way of declaring: 'We're waiting for this repressive régime to fall,' which the authorities were powerless to prosecute; and apropos of *Endgame* Gontarski adds:

> There is a fundamental reality to this work that Beckett always saw and that he revealed most clearly and succinctly as a director working through his own play. His 1967 production in Berlin, for example, was marked by a surprising amount of realistic subtext, and he would often provide 'realistic' motivation. For the line, 'Have you bled?' [*CDW*, p. 95], for example, he told Clov, 'You see something in his face, that's why you're asking.' While trying to kill a flea in his underpants with insecticide, Clov is reminded to ask Hamm, 'What about that pee?' [*CDW*, p. 108]. The associations are perfectly credible. Hamm's 'Since it's calling to you' should be choked out, according to Beckett, to trigger Clov's 'Is your throat sore?' [*CDW*, p. 127]. And Clov's opening speech, the reason for his speaking at all, is driven by some barely perceptible change that he perceives while inspecting his environment. In his director's notebook for the Riverside Studios production of *Endgame*, Beckett wrote: 'C perplexed. All seemingly in order, yet a change.'

Gontarski concludes this fine essay on the subject of self-collaboration – of what he describes as 'Beckett working through Beckett' – with the following point:

> As we credit Beckett with redefining modern theatre in January 1953 in *Waiting for Godot*, which made the theatrical tradition at the time seem positively operatic, we need to understand that Beckett's aesthetic and theatrical development did not stop there. We need to see his redefining of his own theatre with the composition of *Play*, which

drew the performative fully into his creative process for the first time, as at least of equal – if not greater – magnitude. The minimalism and formal simplicity of Beckett's later work makes even *Godot* and *Endgame* seem almost baroque. As Beckett embraced the aesthetics of 'less is more' for his late drama, as he referred to his own 'mania for minimalism', he also seized directorial opportunities to reshape his earlier work according to that principle and to test and re-test the results directly on the stage. Enormous insights are gained by observing Beckett's late aesthetics retroactively applied to earlier work and by watching the changes that result from his self-collaboration, his working through Beckett.

(*BD*, pp. 33–52)

Gontarski's perceptive analysis of the way in which *Play* (1964) represented a turning point in Beckett's career as a the-atrical artist is confirmed by Ruby Cohn's discussion of the productions of *Endgame* and *Krapp's Last Tape* that he staged a few years later, in 1967 and 1969 respectively. After summa-rizing the history of his involvement in the practicalities of drama performance, from acting the part of Don Diègue in *Le Kid* in 1931 to attending the rehearsals of *Waiting for Godot* towards the end of 1952 (after which, she says, his 'grasp of staging was swift'), she reminds us that by the late 1950s and early 1960s his advice was often sought for staging his plays, and his performance concepts dominated several productions directed by others, notably the London *Endgame* and *Krapp* of 1958, the Paris 1961 *Godot*, the Paris 1964 *Play* (as Gontarski has demonstrated), a Paris–London *Endgame* of 1964 (as Clancy Sigal has shown), and the Royal Court *Godot* of 1964. The first piece to bear his name as director was the 1966 Stuttgart telecast of *Eh Joe*. He had taken no public credit for Pinget's *L'Hypothèse* (1965) although, as Cohn explains, he reconceived the entire production after the author Pinget and the actor Pierre Chabert called on him to assist them at an early stage in rehearsals. This valuable hands-on experience was followed in 1966 by his Paris *Come and Go*, and that in turn led naturally to his Berlin stagings of *Endgame* (1967), *Krapp's Last Tape* (1969), *Happy Days* (1971), *Waiting for Godot* (1975), *That Time* and *Footfalls* (1976) and *Play* (1978), in which 'he appreciated the distance from his plays provided by the German translations of Elmar Tophoven', although, as we have seen, that did not deter him from revising them, often substantially, in performance. Cohn continues:

> For production in Berlin, Beckett approached all his plays in the same basic way: (1) meticulous examination of Tophoven's German translation and subsequent revision toward his own English version (since Tophoven, a translator from French, had rendered the French texts); (2) intense visualisation of the play in theatre space – what he calls 'trying to see'; (3) commitment of the revised German text to memory (including stage directions); (4) composition of a director's notebook, to which he does not refer during actual rehearsals; (5) transmission of design ideas to his friend and preferred stage designer Matias Henrioud (known professionally as Matias), who does some preliminary work while they are still in Paris. Only when these steps are completed does Beckett arrive in Berlin, where the casting has already been decided.

> At his first meeting with the actors, he never speaks *about* the play but plunges right into it. Work on scenes begins at once, and Beckett shakes his head at questions that stray from concrete performance. On the other hand, no practical detail is too small for his attention. Sitting or standing, he seems poised to spring to the stage. Early in rehearsals he requests permission to interrupt the actors, and this is always granted. The spoken text must be not only letter perfect, but punctuation perfect; he will stop an actor who elides a comma pause. Yet he rarely interrupts the early run-throughs, and he deliberately absents himself

from a late rehearsal or two, so that the actors may feel freer in their final discoveries; for, although he arrives at the Schiller Theater with the production complete in his mind's eye, he usually makes minor changes during rehearsal.

Endgame being his preferred play, he chose to begin his German directing career (which at the time, of course, he did not anticipate as a career) with this work. While still in Paris, he went over the German text with translator Tophoven, who has acknowledged that their collaboration resulted in a much improved version 'through constant work together, through tightening where this was possible, through expansion where the stage demanded it, through late discoveries and introduction of new assonance and harmony, through elimination of Gallicisms that had been overlooked, and through prevention of undesirable associations and removal of phonetic difficulties'.

For rehearsal purposes Beckett divided his full-length plays into manageable self-contained sections, which in a more conventional work would be called scenes. There are sixteen in *Endgame*, which Ruby Cohn lists as follows (page references to *CDW* are given in parentheses):

1 Clov's dumbshow and first soliloquy (pp. 92–3)
2 Hamm's awakening, first soliloquy and first dialogue with Clov (pp. 93–9)
3 The Nagg–Nell dialogue (pp. 99–103)
4 The excited Hamm–Clov dialogue, with Hamm's first turn around the room, ending on Clov's sigh: 'If I could kill him . . .' (pp. 103–5)
5 Clov's comic business with ladder and telescope (pp. 105–6)
6 Hamm's troubled questioning of Clov, culminating in the burlesque flea scene (pp. 106–8)
7 The Hamm–Clov dialogue, ending with the toy-dog episode (pp. 108–12)

8 Clov's rebellion, giving way to Hamm's story of the madman and culminating in the alarm-clock scene (pp. 112–15)

9 Hamm's story of the beggar (pp. 115–18)

10 The prayer, ending with Nagg's curse (pp. 118–20)

11 The play within the play of Hamm and Clov; Hamm's continuation of his story (pp. 120–23)

12 The second round of the wheelchair (pp. 123–4)

13 The Hamm–Clov dialogue (pp. 124–5)

14 Hamm's 'role' (pp. 125–6)

15 Clov's emancipation, ending with his monologue and exit (pp. 126–32)

16 Hamm's final soliloquy (pp. 132–4)

Glossing this schema, Cohn goes on:

> Concerned with the physical rather than the metaphysical, Beckett's director's notebook focuses on the mobile Clov: one diagram delineates the path of his 'thinking' walk, and another traces his 'winding up' walk. Carefully noted and numbered are Clov's sixteen entrances and exits, his twenty-six stops and starts, his nine repetitions of 'There are no more . . .' and his ten repetitions of 'I'll leave you'.

Turning to the set chosen for Berlin, Cohn comments that 'Beckett's stage was spare rather than "Bare" [*CDW*, p. 92]':

> High curtained windows, one on each side wall, face earth and sea – what remains of nature. Turned inconspicuously to the foot of the left wall is a picture – what remains of art. Downstage left are two adjacent dustbins covered by a sheet – what remains of the older generation. In the centre is an armchair covered by a sheet – what remains of the prime of life. After the opening tableau, action begins with Clov's removal of the sheets (the notebook calls it an 'unveiling'). What is unveiled is a family – ordinary in its memories, attachments and quarrels, but extraordinary since it is the last of the human race. The words 'finish' and

'end' punctuate the dialogue. Both Hamm and Clov utter the last words of Christ on the cross – 'It is finished' – and other biblical echoes abound (in an earlier version of the play Beckett even placed an actual Bible on stage).

Cohn recalls that 'it was the playing theme that Beckett pointed up in directing', especially the motif of chess. In one of his rare élans of explicitness, he told the actor to whom the role of Hamm had been assigned:

> Hamm is king in this chess game that is lost from the start. He knows from the start that he is making loud, senseless moves. That he will not get anywhere at all with the gaff. Now at the last he makes a few more senseless moves, as only a bad player would; a good one would have given up long ago. He is only trying to postpone the inevitable end. Each of his motions is one of the last useless moves that delay the end. He is a bad player.

'Of the month's rehearsal time,' Cohn recalls, 'Beckett spent about half the period on individual roles and half on harmonising the whole':

> Midway during the rehearsal period, after the actors had memorised the text, he held a rehearsal for tone, pitch and rhythm. In the last two weeks especially, he tended to comment in musical terms – *legato*, *andante*, *piano*, *scherzo* and a rare *fortissimo*. Often he spoke of '*reine Spiel*', pure play.
>   Early in the rehearsal period he told the actors playing Hamm and Clov, 'From the first exchange between the two, maximum hostility must be played. Your war is the nucleus of the play.' And he defined the basis of their conflict: 'Clov has only one wish, to get back into his kitchen, that must always be evident, just like Hamm's constant effort to stop him. This tension is an essential motif for playing.'

And, just as others have remarked that Vladimir and Estragon in *Waiting for Godot* form a quasi-conjugal couple, Beckett compared the Hamm–Clov relationship to a marriage in which the two participants are incapable of deciding whether to stay together or to part.

Another point he made to the actors was that 'there are no accidents in *Endgame*: everything is built on analogy and repetition'. (Again, the same thing is true of *Waiting for Godot*.) In this one-act play, analogy and repetition supply the symmetry – two couples, two windows, two sheets, two dustbins:

> Such pairs nourish paired motions. In the opening mime Clov is similarly clumsy at each window. He draws each window-curtain with the same jangle, away from the audience. He removes each sheet with the same jerky motion, and he does not fold the sheets as specified in the text [*CDW*, pp. 92–3], but drags them to his kitchen. He lifts each dustbin lid with the same clatter. Likewise in his opening and closing soliloquies Hamm folds and unfolds his handkerchief with the same four limited, symmetrical movements. Nagg and Nell emerge from their respective dustbins, lids raised to precisely the same height; they never turn their heads, and their eyes rarely blink. Nagg lifts his hand identically to rap twice on Nell's lid, and Hamm makes a similar gesture when he knocks at the hollow back wall. In his recollection of the painter-engraver, Hamm points to the landward window after speaking of corn, and in a mirror-gesture looks to the seaward window after mentioning the herring-fleet [*CDW*, p. 113]. At each window Clov looks through the telescope in the same way, and in the final tableau, the four characters occupy the same position as in the opening tableau, props on the floor. During a late rehearsal, Beckett wondered whether there wasn't too much symmetry, but he kept it all.

Likewise, Cohn goes on, when characters repeat their own words or those of other people, Beckett wanted such repetitions to be spoken identically; he even added extra verbal repeats to the German text; and although under his direction the play went at a smart pace, 'he asked the actors for disjunction between gesture and word: they were first to assume an attitude, and then speak the lines; the macabre humour of the effect was disturbing as though they *could* not move and speak simultaneously'.

In agreeing the set with Matias and in deciding on the costumes, Beckett chose grey tones throughout, in defiance (where the faces and handkerchief were concerned) of what he had himself specified in the published text (*CDW*, p. 92–3):

> The dustbins were grey-black, and their colour blended into the lighter grey walls of the rectangular shelter. Grey curtains shaded small rectangular windows cut into the sidewalls. Hamm wore dark grey and Clov light grey. The red-and-white faces of the published text were monochromed to grey-white, and the handkerchief lost its bloodstains. Cold light, unchanged throughout, shone on door, chair and dustbins.

Similarly, in his 1969 production of *Krapp's Last Tape* in Berlin, Beckett eliminated as a distraction Krapp's clown make-up, and dressed him in shabby rather than comical clothes. While once again separating speech from motion, this time he moved Krapp towards pathos, whereas in *Endgame* the effect had been 'lugubriously comic' until very near the end.

The changes that Beckett made to *Krapp's Last Tape* for his Berlin production subsequently became more or less definitive so far as he was concerned. They were nearly all incorporated, and further refined, in productions he was involved in after 1969, chiefly a 1972 BBC2 television broadcast of the Magee performance, the Paris staging of 1975 in which Pierre Chabert played Krapp, and a 1977 production in which Rick Cluchey took the title role. This was notable for a piece of serendipity, as Ruby Cohn recalls: 'Late in rehearsals Beckett changed Cluchey's listening position. As a result the light now fell in such a way that the metallic rotating tape was reflected on Cluchey's left cheek – a kind of shadow pulse. The technical staff conferred on how to eliminate it, but Beckett told them softly, "I love it"' (*OB*, pp. 291–307). So in this instance too (as I have often had occasion to remark) Beckett accepted and indeed welcomed developments that could not possibly have been foreseen at the outset.

While the Berlin *Krapp* was in rehearsal he was approached by WDR, the Cologne broadcasting station, about a television version of the production. He obliged, and the performance was shown on 28 October 1969. For the director's benefit he wrote detailed suggestions that articulate his attitude to the problem of recording a preconceived stage production for television, but to us they are chiefly interesting for what they leave out rather than for what they contain. Clas Zilliacus, who first published them, explains:

> The ruling principle of Beckett's camera script is elucidative. In being transferred to television, the play as made for the stage is to be clarified. This is effected by switching from one camera to the other, by varying image and distance, and by exploiting a gamut that ranges from fierce motion to sudden immobility. By these means, the syntax of the play is brought out, and a system of italicisation is superimposed on the events as staged. While Beckett's television suggestions are most obliging towards the viewing public, the most striking thing about his script is that which it does not do, that which it refrains from doing. By transferring the play to television, opportunities to move freely in time and space are acquired. This would seem to call naturally for flashbacks, of the punt scene in particular. But no additional material is accepted. Just as *Eh Joe* refrained from visual illustration of stimuli listened to, showing us only their listener, the TV *Krapp* refuses to venture visually beyond the present in which the story unfolds.

Zilliacus thinks that it is perhaps not too far-fetched to trace one cause that motivated Beckett to write his suggestions for a TV *Krapp* as far back as 1963. On 13 November of that year the BBC presented its first teleproduction of the work. Cyril Cusack acted in this version, which was directed by Penelope Fitzgerald. The most interesting aspect of it, from the present point of view, was the flashbacks (consisting of scenes from Krapp's past appearing on the wall), which Fitzgerald and her story editor Harry Moore devised in order to pad out the play. Reviewers were on the whole unimpressed by what one called 'these would-be atmospheric inserts' (the word he used to describe them was 'disastrous'), while another argued that Beckett's playtexts in general 'simply do not work if they are unduly tinkered with', as *Krapp's Last Tape* was in this 'wilful' attempt to make the play 'tele-visual'. 'Conceivably,' Zilliacus concludes, 'Beckett's interest in writing his own TV suggestions was prompted in part by a desire to make it clear that a TV presentation did not presuppose visual extras' (Zilliacus, 1976, pp. 203–8).

Beckett's next foray into directing, the landmark production of *Waiting for Godot*, opened at the Schiller Theater in Berlin on 8 March 1975 and was seen in London in April of the following year. German television made a videotape of it, and his two manuscript production notebooks are now in the Samuel Beckett Archive at Reading University, so we have a complete record of this truly historic theatrical event. As usual Beckett took great pains over his preparations for the occasion. He amended and corrected the German text quite extensively, making it more colloquial and according greater emphasis to the network of motif words, and in the Reading notebooks he gives minute descriptions, illustrated by diagrams, of stage movements (such as specifying that in Act Two Lucky's cord should be much shorter than in Act One, with the amusing result that when the blind Pozzo follows close behind, he knocks into his servant and tumbles to the ground). In ways like these Beckett's annotations amount to a thorough and minute design of the play, even specifying, for instance, that Pozzo should not be completely bald but, like a circus clown, should have a funny tuft of hair on the back of his head. They reveal, too, a strong interest in stage lighting and in the principal props (the stone – which supersedes the 'low mound' of the printed text [*CDW* p. 11] – and the tree), as well as in pattern, shape and the recurrence of themes such as the sky, doubt, reminiscence and sleepiness. And verbal repetitions, of which naturally there are many, find themselves reflected in similar repetitions of physical movements. For example, when Pozzo in Act One lights his pipe, takes a puff and says '*Ah! Jetzt geht's mir besser*' ('Ah! That's better', *CDW*, p. 27), he is echoed a few minutes later by Estragon, having gnawed the discarded chicken bones, burping heavily (an addition not to be found in the printed text), and uttering exactly the same words. This is all the more pointedly comic, of course, because Estragon, unlike Pozzo, has not had the benefit of a full meal.

Estragon and Vladimir's close relationship is stressed throughout, for instance by their whispering in unison, '*Wollen Sie ihn loswerden?*' ('You want to get rid of him?', *CDW* p. 31) from their shared position left, or by their superbly choreographed saunter arm-in-arm down imaginary boulevards as they exchange thoughts about Godot's need to consult his agents, his correspondents, his books and his bank account before taking a decision (*CDW*, p. 20); this is deftly paralleled in Act Two when Vladimir says, 'Let us not waste our time in idle discourse!' (*CDW*, p. 74) and, taking Estragon's arm, walks him round the stage. The closeness of their relationship was reflected not only in the intimacy revealed by exchanged glances, but even in the costumes they wore: Estragon had on a blue-grey jacket with black trousers in Act One and the opposite (black jacket and blue-grey trousers) in Act Two, while Vladimir's dress was identical but exactly the reverse of Estragon's in both acts, as if to underline the fact that they are inseparable. Likewise, the backs of both men's hands were stained dark, as if with the accumulated grime of the ditches and barns they had to sleep in. Nevertheless the two are different, and this was shown in innumerable details, not least the fact that Estragon walked splay-footed whereas Vladimir's toes pointed inwards.

Beckett had seen Klaus Herm (b. 1926) play Lucky in Deryk Mendel's 1965 production in Berlin, and wanted him to take the same part in his own 1975 staging. They then went on to work together on German versions of *That Time* (1976), *Ghost Trio* and *... but the clouds ...* (both 1977), and *Play* (1978). Herm's Lucky differed from most other interpretations of the role in that, with Beckett's approval, the monologue was delivered more slowly and comprehensibly than is usually the case. This, Herm later explained, was 'because Lucky wants to express himself clearly. This is his desperate attempt, now that he is *obliged* to talk: to clear something up. And when one wants to put a thing especially clearly, one invariably ends up rambling without end. So he's always trying to reorganise, to concentrate on the next point, and his aphorisms overwhelm him: he's overrun by them' (*BiP*, p. 201). It is interesting to have it confirmed by Herm that – as I have always argued – Beckett never intended Lucky's speech to be incomprehensible gibberish: Lucky is trying to say something coherent, but like a stroke victim making a slow recovery, he is finding it very difficult, and after a while his companions cannot bear it any longer, so they jump on him to silence him (*CDW*, pp. 42–4).

This much-discussed production of *Waiting for Godot* by the man who wrote it was effectively a re-creation of a (by then) extremely well-known play that had first been put on some twenty years earlier in Paris by Roger Blin, in London by Peter Hall and in the United States by Alan Schneider. When it came to *Footfalls*, however, Beckett's production at the Royal Court in 1976 was the world première: this time, therefore, he started with a clean slate, and there were no precedents either to follow or to avoid. In the play, written for the voice of an unseen actress in the upstage darkness and a figure, May, who paces back and forth across a specified area of ground throughout the performance, Beckett asks for a bare stage dimly lit with the strongest light at floor level (*CDW*, p. 399). In his production Rose Hill took the role of Voice and Billie Whitelaw that of May; the designer was Jocelyn Herbert, who recalls:

In *Footfalls* the swishing noise of May's dress was very important, so I made a taffeta petticoat. After that, I went to the Portobello Road market and bought a very old lace evening dress with long sleeves and a lot of lacy net curtains which I dyed different greys and shredded. I took the sleeves off the dress, leaving a bit at the top to rag, and gradually imposed torn bits of net in layers on top. Originally the shoes were meant to be noisy, but in the end we left it as just the swishing of petticoats.

When I was talking to Sam Beckett about what the character was like he kept crossing his arms over his chest and saying, 'I think she'd be like this, she'd be shrinking back into herself and hiding away.' He asked Billie Whitelaw to incorporate that gesture in her performance, and move her arms from elbow to shoulder in three stages as the play progressed.

(*JH*, p. 92)

Three years later, in 1979, Beckett was back at the Royal Court directing Billie Whitelaw, this time in a revival of *Happy Days*, which he had first staged at the Schiller Theater in Berlin in 1971. For Jocelyn Herbert it was the second time, too: she had designed George Devine's 1962 Royal Court production. Here is how she describes working with the author-director:

The second time I did *Happy Days* the mound was more elaborate and layered. I think Sam Beckett had changed his attitude to the mound too and thought we should have it more broken up with bits coming off it. It's important that the set provides a complete void and gives the impression of unremitting heat. If the mound for the first production was too simple, this one was too elaborate. Sam decided that the parasol should only smoulder and go black rather than go up in flames as it did before, and that was rather more difficult to organise. It was always a terror to know whether it was going to work or not.

(*JH*, p. 55)

By now Beckett was seventy-three years old, and the strain involved in directing his own work was beginning to tell, as he revealed in an interview with Cathy Courtney, the editor of Jocelyn Herbert's *Theatre Workbook*: 'I remember shocking Jocelyn when we did *Happy Days* with Billie Whitelaw. Billie was wonderful as usual, but it is a terribly difficult play and in one rehearsal I said, "I'm beginning to hate this play." I felt I couldn't bear the text any more. Jocelyn reproached me for saying that in front of Billie' (*JH*, p. 55).

After that, his role, at least where stage plays was concerned, was largely advisory, as in the theatrical version of the prose work *Company*, which Stanley Gontarski prepared in 1984 with his 'permission, encouragement, cooperation and participation' (*BD*, p. 45) for performance at the Los Angeles Actors' Theatre in February 1985. *Company*, Gontarski explains,

> is divided between a series of more or less autobiographical vignettes in the second person and the fictive musings of a hypothesising voice in the third person. Almost all the incidents that the second person relates are potentially painful. They suggest a loveless childhood in which the boy was rebuked or derided by his parents for his comments on the perception of the sky or for his report of being able to see the mountains of Wales from his 'nook in the gorse' in the Wicklow Hills of Ireland. There is the lovelessness of parents 'stooping over cradle', the lack of parental concern for a child in such desparate need of attention that he throws himself from 'the top of a great fir', or the embarrassment of a child's being on exhibition, standing naked at 'tip of the high board' before the 'many eyes' of his father's cronies as he is urged to 'be a brave boy' and dive into the Irish Sea. The child in these 'memories' seems never to have been the boy his parents wanted. This second-person voice recounts other embarrassing and naive incidents: a boy who believes he can play God by intervening in the life of an ill

hedgehog, unwittingly causing its death, or a young adult who hints at the disastrous end of a love affair in the closing line 'all dead still'.

'When I was preparing the stage version,' Gontarski goes on, 'Beckett discussed the contrapuntal, fugal nature of these two voices.' (As was his wont, he thought in musical terms.) The third-person voice, the author noted, was

> 'erecting a series of hypotheses, each of which is false'. The second-person voice was 'trying to create a history, a past for the third person'. The third person resists the intrusions of the second person for numerous reasons. The memories are, of course, painful for the most part, but 'he' also resists the simplified notion that a sum of memories (or stories) will add up to a history, a life. And even if the second-person voice recounts incidents from the past more or less accurately, memories are not historical but fictive: selected, reordered, reemphasised versions of past incidents.
>
> (OB, pp. 8–9)

This is what Beckett wanted brought out in the stage adaptation. The parallels with his reading of *Krapp's Last Tape* are striking, and hardly likely to have been fortuitous.

In 1986 the world marked his eightieth birthday, even if he, in common with his Krapp, did not feel much enthusiasm for celebrating 'the awful occasion' (*CDW*, p. 217). He did, however, give the seal of his approval to BBC Radio 3's idea of devoting the day to repeats of *All That Fall*, *Embers* and *Rough for Radio* and to a radio adaptation of *A Piece of Monologue*. Asked to nominate an actor for the monologue (which begins memorably – and in the circumstances, appropriately – with the words 'Birth was the death of him', *CDW*, p. 425), Beckett chose Ronald Pickup, whose performances in *Play*, *Ghost Trio* and *. . . but the clouds . . .* had greatly impressed him.

After that, 'Little is left to tell' (*CDW*, p. 445). Beckett died a few months before his eighty-fourth birthday, having secured a unique place in the history of Western theatre, not only as a writer of plays, but also as an inspirational director of those plays. We shall not see his like again.

Collaboration and Resistance

This chapter is in two parts. The first deals with the many thea-tre people who have worked with Beckett and/or who have sought to follow both the letter and the spirit of his dramatic texts. The second covers a smaller category, but not by any means an insignificant one: those who took an independent line with both the man and his works.

Survey of interviews with, and comments by, Beckett's collaborators

Peggy Ashcroft (1907–91)

Dame Peggy was by far the best-known British actress to have worked with Beckett. The highlight of her long and distin-guished career on stage and screen was perhaps her perfor-mance as Desdemona in 1930, when she was cast opposite the great black singer, actor and civil-rights campaigner Paul Robeson (1898–1976), who played Othello and with whom she had an affair, proving, in that more conventional era, that she was no docile conformist.

In 1962 she was considered for the role of Winnie in the London première of *Happy Days* but, according to James Knowlson, George Devine 'did not consider her right for the part' (*DF*, p. 499). Knowing Beckett as well as he did – and particularly how stubborn the playwright could be – Devine was probably not mistaken in that view. For the revival at the National Theatre in 1975 she was the choice of the director Peter Hall, but (Knowlson recalls, *DF*, p. 604), there was a clash of personalities between Beckett – who came over from

Paris for the occasion – and Dame Peggy. Although he liked and admired her, he was annoyed by 'her reluctance to give herself up to an emotion-free reading of the part', and she was unwilling to give way on this, because (as she later told Michael Billington) she felt that she needed to find the 'absolute reality' of the character. As we know well enough by now, Beckett did not take kindly to actors who wanted to get under the skin of his characters: he just wanted them to play the parts as impersonally as possible. Anthony Cronin puts it more bluntly, recalling how Harold Pinter once assured Beckett that, when it came to delivering the closing lines in his own play *Landscape*, Peggy Ashcroft could be trusted to 'get it right'. Beckett would have none of this:

> Such an attitude was anathema to him. He simply did not trust actors to get it right. For all his gratitude to and occasional enthusiasm for actors, Beckett felt that both directors and actors were an unfortunate necessity and that the ideal dramatic executant would be one totally subservient to the author's ideas about production and prepared to abandon his or her personality and character in favour of the text. The ideal actor would be, as a person, invisible.
>
> (Cronin, 1996, p. 525)

No wonder, then, that such a highly esteemed and experienced actress as Dame Peggy is reported as having 'disagreed vociferously' (*BD*, p. 13) with what she was being asked to do by Beckett in *Happy Days*. She largely got her own way, however, notably over her wish to adopt an Irish accent. He did not approve of this, but she insisted, on the grounds that it enabled her to speak the words with the rhythms in which she felt they had originally been conceived. 'I know what Winnie's voice sounds like,' she told him: 'like you' (*WiB*, p. 12).

When she described their association later she expressed herself tactfully – or was she simply, like Winnie, putting a brave face on things? – in putting her side of the story in an interview with Katharine Worth:

Have I enjoyed performing and reading from Beckett's work? Oh yes, it has been a very great experience to be involved with writing of such quality. I respond very strongly to the rhythm and I love the humour. Playing Winnie in *Happy Days* was a major event for me. I had always wanted to play the part; in fact, I was slightly miffed that George Devine didn't ask me to do it when he directed the play at the Royal Court Theatre, the first British production. I learned later that he had thought I wouldn't want to. So I was happy when the opportunity came my way later, with Peter Hall's production at the National Theatre. Winnie is one of those parts, I believe, that actresses will want to play in the way that actors aim at Hamlet: a 'summit' part.

Beckett himself took an interest in the production, coming over from Paris to see the rehearsals. I'm not sure if he altogether approved of my interpretation. He might have thought it too 'humanised'. When he directed Billie Whitelaw in the part, he gave the rhythmic structure priority. I couldn't have worked on the 'metronome' principle, though of course Billie achieved wonders. I was always, of course, very conscious of the rhythm, and let it carry me along to some extent. But I felt the need to work in terms of character: *why* did Winnie use certain rhythms, what did it tell about her? Beckett would answer questions like 'Why does she gabble as she does at a certain point?' by saying 'Because it has to go fast there.' The emphasis was really musical in his approach, though obviously he has created characters which have an extraordinarily strong life of their own.

Incidentally, after the production moved to Canada there was a frightful moment when I cut five pages and had to find my way back; not easy, with so much repetition in the text. I knew I had to get to the revolver, establish its presence: somehow I managed it and was able to go on. So the revolver was my lifeline on that occasion!

I couldn't play *Happy Days* again. But it is one of my most intense theatre memories. There's no doubt that

Beckett has a strong appeal for actors, if once they sense the style, the tune of his writing.

(*WiB*, pp. 11–14)

Whatever the author thought of this production, Irving Wardle – always a perceptive critic – liked it, noting that in Peter Hall's version the revolver 'takes on a much more explicit meaning: where the other objects stand for habitual, unnoticed actions, the revolver implies the possibility of a conscious and unrepeatable act', that is, murder or suicide. 'The crucial question facing any Beckett actor', he went on,

is the degree of self-consciousness that he or she can allow the character. I have seen Winnie played as a bovine, matter-of-fact lady who really does seem to be having a happy time, surrounded with all her favourite things. Neither that, nor Madeleine Renaud's Racine-like lyricism, is the approach favoured by Peggy Ashcroft and Peter Hall. Their method is to stretch to the limit the distance Winnie travels during the play.

In the first act, Dame Peggy plays her as if anaesthetised by habit. She seems almost rich, with all those playthings, plus her expanding parasol, and converses cheefully with Willie's back like a housewife out for a day on the beach. Sometimes her mood darkens, and her mouth sets in a thin crooked line, but she can always recover her spirits for another radiant burst of thanksgiving to the merciful Creator who has sadistically buried her up to her waist in the mound. Even when she comes to echoing references to 'the old style', she pronounces them with gentle wistfulness; and her delivery is full of Ashcroft music: she floats sentences off into the air with a soaring lift at the end. With the second act, robbed of her habit-sustaining props, she reappears as an immobilised head with eyes trying to burst out of their sockets. The face, still framed in a tasselled straw hat, is barely recognisable. And when she speaks, it is with a continuous undertone of terror that the words may run out.

Were that to happen, Wardle says, the silence that is an ever-present threat where the Beckettian hero is concerned would engulf Winnie also, an outcome she wants at all costs to avoid.

As we have seen, this critic was particularly impressed by the way the relevance of the revolver was brought out in this production, and he concludes:

> When Dame Peggy launches into Winnie's long-delayed song, it is not delicately pathetic [as in the original *Merry Widow*, Franz Lehár's famous operetta of 1905], but harsh and out of tune. Willie, in the attitude of a suitor, goes crawling up the mound. 'Is it me you're after, Willie . . . or is it something else?' [*CDW*, p. 167]. The revolver is almost in his grasp; but the curtain falls before she finds out. The ambiguity of the play remains intact; but it has acquired a fearsome new cutting edge.
>
> (*The Times*, 15 March 1975, p. 11)

The relevance, from the present point of view, of the staging of the Hall–Ashcroft *Happy Days* is that it shows how, despite his reputation for intransigence, the author by no means always got his own way. Theatre is, after all, a matter of give and take: it is rare for any single person involved in a production to be able to make all the decisions regardless of the views of others. Everyone has to be prepared to compromise, and Beckett, faced with a talent as impressive (and a personality as formidable) as Peggy Ashcroft's, was no exception. No wonder he left London before the end of rehearsals. Knowlson tells us (*DF*, p. 604) that he did so out of irritation; but what Dame Peggy (perhaps like Winnie, as I say, looking on the bright side) concluded was, 'I suppose he must have been reasonably pleased with what we were doing: he left it to us in the end' (*WiB*, p. 12). The account in Peter Hall's diaries, too, is upbeat:

> Exciting to be working with an absolute genius. Sam continuing to talk us through the text, giving meticulous physical and verbal instructions. It sounds beautiful, balanced,

rhythmic, incantatory, in Sam's gentle Anglo-Irish brogue. To hear him say the lines is to understand their texture. 'All true grace is economical,' he observed.

But the same problem kept emerging – unless Peggy is allowed to feel it all very strongly, she will never know what she is hiding. But the slightest sign of feeling disturbs Sam, and he speaks of his need for monotony, paleness, weakness. This is where, unlike Harold Pinter, he is not finally a theatre worker, great director though he can be. He confuses the work process with the result. But an actor takes weeks of work to explore and then realise a few minutes of text.

(*PHD*, pp. 124–7)

Hall's diaries make it clear that in the personality clash with Beckett, Dame Peggy was not blameless. She could be 'very obstinate' with Hall himself, who for his part suspected her of becoming tearful as a way of getting a director 'off her back'. Still, even if she could be manipulative, come the first night, like a true pro, she 'rose magnificently to the occasion' and 'acted with fluency and precision' (*PHD*, pp. 131–2).

Walter Asmus (b. 1941)

At the Schiller Theater in Berlin Walter D. Asmus was assigned to work with Beckett on his production of *Waiting for Godot*, and with the author's support and encouragement subsequently staged it himself in the United States. In 1984, in association with the San Quentin Drama Workshop, he took the play on an Australian tour. He next directed it in Dublin, first in 1988, and then in 1991, touring the States with this production too. His major contribution, from the present point of view, lies firstly in the diary that he kept during the 1975 Schiller Theater rehearsals of the play and that contains the author's invaluable analysis of Lucky's speech (*OB*, pp. 280–90), secondly in notes compiled the following year during preparations, again at the Schiller Theater, for *That Time* and *Footfalls* (*OB*, pp. 335–49), and thirdly in descriptions of Beckett's work on German productions of *Play* and *What Where* (in *Theater Heute*, December 1978 and April 1986). He has also given interviews about his association with Beckett, including one in 1987 while the author was still alive to Jonathan Kalb, and another in 1992 after his death to Lois Oppenheim.

In the first, Kalb began by asking Asmus what, in general, Beckett expected of his assistant director at rehearsals:

ASMUS: With *Godot*, not very much. At the beginning there was for me a feeling of being overawed, but by and by it became a normal working relationship, that is to say we developed a mutual respect and got to know one another better and better. And there grew up between us a sort of truthfulness where he knows that he can rely on me and I know that I can rely on him.

KALB: *You once commented that there was no discussion of psychology in his rehearsals. How then did the actors resolve their need for motivation?*
ASMUS: He gave them images for understanding their relationships. For example, Gogo belongs to the stone and Didi to the tree. That means they are connected, and at the same time there is always the tendency to go apart. He used this image of the rubber band: they pull together by means of a rubber band and tear apart again, and so on – which makes sense if you have to make crossings onstage.

What did he want to achieve with the clown-like costumes in Godot? Didi wore striped trousers and a black jacket too small for him, and Gogo wore black trousers and striped jacket too large for him, then they switched during the interval.
That has to do with the close connection between the two characters: being the same and not the same. It doesn't fit and at the same time it does. It was a stylised thing.

How did these actors develop what they needed in terms of a human relationship? Did they perhaps make use of a friendship that existed beforehand?

Yes, in the Schiller Theater *Godot* at least, Gogo [Horst Bollman] and Didi [Stefan Wigger] had their own friendship. And they played these games in private, too. You know, all the ping-pong, ball-throwing and teasing between them – they did that. Being colleagues for decades, they had this personal relationship, and also a feeling for irony and sarcasm. They knew exactly when they were hurting one another while pinching, torturing and teasing in private, too.

The actors would not have been as accepting with another director, so why with Beckett?
I'd say they loved him as a person. But of course it had also to do with Bollmann [Estragon] having worked with Beckett before on *Endgame*, and both he and Wigger [Vladimir] knowing *Godot* very well, having done it ten years before. And it is no secret that Beckett has had greater difficulties with other actors. In *Footfalls*, for example, the actress Hildegard Schmahl had a very difficult time. There was a strange relationship between the two. She adored him as a man, I would say, as a woman adores a man – of course I don't know any woman who doesn't. So it was really a love thing, and it was all the more frustrating for her not to fulfil his obvious demands, which he had as a director. She wanted to fulfil all the things that she sensed he wanted, but up to the very last rehearsal she used to break down in tears and would have to give up. But she found her way in the end, she succeeded somehow, she is a great actress.

(*BiP*, pp. 173–84)

In the second interview, with Lois Oppenheim, Walter Asmus had more to say about his own productions, staged in the manner of Beckett, after his death, respecting as far as possible the spirit of the author's direction. Of course things had to be different, if only, Asmus said, because 'for most actors who worked with him Beckett was the absolute authority. They took the trouble to find out themselves what his line readings meant for the character they played. Or they understood intuitively. Billie Whitelaw, for example, did. She claims to have been his medium, and I believe she was.'

OPPENHEIM: *Of all that you must have gained as an independent director from working as Beckett's assistant, what would you say remains the most significant for you today? What did you learn most from working with him?*
ASMUS: To strive for precision. To strive for simplicity. In both you find a lot of truth. To encourage actors to be simple with their means, to trust simplicity, to dare *not* to act. To act concrete and functional. Art is reduction. Most of all I think I learnt – as he famously put it – to 'fail better'.

Why do you use the word 'choreography' in connection with Beckett's plays?
Because Beckett himself, when directing *Godot* in Berlin, used the word 'balletic' in the context of the actors' movements. But I think the words 'balletic' and 'choreography' shouldn't be overvalued. It was not that Beckett wanted them to *move* like ballet dancers. It was simply to express the exactitude, and that there was a design in the blocking that had a meaning. Movements step by step on a line or a word, or a crossing in silence, had to do with the reunification or separation of Estragon and Vladimir, for example, who belong inseparably together. The design of the movement structure tells the story of the relationship of the characters to one another. The 'lessness' of Beckett's later plays caused him to shape the earlier ones more strictly, especially *Godot*, which he regarded as disorderly. But *Endgame* and *Krapp* also. His development as an artist is certainly to be seen in the way he treated his own earlier plays while directing them. He got rid of a lot of redundancies.

Have you worked with other than a proscenium stage? Can you envision doing Beckett in some non-traditional space, such as in a factory?
I could. I haven't.

You wouldn't be adverse to that?
No, not at all, especially with the later plays.

Did you ever violently disagree with Beckett?
No. I saw his vision. That's why we got on so well. Once or
twice I did get a sneering remark, but that was his way of dealing with matters at times.

(*DB*, pp. 40–47)

Roger Blin (1907–84)

The first and most famous of all Beckett's directors, Roger Blin
gave several interviews. As early as 1950, when he was still trying to find a theatre in Paris to put on *Waiting for Godot*, he
declared:

> What is a director? Nothing; he shouldn't be talked about;
> his personality shouldn't exist; he shouldn't seek a style; he
> should be rigorous about rendering the thought of an actor,
> without adding anything. For that matter, authors should
> direct their own works; unfortunately, most of them can't
> do it. In the old days the director was an actor in the com-
> pany who did the blocking; there was no talk about it. I put
> my name as director only because I was asked to, but I
> don't like it. I have no theory, and I try to have no charac-
> teristic style.
>
> (*Arts*, 24 February 1950)

No wonder that Blin was the ideal director from Beckett's point
of view. They got on well from the start; there was between
them, Blin said, '*une solidarité entre maigres*', 'the fellow-feel-
ing of two thin men' (*Arts*, 3 July 1953).

The story of the three-year wait endured by Blin before he
could find a theatre prepared to take the risk of staging *Waiting
for Godot* has been told many times, so I shall not repeat it
here. His account of the actual production is, however, less well
known:

> At the time *Godot* went into rehearsal Beckett did not yet
> have much experience in the theatre, but he already had a
> very precise knowledge of the theatre as spectacle – that is

to say, as an event unfolding on a stage. He did indicate in his text the motion, the timing he desired, but those indications were meant especially for the reader; once on the stage things change. Beckett soon realised on the spot which things were 'intellectual', and accepted my suggestions with good grace. Looking first and foremost for stylised action, he gave his approval whenever adjustments were required for its achievement. For instance, at the end of the first act, to stress the derisory character of the Pozzo–Lucky couple, I made them walk round and round, one dragging the other, as clowns would do in the circus. And again in the second act when Pozzo and Lucky are prostrate and Vladimir discusses with Estragon the possibility of picking them up, they walk around the set while talking and, at the moment of Vladimir's great discourse, they step as if unaware on the bodies of Pozzo and Lucky, the words 'all mankind is us' [*CDW*, p. 74] being accompanied by vigorous steps on Pozzo's back. Beckett accepted these suggestions because here he saw pieces of stage business which were not contrived. The same is true of Lucky's costume: he had originally envisaged the character wearing the uniform of a station porter, but yielded to the way I saw him dressed. He did not yet have the fussy desire for precision he has acquired since, and while following the rehearsals actively, he left the director his share of freedom, as long as he did not impose on him anything he did not approve. As for me, I have always believed that the attitude of the director towards the author must be one of humility, but an active humility.

It is probable that while writing *Godot* Beckett was, as far as his four leading men were concerned, under the influence of the great American comic film actors of the time. For me they were, ideally, Charlie Chaplin for Vladimir, Buster Keaton for Estragon, and Charles Laughton for Pozzo, because Pozzo, a miserable loudmouth, has to be played by a fat man. (All Beckett himself would say was that his characters wore bowler hats.) There is a great deal of Irish sense of humour in Beckett's theatre. For that reason it is a mistake to play *Godot* as a tragedy; for him it was a very active play, a kind of western. It must not be interpreted tearfully; it is not a theatre of tears but of humanity, a 'theatre of cruelty' in Antonin Artaud's sense of the word.

(*BTh*, pp. 68–9)

I myself was extremely fortunate to be able to interview Roger Blin and watch him at work. This was in 1964, when I was studying for my PhD at the University of Toulouse. Here is what I wrote soon afterwards:

Beckett's French director and close friend, Roger Blin, was in Toulouse, in southern France, recently, spending about a month with a local company, Le Grenier de Toulouse, rehearsing *Waiting for Godot*. The group then took it on tour around the sub-prefectures and market towns of Languedoc.

This is the fourth or fifth time he has staged it. Each time he approaches the text afresh, because although he has his own idea of how the play should be performed (an idea worked out in close collaboration with the author), he must inevitably adjust that idea in accordance with differing circumstances and different personalities in his actors. This time, for instance, he had as Pozzo a bulky, slow actor in his sixties, Jean Hort, with a booming voice and a tendency to grunt and gurgle in his throat – the ideal man for the part, as Blin admitted, saying that Hort would be the best Pozzo the French stage had seen. During rehearsals he addresses him formally as '*vous*', whereas he says more familiarly '*tu*' to the other actors, no doubt in deference to Hort's seniority in years and theatrical experience. The others in the cast are Jean Bousquet (Vladimir), Claude Marcan (Estragon), Louis Granville (Lucky), with Michel Boussières as the boy. More than one of them has a perceptible southern twang in his voice, which does not detract from this production, set firmly as it is deep in the French countryside.

The early rehearsals are slack and informal, with Marcan tending to crack feeble jokes that contrast with Blin's smiling manner and preoocupied air. His presence is impressive: tall, gangling even, full of tics and facial twitches, with a tendency to stammer when he speaks, blinking all the time and often rubbing his eyes, but transformed the moment he acts, in order to demonstrate a moment, in order to speak a line. Then, all at once, all the twitching and stuttering goes, his deep, melodious voice breaks out clear and unhurried, his body under complete control. The differences between Blin off-stage and Blin on-stage could not be more striking. He is another man altogether.

His manner of directing actors is strangely detached. He stands watching them sometimes, moving little, infrequently smoking short black cigars that are thin and insubstantial-looking; despite his nervousness, he is no chain-smoker. More often he sits slumped in a chair, with his legs interwoven, his hands dangling, his eyes closed. He intervenes rarely, and when he does, it is only after a preliminary stutter. When he has to interrupt, he prefers going on stage to demonstrate the actions and speak the words himself. I watch him now burping contentedly on his stool as Pozzo, now waddling painfully as Vladimir, now shaking with Lucky's palsy. 'You need to be very fit to play Beckett's decrepits', he tells me, and noticing Bousquet drenched in sweat towards the end of a rehearsal I have to agree with him.

Each time that he demonstrates something, his authority is undeniable; and one sees his familiar production coming to life before one's eyes. Blin has this play in the palm of his hand; he reveals new facets every moment one watches him at work on it. As he teaches Granville to shake and puff and pant like Lucky, a question occurs to me. How did the original Lucky, Jean Martin, come by that frightening but unforgettable ague? He thought it up himself, and adopted it from the start, and neither author nor producer felt any need to ask him to modify it; the only trouble was that it affected him deeply, and he took months to lose the fidgets that prevented him taking other parts after the end of *Godot*'s run. Blin shows Granville how to do it, without of course insisting on an exact imitation; he respects each actor's characteristics. In particular, Granville has not Martin's high-pitched voice verging on a scream, and so Blin lets him deliver the speech at a normal speaking level.

As rehearsals progress, Blin tightens things up, but ever so gradually, with elaborate politeness; always slightly withdrawn, he never orders, only requests, and is never familiar. He is evidently too shy to impose himself or become 'chummy'. Reheasals begin after lunch and last all afternoon, recommencing after a break for dinner; they then go on until midnight. For practical reasons of availability of stage space, the afternoons are given over to working mainly on the text and on enunciation in an empty cinema, with the actors either standing on the narrow stage or reclining in the red plush seats. In the evening, in a large barn-like hall with a big stage at one end and Grenier posters everywhere, actors and director get down to the concrete details of the movements. As the days pass, the initial hesitations are resolved, the untidinesses ironed out. The actors have learned their words, and their movements, even the complicated clown-games demanded of Vladimir and Estragon, are becoming more automatic. The play starts to exert its power. Hort has fully mastered his role as Pozzo, and true to the author's direction is 'suddenly furious' when, in Act II, he rails at the two men for 'tormenting me with your accursed time' – and then his anger subsides, his voice takes on the accents of poetry as he utters the famous words, 'they give birth astride of a grave . . .' [*CDW*, p. 83]. The play, with all its drama and its farce, its pathos and its humour, is ready to take the road, and Blin's work is nearly done. In his free mornings, and even in odd moments during rehearsals, he (unlike the author) is ready to talk to me about himself.

He speaks of his past, of the strong influence Surrealism had on him, of his friendship with the tortured genius Antonin Artaud, an association which lasted from 1928 to the poet's death a couple of decades later; he remained in contact with him throughout the long years which Artaud spent in a mental hospital. Curiously enough, he does not believe that the theatre has been as much affected by Artaud's theories as critics usually maintain, and declares himself to have been more deeply influenced by the writer's lesser-known poetry than by the famous tract *The Theatre and Its Double* (1938), much of which, Blin insists, is unrealisable in normal stage conditions.

(*Modern Drama*, February 1966, pp. 403–8)

Roger Blin's name will for ever be linked to Beckett's great early plays: *Waiting for Godot*, *Endgame* (which is dedicated to him and in which, with more than a sidelong glance at *King Lear*, he gave a landmark performance as Hamm, a part he played almost 300 times), *Krapp's Last Tape*, and *Happy Days* (made all the more memorable by the interpretation of the role of Winnie by his choice for the part, the great actress Madeleine Renaud). He revealed to me in Toulouse, however, that he was a little disturbed by the way Beckett was developing theatrically: he felt that there was less and less scope for the director in the carefully annotated texts that the author was beginning to write. One has only to compare the text of *Godot* with that of *Play* (which was then in production, significantly without Blin at the helm) to see what he meant: the minutely detailed instructions in *Play* would daunt any independent-minded producer. In *Godot*, however, Beckett was much more open to suggestion, even allowing Blin, in one place, to correct a non-idiomatic French phrase which, through an uncharacteristic lapse, had been overlooked.

Blin showed at the Toulouse rehearsals that he too could be flexible. One of the actors suggested that instead of the 'Bye bye bye bye' given by Beckett (*CDW*, p. 65), Vladimir should sing a lullaby of Languedoc in dialect, '*Soun soun soun / Veni veni doun*' ('Come, then, slumber'), in order to send Estragon to sleep in Act Two.

He had several things to say about the author of the play. The cruelty in his work was, he maintained, a form of self-defence against an acute sensibility, and he told how, passing through the wholesale meat market in Paris with Beckett one day, he had noticed how his companion flinched at the sight of animal heads and offal in a cart, and how much the view of spilt blood affected him.

Blin was interviewed in 1975 by Joan Stevens. After asking him to recall the events leading up to the Paris première of *Waiting for Godot* – 'What attracted me to the play, and why I still like it so much,' he told her, 'is its human quality and the humour of the writing' – she wondered about the bowler hats: were they suggested by Laurel and Hardy? Blin replied:

> Yes, and Chaplin, too. And it signified dignity. Also, it was common in Ireland. If you look at photos taken in Ireland even thirty years ago, people wore bowler hats on Sundays. They still do, I'm sure. I saw Pozzo as a kind of lord. For his costume I looked at some English hunting sketches, pictures I'd seen of gentlemen farmers, John Bull types, so that's how he was dressed, in a colourful cape with quite a lot of red in it. I put Lucky in an old red and gold dress coat, the sort of livery footmen used to wear in France, and a knitted sailor cardigan with stripes, and very short black trousers, big shoes, and long hair, as Sam wanted. He was an old valet, an old servant, a miserable creature who was rich once, and he cringed like someone who had long been in the service of an old lord of the manor. I dressed Vladimir, who loves to talk, as a teacher, in a shabby morning coat and crumpled black trousers, with a broken, stiff

collar, a bit of string for a black tie, and then a starched pink shirtfront, which kept riding up, revealing his dirty underwear beneath.

Beckett knew nothing about the theatre. His play is a wonderful piece of theatre, but all his instructions, silences, pauses, and so – he said these were more for the reader. You can't just determine the length of a pause. One silence has to be relative to others. The pauses, the silences, relate to each other. You can't say in advance how long they should be – the director has to determine the pace of the play from the rhythm and, from this pace, incorporate the silences to make them as meaningful as possible. When you're working with actors, I think you should be as relaxed as you can with them.

In *Godot*, the circus element must be implied, not shown. I started from the characters' physical peculiarities. Estragon's feet hurt and stop him sleeping, so he's always tired, he keeps dropping off. And Vladimir, who has prostate trouble, who wants to pee all the time, moves around a lot; he can't stand still. Pozzo is fat, with a swollen heart; he's breathless, and he's carried along by his stomach. Lucky represents a kind of wicked senility. He is the most evil. He's a kind of scapegoat, and he gets his revenge: there is a build-up of hatred throughout the play, and he unburdens himself in the end, through words, in a speech that is actually very clear, though it's broken up, like a puzzle. From the first rehearsal Jean Martin started to play the role shaking; he managed to clench his legs and his feet and to tremble naturally. I didn't ask him to do it. I hadn't seen it like that, but when I saw him do it, and do it so well, for me he gave the play its truly cruel dimension which it might not have had without that. Yes, it is cruel: Lucky's trembling counterbalances, in relation to the audience, to the balance of the play, the possible sentimentality of the other actors. I ask my performers, because they are also clowns, to be careful not to be overly sentimental.

155

They must not burst into tears. And you must not play the second act as though it's the end of the play. It's not the end of the play.

For *Happy Days* the designer Matias produced something really good, because if you want to give the impression of all that weight – the sky, the heat – it would be a mistake to have a blue sky. He decided on a completely orange sky, which gets lighter, violently so, at its highest point, and which fades, bit by bit, until it becomes a kind of greyish pink around the actress and her mound. And the ground is a mixture of oranges and browns, too. That makes the audience – should it be tempted to look elsewhere, to look up at the sky – upset by this orange, and it forces it to look back again at this point, at this little head, which had so much presence that it might as well have been nine feet high. Each member of the audience was forced to sort of zoom in on her. It's a horrible and yet a marvellous play.

I did not take the part of Krapp in *Krapp's Last Tape* because I was tired, and a bit frightened of all the old men in Beckett's drama that I had had to play. I think he was a bit annoyed with me because I didn't do it. It's probably the work that moves me least. Maybe it's the sentimental side of the play that I don't like.

In fact Blin told me in Toulouse that his favourite Beckett work was the relatively little-known radio play *Embers*; I thought this somewhat perverse at the time, and I still do.

It is clear from interviews with Roger Blin that, while he and Beckett never had major disagreements, all was not unmitigated sweetness and light between them. It is common knowledge, for instance, that the author was much more self-assertive over *Endgame*, but Blin did not always let him have his own way. He told Joan Stevens that 'he made us start the play far too loudly by shouting "Clov" several times': 'It was too much. Consequently, after three or four days I felt we shouldn't overdo it, that the main interest of a play is to reach an extraordinary intensity, that this intensity must not reach its high point at the outset. If you bring it out too much at the start, you risk saturation and boredom' (*DB*, pp. 301–14). I can confirm this. As I have said, I managed to get a ticket for the première at the Royal Court Theatre and was a member of that first-night audience on 3 April 1957. The effect was indeed oppressive: Blin was right to insist on toning it down in later performances. In another interview he revealed that the *King Lear* aspect was his idea; Beckett was not able to veto it at the time, but he made changes as soon as he could:

> *Endgame* is for me a tragic play, but Beckett denies this. I saw in it the theme of the death of kings. I deliberately slanted it towards *King Lear*. From the set designer I requested for Hamm an armchair evoking a Gothic cathedral, a dressing-gown of crimson velvet trimmed with fur, and a gaff like a sceptre. Whatever was regal in the text, imperious in the character, was taken as Shakespearean.

When the production moved from London to Paris, however, the regal aspects of the set and costumes were played down at Beckett's insistence. A worn coat replaced the velvet robe, and the throne-like chair was changed to a simple wooden one on wheels (*BTh*, pp. 169–71).

When Blin directed the French première of *Krapp's Last Tape* in 1960, his background in radio enabled him to come up with a rather nice touch, as he told James Knowlson in an interview recorded a couple of decades later:

> My own innovation was – I don't know whether Sam liked it or not – that at a certain point, as Krapp is searching for the story of the girl in the punt and goes back on the tape, I got the actor to do this manually. He turned the tape backwards with his fingers and so the sound was backwards too. I've done a lot of radio, and during the editing sessions when you go backwards it makes a sort of sound *ooo-ooo-*

ooo-oh, so that as Krapp goes backwards, he can tell by listening to the sound where he's got to, ready to start it
again. I found it quite moving that he searches, using his
fingers, with the sound backwards – as I've done with radio
tapes.

(*KLTWb*, p. 66)

Barbara Bray (b. 1924)

In the present context, Barbara Bray is significant on two
counts. She was associated professionally with Beckett in the
late 1950s when she was Script Editor in the Drama
Department of BBC Radio and responsible, along with Donald
McWhinnie, for revitalizing the stage-oriented routine of the
department by bringing into radio such writers as Pinter, Giles
Cooper, Robert Bolt and, of course, Beckett himself. Not long
afterwards she began an intimate relationship with him that
lasted until his death, despite occasional infidelities on his part,
and notwithstanding the fact that he went ahead with his plan
to marry his long-term partner Suzanne Deschevaux-Dumesnil
in order to provide for her financially should he die before she
did. Beckett's divided loyalties between Suzanne, to whom he
felt he owed everything – particularly his literary success – and
the younger Barbara, with whom he got on much better, lie
behind the half-comic, half-tragic sufferings of the trio in *Play*.
With coarse humour and sardonic wit – 'Adulterers, take warn-
ing, never admit' (*CDW*, p. 310) is a typically acute (and
astute) comment – a weak, indecisive man (M) is shown as incapable of either leaving his wife (W1) or dropping his mistress
(W2):

W2 One morning as I was sitting stitching by the open window she burst in and flew at me. Give him up, she
screamed, he's mine. Her photographs were kind to her.
Seeing her now for the first time full length in the flesh I
understood why he preferred me.
[*Spot from* W2 *to* M]

M We were not long together when she smelled the rat. Give up
   that whore, she said, or I'll cut my throat – [*Hiccup.*] pardon
   – so help me God. I knew she could have no proof. So I told
   her I did not know what she was talking about.
[*Spot from* M *to* W2]
W2 What are you talking about? I said, stitching away.
   Someone yours? Give up whom? I smell you off him, she
   screamed, he stinks of bitch.
[*Spot from* W2 *to* W1]
W1 Though I had him dogged for months by a first-rate man,
   no shadow of proof was forthcoming. And there was no
   denying he continued as . . . assiduous as ever. This, and his
   horror of the merely Platonic thing, made me sometimes
   wonder if I were not accusing him unjustly.

   (*CDW*, p. 308)

In the light of what we now know about the Beckett–Bray
love affair, the press-cuttings of the period make intriguing
reading. In the *Observer* of 28 May 1961 the widowed Mrs
Bray reported from Paris, where she had moved with her
daughters: 'Beckett has just completed a new play' (this was
Happy Days). On 26 November of the same year, she reviewed
an exhibition by the Dutch painter Bram van Velde, whom
Beckett had championed for decades, and her somewhat
opaque language – 'There is another kind of writing that never
appeared on any wall, and this graver meaning, which has
nothing to do with semantics, fills the work of Bram van Velde'
– sounds as if it could have come from conversations with him;
it certainly bears an uncanny resemblance to the manner in
which he expresses his enthusiasm in his own writings on the
painter. The most poignant *Observer* piece, however, is her
review of *Play*, which she describes as 'one of the most remarkable works of Samuel Beckett':

The story itself is superficially the most banal tale imaginable:
a triangle – man, wife and mistress – which comes to grief.
And not only is the basic situation itself abysmally conven-

tional and trite, but Beckett does everything possible to render it ludicrous in its details. All three characters are ordinary, mediocre, lamentable: in short, painfully familiar. The man, scooting breathlessly back and forth between the two women, is perhaps the worst of the bunch: all need and weakness and feeble, if amiable, duplicity. This intentionally commonplace and in current terms despicable material Beckett transmutes into an astonishing, hilarious and moving experience. The most ingenious and complex irony is extracted from this triple counterpoint. Of all Beckett's works so far, this is the one which most openly approaches the everyday experience of any audience, yet at the same time makes the fewest concessions. The language is of classic simplicity – a single touch gives tragic resonance to the ridiculous: 'He went on and on. I could hear a mower' (*CDW*, p. 310). Beckett's inventiveness, formal mastery and poetic power are now so rich and intense that these three suffering heads conjure up not only three whole lives, but also awaken the reverberations that transform them from the trivial to the universal. Here are people in all their funny, disgraceful, pitiable fragility, and all the touchingness, in spite of everything, of their efforts to love one another, and endure.

(*Observer*, 16 June 1963, p. 29)

This is criticism of a high order – all the more impressive for being, as we now know, uncomfortably close to home.

Bray was interviewed by Randolph Goodman for his book *From Script to Stage* (1971) on the subject of her production of Beckett's adaptation of Pinget's play *The Old Tune*, broadcast by the BBC Third Programme on 23 August 1960. 'The characters are beautifully observed,' she said, 'and for all their seriousness are extremely funny. They are a good example of Pinget's special kind of comedy.' She found that the play presented some difficulty in production because the thought patterns and transitions are often submerged, and she was in no doubt that it would not have worked without the complete collaboration of the actors (two old Beckett hands, Jack MacGowran and Patrick Magee), not only with each other but with her: they made excellent, imaginative suggestions for the development of the characterization and for the handling of the dreamlike dialogue. She kept the conception fluid and her ideas changed as the rehearsals progressed, particularly since the programme was done collaboratively. She went on:

> The director interpreting a radio script is like a conductor following a composer's score: the means at his or her disposal are tempo, rhythm and volume, and a sensitive use of the pause for the dramatic handling of silence as well as of sound. The radio director must create aural patterns that are exactly right; a 'beat' too long can be as disconcerting as a wrong note in a musical performance. One great difference between the musical conductor and the radio director is the amount of technical knowledge and equipment that the director must work with. There are complicated light and hand signals which the director must use to cue in voices, music and sound effects, and to indicate pauses. And the sound effects as well as the music must be selected and timed.

The music in question, played on a barrel organ, was a tune chosen by Beckett, 'The Bluebells of Scotland'. The patterns in measured sound were not timed mechanically but were felt, and grew out of the emotions and tensions of each moment of the play. Bray believed that no medium was better suited than radio to the presentation of 'poetic-musical drama', in which the imagination is given free play. No wonder that her professional relationship with Beckett developed into a personal one: apart from anything else, they saw eye to eye on the potential of radio to convey his vision (he was to write four more plays for the medium after translating *The Old Tune*). And long after they both ceased to have much to do with radio, their collaboration continued: as James Knowlson records (*DF*, p. 703), one of the last things she did for him was type and print out for his

signature a text called 'What is the Word' that he had painfully and with difficulty translated from his original French.

Brenda Bruce (1920–96)

In 1962 George Devine, the director of the London première of
Happy Days, asked the experienced but not particularly well-
known actress Brenda Bruce to take the role of Winnie after
Joan Plowright, the wife of Laurence Olivier, had to pull out
because of impending maternity leave. As he had promised
Devine, Beckett came over from Paris to help. At first things
went reasonably well: he confided to a friend that Bruce was
about the right age for the part, 'small, blonde, quite pretty,
with a very fetching smile, [if] a little too thin'. Their personal
rapport was good and they enjoyed 'a jolly couple of hours'
together shopping to buy Winnie's spectacles; but he soon irritated her by replying, ''Tis of no consequence,' whenever she
asked what something meant (*DF*, p. 500). He did, however,
tell her how he came to write the play:

> He said: 'Well, I thought that the most dreadful thing that
> could happen to anybody would be not to be allowed to
> sleep, so that just as you're dropping off there'd be a
> "Dong" and you'd have to keep awake; you're unable to
> move, sinking into the ground alive, and it's full of ants; the
> sun is shining endlessly day and night and there is not a
> tree; there'd be no shade, nothing, and that bell wakes you
> up all the time; there is a man you can't see and who is of
> no help whatsoever; and all you've got is a little parcel of
> things to see you through life; and to have the means in
> sight to kill yourself but not the will to do it because inside
> you've always got that slight ray of hope.' Then he said:
> 'And I thought, who would cope with that and go down
> singing? Only a woman.' So he wrote it for a woman to
> perform.
>
> (*DF*, p. 501, and *JH*, p. 221)

The rehearsals were, however, literally torture for Brenda

Bruce. Although he tried to be nice to her, bringing her beautiful yellow roses, for instance, when he came to say goodbye just before the opening, Beckett was inflexible over the way he wished the part to be played. He even brought along a metronome – an instrument common enough in the music-room but unheard of in the drama studio – to demonstrate the rhythm he wanted. When she finally broke down in floods of tears he was prevailed upon to leave her alone for a week to give her time to master the part in her own way. Let her take up the story from the beginning:

When I read the play I was very irritated by all the lines of dots Beckett had put in between the words; my husband told me not to worry, though, because it would all get ironed out in rehearsals. But of course when I started working with Beckett I found that the lines of dots were absolutely part of the play and that if I didn't attend to them on the split second I had to go right back to the beginning again. So when he produced the metronome I just got absolutely hysterical. It wasn't that he was being nasty to me, it was just that he didn't really understand how actors work. I was aware that it was a tremendously important play, and that in itself was scaring. I was so nervous on the first night that my hands were shaking too much to put my make-up on and the tears were just rolling down my face. Jocelyn Herbert came in and said, 'I really think you should have a brandy.' My heart was hammering so hard that it hurt. She and George Devine helped me downstairs and then they put me in that mound and the stage manager came and shut it behind me and put the bolt in. It was dreadful. There was the claustrophobia of sitting there trapped, I couldn't ease it by walking across the stage. It is complete exposure because with the lighting there is no shadow anywhere. You begin to get mesmerised by the lights. As for Beckett, he'd gone off to write some more torture for somebody else.

(JH, pp. 219–20)

True enough: *Not I* was still to come, and with it the torment of another actress, Billie Whitelaw. Still, after feeling that Beckett was trying to dehumanize her, Brenda Bruce did eventually come to love *Happy Days*, and she had the consolation, when touring South America with the play, of winning an award in Brazil for her performance.

Pierre Chabert (b. 1938)

The distinguished French actor and director Pierre Chabert appeared in Paris productions of *Endgame* (as Hamm) and of *Krapp's Last Tape*, the latter staged by Samuel Beckett, and himself directed French versions of *Happy Days*, *Rockaby*, *Ohio Impromptu*, *Catastrophe* and *What Where*. He has also written extensively and with considerable insight about the issues involved in putting Beckett's works on the stage, not least two texts originally conceived for other media, *Mercier and Camier* and *Company*, which he adapted with Beckett's cooperation and consent. In a thoughtful interview with Lois Oppenheim that took place after the author's death he spoke first about these, pointing out that Beckett was not consistent in his attitude to 'cross-overs': he would go along with them out of 'friendship or weariness', but he never really liked the idea; for him, 'The theatre plays were written for the theatre, the radio plays for radio, the television plays for television, and the novels for a narrative voice speaking "out of the dark".' Oppenheim then asked Chabert what he had learned from Beckett about directing: 'Everything,' he replied, and went on to elaborate this very interestingly:

He taught me artistic *necessity* and the necessity of the text to its staging. He taught me respect, respect for the text, as for any other living form. He taught me to strive for the highest standards. He taught me love. Not by words but by example. What does it mean to 'make theatre' if all that isn't there? He taught me that fundamental thing of the absolute connection between aesthetics and ethics: the passionate search for truth, the refusal of all facile effect and vulgar gratuitousness, insulting to oneself and to others. I learned everything from him. On a more practical level he taught me precision and simplicity, the most unequivocal simplicity. And I learned to play a lot on the music and not on the superficial meaning.

But I must also say that you have to be very careful with Beckett's own stagings. He had genius, and he had it also as a director. I found him brilliant. But one must not try to imitate it, because one risks only imitating the surface, catching only the mannerisms. Also I believe he could demand certain things of actors. He could demand anything of them because he was Samuel Beckett, he was the playwright and the director. He could require that the actors conform entirely to what he wanted and to the way in which he understood his text. But we can't do that. We have neither the authority nor the right.

Naturally, Beckett's productions are always a point of departure for my own. That is to say that, having known Beckett as I knew him, knowing the value of his work as a director, if I didn't consult his directions, his notes or the videos of his work, I would be a philistine, an ass. I believe all of that to be an enrichment which I don't have the right *not* to make use of, but I also believe that one must go further. I know that there are little things that bother me in Beckett's productions, so I do something different. In particular I part company with him over his tendency, through his desire to be always extremely musical, to 'mechanise' the actors somewhat. In his productions, due to his desire for musicality, its preeminence, there is something that runs counter to the natural and that sometimes evokes something artificial.

I felt this watching the video of his *Happy Days* with Billie Whitelaw, which is an absolutely fantastic production. At certain moments, however, I find that Billie Whitelaw (who is an actress whom I like and profoundly admire) is a little affected, not natural. She appears somewhat like a mechanical puppet whose strings, one knows, are being pulled by Beckett himself. But there is also something very moving in that. To see that woman who is basically a sort of doll – that also has its beauty, and most of the time it is sublime. And yet, personally, I am inclined to try and find a certain balance between this form, this musicality, and something more natural, something closer to life. Of course, Billie Whitelaw is a person who had sufficient experience with Beckett and who had enough modesty, admiration and savoir-faire to be able to achieve exactly what he wanted. Few actors have gone so far towards attaining what he was after, towards achieving his theatrical vision. Beckett heard, very precisly, the words, the sentences, that he had created: he knew exactly how they had to be said. But we must absolutely avoid doing to him what was done to Brecht. A sort of Brechtian convention developed which gave rise to productions of disgusting conformity after his death. They were nothing but copies, and there was, basically, only one schema, which was hollow, because what Brecht did only Brecht could do. People took piles of photos and tried to reproduce Brecht's productions. That just doesn't work.

I believe that to reproduce exactly what Beckett wanted is impossible, but I make a distinction with regard to the principal stage directions, which are fundamental and inviolable. For example, in *Happy Days* there is Winnie buried to the waist and then Winnie buried to the neck. That must not be changed. I was therefore led to distinguish that principal stage direction, which must be respected to the letter, and the secondary directions – for example, the 'very pompier trompe-l'oeil backcloth' (*CDW*, p. 138), which is very difficult to create, and has to be interpreted in order to find a subtle equivalent. In my version this equivalent is a frame set on the stage. The aim of this frame is, first, to concentrate the audience's attention on Winnie. Also, it gives a certain mystery to the mound that emerges from the frame, its lower part. By not letting the audience see that it rests on the ground, the mound appears suspended. But this frame also combines several ideas or images: that of a theatre stage, that of a theatre 'box', that of a painting, or that of a film screen. In short, the frame suggests to the audience: you don't have reality before you but, instead, a representation. So, it is an interpretation of 'very pompier backcloth', but in my opinion it is very close to the stage direction of the text.

(*DB*, pp. 66–79)

This production opened in the autumn of 1992 with Denise Gence in the role of Winnie, one that Madeleine Renaud, who was still alive, had made her own. With endearing modesty, Chabert said that he approached Beckett's 'great plays' with diffidence, because of 'presences' like Renaud's; and, as of that date, he had not even attempted to direct *Godot* or *Endgame*, because he felt that the ghost of the great Roger Blin still haunted the Paris stage.

Rick Cluchey (b. 1933)

Perhaps at first glance the most unlikely of Beckett's collaborators, Douglas (known as 'Rick') Cluchey is a former convict who achieved rehabilitation through his encounter with *Waiting for Godot*. His heart-warming story is well known, and I have already referred to it, but it bears repeating, especially in his own words, as here:

I began first to act in Beckett's plays in 1961 while serving a life sentence for armed robbery and kidnapping at San Quentin prison in California. Although many of my fellow convicts had a similar interest, as early as 1958, we were all nonetheless required to be patient and wait until the Warden of that day decided to allow us the special sanction of an experimental workshop, where such plays might be performed. So in 1961, with the advent of our own small theatre, we began to produce a Beckett trilogy, as the first works to emerge from this little workshop.

Thus our first effort was *Godot*, then *Endgame*, and lastly *Krapp's Last Tape*. In all we gave no less than seven productions of Beckett's plays during a three-year period. All the plays were acted and directed by convicts for a convict audience. And so every weekend in our little theatre at San Quentin, it was standing room only for imprisoned Americans; and rightly so, because if, as Beckett has stated, his plays are all closed systems, then so too are prisons. I personally can say that San Quentin is a closed system, a very tightly closed system!

If the critics are right when they proclaim that all of Beckett's characters are drawn from his early life in Dublin, that is, the streets, bogs, ditches, dumps and madhouses, then I can only add that the most informed, knowledgeable and qualified people to portray Beckett's characters would be the inmates of any prison! For here, more than any other place in the world, reside the true Beckett people: the castoffs and loonies, the poets of the streets, and all of the 'bleeding meat' of the entire system. The real folk of our modern wasteland.

And may I say that it was of special interest to us at the time that, while all over the world audiences were puzzled and fascinated and the critics astounded by the plays of Beckett, we, the inmates of San Quentin, in fact found the situation normal. Yes, we did understand about waiting, waiting for nothing. Our 'affinity' with the works of Beckett has perplexed many critics, but never our audiences.

During my work with the Beckett plays at San Quentin the first role was that of Vladimir in *Waiting for Godot*. I was then and am now struck with the simple situation of a man waiting in 'fear and trembling' as the philosopher Kierkegaard put it – certainly my own situation at that time in San Quentin prison. I felt very close to the character of

Vladimir. I took up the mask of Beckett's people. And I wondered about the man who could create these plays which seemed so much about my own life. In these works I was to feel secure with the characters, perhaps because they were so like the people of San Quentin: extensions of disconnection, decay and uncertainty. 'Can it be that we are not free? It might be worth looking into.' Well, in the end it was Beckett and not the Warden who gave me my freedom, a freedom of mind if not of body.

I never had the slightest notion I would ever meet Samuel Beckett, yet I felt that I knew the man. When eventually, in 1966, I was paroled after serving twelve years, I decided to come to Europe and quite by chance met Beckett in Paris. It was the beginning of a long and lasting friendship, one which in due course would bring me into greater artistic contact with Beckett the director. As a director he inspires awe. He is so much his own master, completely in control of his stage, knowing each step of the way exactly where it is he is going. His Schiller production of *Godot* has set standards for all other productions, by virtue particularly of its shape and style, its musicality and mime, its beauty of tone and sound, its movement and silent landscape merging, flowing richly, gracefully, like the form of a fine mobile at play in the wind.

(*KLTWb*, pp. 120–23)

In 1977 Cluchey was directed by Beckett in *Krapp's Last Tape*, a play that he himself had produced, and performed in, more than once while at San Quentin. He was impressive in the part. The critic James Fenton commented: 'He has a face which, when it relaxes into sorrow, is able to command the silence of a large audience for a considerable length of time, and he brought off the evening with great consistency and skill' (*Sunday Times*, 3 August 1980, p. 38). Extracts were shown in an arts programme on Channel 4 on 29 July 2001, and the anguish on old Krapp's face as he listened to the memory of the

girl in the punt was indeed quite moving. Not all critics, however, have been equally enthusiastic about Cluchey's acting.
Beckett himself did not have a particularly high regard for it –
unlike, say, his opinion of the work of Patrick Magee or Billie
Whitelaw; but he was intensely loyal to Cluchey and his colleagues in the San Quentin Drama Workshop (the troupe took
its name, of course, from the prison where it all started). He
assisted them financially, and showed his gratitude for their
devotion to his work in other ways, for instance by agreeing to
be godfather to Cluchey's son – a remarkable concession from
a man who had been an atheist since his student days. They
repaid him in kind by performing the texts exactly as he wanted, perhaps a shade too slavishly and uncritically for some
tastes. Certainly Rick Cluchey, with his hero-worship of
Beckett, stands at the opposite end of the spectrum from an
independent spirit like JoAnne Akalaitis, as we shall see later in
the chapter.

George Devine (1910–66)

Actor, director, and founder of the English Stage Company (the
troupe in residence at the Royal Court Theatre, London),
George Devine has earned a permanent place in theatre history
for his remarkable achievement in bringing ground-breaking
plays such as *Look Back in Anger* (1956) by John Osborne (b.
1929) to Sloane Square, thereby revitalizing British drama. He
scored a real coup when, on hearing that Roger Blin was having difficulty raising money for the Paris première of a new play
by Beckett, he set about acquiring this production to open the
1957 season at the Royal Court. This led to his first meeting
with the playwright, and he described what it meant to him in
a note dictated a few days before he died:

> To meet Beckett for the first time must be described as the
> experience of a lifetime. But what does that really mean? It
> means an experience, the like of which one has never had
> before, and which remains with one for ever in the memory.

So it was with me. I spent half an hour with him in his flat in Paris. We talked, drank whiskey, and decided nothing. In that half hour I felt I was in touch with all the great streams of European thought and literature from Dante onwards. I just knew about all that by contact with this extraordinary mind and poetic vision, at the same time so rich and so simple. This man seemed to have lived and suffered so that I could see, and he was generous enough to pass it on to me. Generosity is the word that springs first to mind when thinking about this remarkable man.

(B60, p. 99)

As Irving Wardle says, this friendship was shaped by Devine's humility towards one whom he regarded as wiser than himself: his attitude to Beckett and his work was one of reverence. Beckett repaid the compliment by giving him control over the English productions of *Endgame*, *Krapp's Last Tape*, *Happy Days* and *Play*, and that put the playwright in touch with the *crème de la crème* of the British stage. The great Alec Guinness (1914–2000), of *Bridge on the River Kwai* fame, the finest English character actor of his generation, was approached to play the role of Hamm, but was not available. John Gielgud (1904–2000) was offered the part, as we have seen, but having found *Godot* 'a load of old rubbish' (Cronin, 1966, p. 437), perhaps not surprisingly turned it down; he made amends later, in the last year of his life, when he took the role of Protagonist opposite Harold Pinter's Director in the filmed version of *Catastrophe* shown on Channel 4.

As we saw with Rick Cluchey, devotion to the great writer was not, however, always an unmixed blessing. Beckett supervised the final rehearsals of *Endgame* at the Royal Court in 1958. Devine had taken the role of Hamm, and he and Jack MacGowran (Clov), Wardle writes,

up to that point had been working on extracting the ghastly comedy from the Hamm–Clov relationship. But Beckett did not approve what he saw and asked for stylistic corrections.

Another director might have asserted his own authority, but Devine accepted Beckett's instructions, with the result that when the production opened the cast were still striving to achieve the 'toneless' voice required by the author. One cannot say that the production would have been 'better' without Beckett's assistance, though perhaps it would have been more popular. But what the episode illustrates is that Devine's respect for Beckett and his work was such that he would surrender professional control in Beckett's presence. Believing the play to be a masterpiece and well aware of the derision it might arouse, he was exceptionally nervous of his responsibilities towards it. He sensed that his performance was not right, and in trying to correct it he became more nervous than ever. Preparing for the show was a nightly ordeal and he would be shaking with fright as the curtain went up. The sound I remember from his performance is one of grating determination. He himself felt that he had failed in the part.

As we have seen, the same situation recurred in his production of *Happy Days* in 1962, where, according to Wardle, 'Devine stopped directing and virtually handed the show over to the author,' leaving Brenda Bruce to the latter's tender mercies. However,

as it turned out, *Happy Days* was an artistic success and Devine's trust in Beckett was vindicated. It is easy to recognise that now. We have the testimony of Martin Held, Madeleine Renaud, Alan Schneider, Billie Whitelaw and other artists on the enormous value of Beckett's participation in rehearsal. And his Schiller Theater production of *Waiting for Godot* (which reached the Royal Court in 1976) conclusively proved him a master exponent of his own work. But at the time of the early Court productions he had no such credentials to offer and lacked the confidence to take on the full responsibilities of directing a show himself. Actors like Peter Duguid [who played Willie opposite Bruce's Winnie], accustomed to the straight professional transactions between cast and director, were apt to view him as a meddling amateur. But Devine from the start believed that Beckett was the best guide to staging the plays.

So much so that he stood up to Kenneth Tynan, the great theatre critic and literary manager of the National Theatre, when in 1964 the latter, backed by Laurence Olivier, tried to get *Play*, which Devine had agreed to lease to that official institution, performed more audibly, in defiance of the stage directions ('Voices toneless except where an expression is indicated. Rapid tempo throughout' *CDW*, p. 307). Devine's rebuttal of Tynan's argument for adopting a more audience-friendly approach was characteristically robust; it was always his intention, he said, to achieve precisely what the text specified, since there was only one way to perform the play: as written.

> Any other interpretation is a distortion. You do not seem to realise that rehearsing a play is an organic process. To play it as you indicate would be to demolish the work's dramatic purpose and turn it into literature. You'll have to have a bit more guts if you really want to do experimental works, which, nine times out of ten, only come off for a minority to begin with. I certainly would never have leased the play to the National Theatre if I had thought the intention was to turn it into something it isn't, to please the majority.
>
> (Wardle, 1978, pp. 204–8)

Devine died a couple of years later of coronary thrombosis. Beckett was present when the director to whom (along with Peter Hall) he owed his reputation in the United Kingdom was cremated. There were to be many such funerals. He was particularly sad on this occasion, writing to a friend: 'Giacometti dead. George Devine dead. Yes, take me off to the cemetery, jumping all the red lights' (*DF*, p. 543).

Peter Hall (b. 1930)
As I have just mentioned, Beckett owed a lot also to Sir Peter, one of Britain's greatest director-managers, who, at the tender age of twenty-four, not long down from Cambridge, staged the first English-language *Godot*. He told a radio interviewer how this came about:

> I'd been director of the Arts Theatre in London for a few months, and during that time I'd been looking out for new experimental plays, when the script of *Godot* arrived – a bit dog-eared, I must confess, because it had been the rounds of the West End managers who'd expressed interest, and many leading actors had expressed interest too, but no one had quite dared to do it. We decided that we would, and we set about casting it, and a wonderful cast we had. We were under such stress and duress: the play was so difficult – we didn't understand it – that we absolutely had to pull together. Perhaps it's a help to a director when a play is obscure. The actors can't have their own pet theories or argue too much. Mine didn't anyway. They trusted me, and off we went. The director of course shouldn't waver or doubt or not know his own mind. Or at least if he does, he shouldn't show it to the actors. I must admit I didn't really know all of *Godot*, and I couldn't say in precise or literal terms that I understood it, but then I don't think one can say about this kind of writing or this kind of play that there is a literal or final meaning.
>
> I remember that I read it first between two dress rehearsals of a previous play at the Arts. I was immediately struck by the enormous humanity and universality of the subject, and also by the extraordinary rhythms of the writing, and it was these rhythms and almost musical flexibility of the lyricism which communicated itself to me and which I tried to pass on to the actors. I'm an instinctive director. A play like this I respond to very much, and my actors responded with me.

Looking back on the production, some of the things make me feel very hot and embarrassed. I used a lot of music, and I believe that I shouldn't have. Also, the stage had too much scenery on it; it should have been much more bare and barren. But anyway the play worked and was a great and significant success. It was the happiest experience of my early years as a director, and I've often thought that I would like to revive it.

(BBC Third Programme, 14 April 1961)

He got the chance many years later, in 1997, at the Old Vic Theatre, London. This time he avoided what he now saw as his mistakes of 1955: an overcluttered naturalistic set, an over-complicated tree, an oil drum as opposed to a boulder for Estragon, and the playing of music by Bartok as the lights went down. Beckett had objected to these things at the time and made sure (as we shall see) that the director of the American première, Alan Schneider, benefited from his point-by-point critique of Hall's interpretation. Later on he made his peace with his first British producer, as the latter recorded in his diary for 11 May 1976 (by which time he was running the National Theatre):

Sam Beckett came over this afternoon. His face is even more extraordinary: dark *Endgame* spectacles, the eyes pale and watering, the appearance sometimes hawk-like, sometimes child-like, but definitely a bird – a bird in his movements, his shyness, and because of occasionally a certain predatory hauteur. But he was warm, charming, smiling and affectionate. No distrust, no uneasiness: very free. He wants us to do *Godot*.

(*PHD*, p. 232)

A lot of water had, however, to flow under Waterloo Bridge before Hall was able to do *Waiting for Godot* again. This time he used the revised and annotated text in *The Theatrical Notebooks of Samuel Beckett*, a monumental piece of literary scholarship to which I have already had occasion to refer. Eric Prince interviewed him after the Old Vic production had achieved a resounding critical and popular success, and began by asking him if he felt at all surprised by the obvious accessibility of his production and by its reception:

> I am not surprised about the potency of the play because ever since I met Beckett in the mid-1950s I thought it was *the* play of the mid-century. I still think it is. I think it changed theatre and I think it changed our apprehension of what theatre is. What Beckett stands for has now gone into international consciousness. What is wonderful is to see young people coming to see this production of *Godot* who do not find it in the least mystifying or in the least peculiar. They see it as a metaphor of human existence and they laugh and they cry at it and they go out feeling joyous, which I think Sam meant and always wanted. I have always found Beckett a profoundly comic writer; at the very moment of greatest despair he found something funny.
>
> In 1955 nobody would do the play, nobody would be in the play, and a lot of the initial critics said it was twaddle and rubbish. I always knew that it was a great play, but how to do it, I didn't know; it was new, uncharted terrritory and I was finding my way.

In the Prince interview Hall goes on to contrast the fortunes of two plays that in the mid-1950s revolutionized the British stage: *Look Back in Anger* – which I have already mentioned – and *Waiting for Godot*. If you consider *Look Back in Anger*, he says, 'it is creaky, old, a very dated piece of journalism now, whereas *Godot* is an unmatchable masterpiece that has not dated at all: it doesn't say "I am 1950s", it really doesn't.' Hall is equally damning about what he calls the 'so-called poetic revival' started in the theatre by T. S. Eliot (*Murder in the Cathedral*, 1935) and Christopher Fry (*The Lady's Not for Burning*, 1948), which, he says, 'we were still in the fag end of' in 1955:

I was always very sceptical. It seemed to me that it was rather conventional drama that had poetry with a capital 'P' pinned on it like sequins. It was not in any sense organic writing. The extraordinary thing about Beckett, and I really did respond to this, was the rhythm, the precision of the language. It is truly poetic writing and yet it is never pretentious, unlike Eliot's.

Asked what he perceived to be the chief differences between his approach in 1955 and in 1997, Hall replied:

I suppose the main difference about coming back to the play is that my aesthetic as a theatre director has been honed over the years into really believing that you shouldn't put anything on the stage unless it is really necessary. That 'less' is really 'more' in the theatre, that decoration in the theatre is dangerous and misleading. Back in the 1950s when I first did the play I felt that, even then, but I don't think I had the courage. There was too much scenery in the first production, but people expected it in those days. Now we accept theatre as actors on a bare stage. So when I came to do Godot again I said to myself, well, what do we need? Two entrances, a moon, a tree and a boulder for Estragon to sit on. We don't need anything else. I did have a kind of road in this second production, a path across from one side of the stage to the other that they travelled on, but I took that away. It was not necessary.

In reponse to Prince's comment that this was a 'physically natural production, not at all stylised or abstract', Hall agreed:

It was a conscious decision to strip everything down to the actors and the language. I don't think Sam liked stylisation. He liked concentration. He started me off on the road of concentration, where I still reside. This second production of Godot is a bolder, more intriguing, more amusing one to watch. The only thing he said to me about the original Godot was that he thought it perhaps too emotional and

177

perhaps a bit sentimental. I think it was. It was not tough enough or hard enough. Sam was impatient with actors' sentimentality. That applies crucially to Pozzo who can, for example, be played simply as a strange kind of duffer like the Mad Hatter in *Alice in Wonderland* when actually there is a dreadful coherence to Pozzo.

(*Journal of Beckett Studies*, VIII, 2, 1999, pp. 50–57)

Martin Held (1908–92)

The second time Beckett went to Berlin to work with the Schiller Theater was in 1969, and the invitation on this occasion was to direct Martin Held in the German version of *Krapp's Last Tape*. Held gave a truly electrifying performance as Krapp: it was universally admired, and has been preserved on videotape. Held was a big man, and at first Beckett thought him 'too large and lumbering for the part' (*DF*, p. 567); but in fact good use was made of his 'corporeality' (*BiP*, p. 217), and the two worked very well together, in spite of getting off on the wrong foot. Somewhat insensitively, certainly rather tactlessly, Beckett tried to get Held to walk with the banana in his hand exactly as Patrick Magee had done. Held did not actively resist, but he did manoeuvre Beckett into letting him play the part his own way:

> When I noticed that Beckett always came very early to rehearsals and sat sometimes for half an hour in the auditorium with the stage designer, I used this opportunity and, since I rehearsed right from the beginning with these big down-at-heel plimsolls, I pretended that I had to get used to them and kept walking across the stage with that shuffling walk. I did that for three days and on the third day he said to me: 'That is exactly the walk you should have,' and then the problem was solved.

After that Beckett 'gave him his head a little', and finally 'a completely free hand'. In the evenings they drank wine together and talked a lot about Joyce. 'From there we got back again to the play':

For me among the best things in our collaboration was that he sometimes said: 'Let's save this situation up for the last few days of rehearsal. We haven't got so far yet that we can be completely clear about this.' This was a lovely flexible way to work; I find it the most ideal method of direction. He often went into detail, for example in those glances to the rear, when Krapp is listening or he wants to switch the tape on, and he jumps, and turns slowly round. Beckett rehearsed these things exactly. They were more than just stage directions.

I did something whereby I was afraid that I might hurt his feelings. When I have my hand on the table – and Krapp crooks the knuckle of one finger – then this is Beckett. He can't move his hand. I gradually worked towards it and made it more each time. And he looked at it once and just said: 'Good.'

He speaks very good German, so I always understood what he was getting at. For instance, I knew what he meant when he said that Death the Reaper, whom Krapp has been looking for unconsciously, is standing behind him. It is the finish, the end. Krapp sees very clearly that he is finished with three things, with his 'opus . . . magnum' (*CDW*, p. 218), with love, and with religion. All this is done without sentimentality.

Meeting Beckett was an inexpressible happiness for me. It belongs to those encounters in my life which can help one to develop inwardly.

(*KLTWb*, pp. 67–70)

Unfortunately the friendship ended acrimoniously. Beckett wanted Held to play Pozzo in his 1975 *Godot* at the Schiller, but despite having exactly the right build for the part the actor cried off, pleading ill health. Beckett did not believe him, felt let down, and 'never really forgave Held for what he saw as a lack of loyalty' (*DF*, p. 608). This was sad, because Martin Held was perhaps the greatest Krapp of them all.

Jocelyn Herbert (b. 1917)

There were no such problems with the British stage designer Jocelyn Herbert; she first met Beckett in 1957 and they remained friends as long as he lived. Working closely with her partner George Devine until his death in 1966, and then alone, she did the set designs not only for plays staged at their Royal Court Theatre (including *Endgame*, *Krapp's Last Tape*, *Happy Days*, *Come and Go*, *Not I*, *Footfalls* and *Play*) but for many other works (opera as well as drama) at other venues in this country and the United States. She was a great innovator, as Peter Hall explains:

> I think Jocelyn is one of the designers who absolutely changed the course of British theatre design. Before her most designers were encouraged to wrap up the pill with a lot of fancy paper, but Jocelyn affected a whole generation of designers and directors and made them insist on the question, 'It may be nice, but is it necessary?' She removed everything from the stage that didn't fulfil a function and made something beautiful out of that minimalism. Her influence is very strong. At her best I don't think her minimalism is ever arid or dry or abstract because what there is can be breathtakingly beautiful and very colourful. She doesn't eschew colour but it has to be used with real meaning, not for effect. There is something puritanical about her minimalism, but it's passionate, very strong, and not at all repressed. Sometimes I've felt she carried minimalism to a point where it was almost too modest, but that would be the most I would fault her for. I've never seen anything of hers which has been over-designed or over-decorated.
>
> (*JH*, p. 223)

No wonder that she and Beckett saw eye to eye. 'For me,' she said, 'there seems no *right way* to design a play, only a *right approach*: one of respecting the text and not using it as a peg to advertise your skills, nor to work out your psychological hang-ups with some fashionable gimmick' (*JH*, p. 15). As for him, we saw earlier what he thought: 'She doesn't want to bang the nail on the head; there is a tendency on the part of designers to overstate, but this has never been the case with Jocelyn' (*JH*, p. 219).

Jack MacGowran (1918–73)

Even for those who, like myself, knew him only superficially, Jack MacGowran was a person one took to immediately; but in those who were much closer to him, as Beckett was, it is hardly an exaggeration to say that he inspired love. Although probably best known to a wider public for his performance as Burke Dennings in *The Exorcist* (1973), the most talked-about horror film of all time, from our present point of view he will for ever be associated with Beckett's tortured heroes, especially Joe (in the 1966 television play *Eh Joe*, which was written for him). Joe stares in increasing anguish at the camera as the off-screen voice of a discarded lover whispering in his head reminds him painfully of his callous treatment of another woman: 'You know the one I mean, Joe . . . The green one . . .,' who committed suicide out of unrequited love for him (*CDW*, p. 365); but he was also a fine mime in *Act Without Words I*, a memorable Vladimir and Lucky in different productions of *Godot*, the first British Clov (1958), Krapp in Alan Schneider's 1971 television version of *Krapp's Last Tape*, and the director of a 1962 production of *Happy Days*. His second go at Clov, in 1964, opposite Patrick Magee's Hamm, in the Michael Blake production that I mentioned earlier, was as near to definitive as anyone is likely to get: in Peter Lennon's striking words, 'The actors are unerringly typecast, working together like old, slightly putrid pub pals. They are consistently alert to each other's moods and project a relationship which is a mixture of reluctant affection and animosity, desperation and sullen dependence, seasoned with some coarse guffaws at life. They are King Lear and the Fool speaking in Irish accents, in a bad way in a dosshouse by the Liffey'(*Guardian*, 21 February 1964, p. 11).

Those were some of the highlights of his Beckett career, but he was involved in much else: he had a small part in the original 1957 radio production of *All That Fall*; he compiled (and performed) an anthology of extracts from the author's works, which Beckett asked me to translate into French so that it could be submitted for a European prize to earn his friend some much-needed money; and he read beautifully two selections of Beckett's poems that I introduced on the BBC Third Programme in 1966. At the recording of the first of those broadcasts Beckett was present, and one of my happiest memories is adjourning at lunchtime, in hallowed Third Programme style, to a pub near Broadcasting House with the author, the actor and the producer Martin Esslin.

In an interview that is full of insights into the work from an actor's perspective, MacGowran spoke of the impact that the encounter with Beckett had on his career:

> Up to that point, I was an average working actor, making a reasonable living doing movies, television shows and plays. But as a result of playing Beckett, my whole attitude to life changed – he expanded my potentialities as an actor very, very much.
>
> When I got to meet him I discovered he was a Dublin man, born three miles away from where I was born. A lot of the rhythms he uses in his work are native to my ear, because we not only come from the same country, but from the same city which has its own recognisable idiosyncracies of speech.

'He writes about human distress, not human despair,' added MacGowran in a telling remark that could be set as an examination question, in the hallowed phrase, 'to discuss'. He is equally perceptive about Vladimir and Estragon, who are usually seen as the 'intellectual' and the 'non-intellectual' person respectively:

> I sometimes think that the roles are reversed: Estragon is the one who has read and known everything and thrown it

away and become completely cynical. Vladimir, who appears to be the brighter of the two, is in fact the half-schooled one, madly trying to find out answers and pestering Estragon the whole time. Otherwise, Estragon couldn't remember Shelley's 'To the Moon' and deliberately misquote the lines to fit their situation as he does [*CDW*, p. 50]. This tells you that Estragon has read everything and dismissed it.

MacGowran points out that, although Beckett would evade a 'casual' enquirer's questions about the 'meaning' of his work, he was usually willing to explain things in a production context. For instance, the two tramp-clowns in *Godot* were, he said, 'interdependent', the one needing the other: Estragon has so many nightmares he cannot bear to be alone, and Vladimir must have someone to talk to because he cannot find answers to the questions that trouble him. Pozzo and Lucky are interdependent too. Lucky is a 'damaged person mentally – his speech disintegrates because his mind is disintegrating'; Pozzo cannot get rid of Lucky because he's blind and needs the halter to hold on to. Likewise with Hamm and Clov's 'love-hate relationship' in *Endgame*:

> The reason Clov doesn't leave at the end is because Hamm puts a doubt in his mind whether he does see life outside or not. If he did see life outside, Clov would escape, and Hamm wouldn't worry because he would take in the new life to help him. Beckett wanted to leave a doubt about the existence of human life so as to make Clov less sure of going. When Hamm says, 'I don't need you any more' [*CDW*, p. 131], Clov doesn't like the fact that he's not needed – he must be needed. That is why he never leaves. Beckett's attitude towards it was that Clov will not go because he cannot face what's outside without anybody, so he's still dependent on Hamm: man must depend upon his fellow-man in some way, no matter how awful. As for the business of Hamm's narrative, we played it as if Clov was

the baby brought there by the starving man, so that the story is not really fiction at all. It's a retelling of those early years, which Clov may or may not remember because he has been there so long.

Another puzzle that Beckett was happy to clear up concerns a moment when Clov realizes that he has had a little victory over Hamm and he starts humming. Hamm says, 'Don't sing'; Clov asks, 'One hasn't the right to sing any more?' Hamm replies, 'No,' and Clov asks, 'Then how can it end?' [*CDW*, p. 127]. When MacGowran said to Beckett, 'I'm really not quite sure what that means,' this was the reply: 'That was a difficulty in translation I had. When I wrote it in French, there is a French proverb which is well known, "Everything ends with a song," and I could not translate that proverb, which is particularly French, into English unless I did it that way. It was more readily understood in French, Clov intimating that this is the end of their relationship.' The last point MacGowran made in this interview is one that we found Peter Hall making too: that 'the easiest audience to play to are students and young people who just seem to know what Beckett is talking about, whereas the middle-aged group are not so tuned in on him' (*OB*, pp. 213–24).

The 'waif-like' MacGowran, 'trailing memories of Charlie Chaplin', had the 'odd idiosyncratic look of a gnarled elf' (Worth, 1999, p. 147), and this 'quintessential Beckett interpreter' (Zilliacus, 1974, p. 9) established with the playwright the sort of rapport few others achieved (with the notable exception of Billie Whitelaw, as we shall see). Michael Ratcliffe watched them at work rehearsing MacGowran's one-man show (the anthology programme I mentioned earlier), and was struck by the 'true collaboration between player and author'; MacGowran's brilliance, he wrote, 'shines brightest when Beckett is present; they are like brothers', especially when 'Irishly, they discuss the proper pronunciation of "ordure" – the result sounds not unlike "orgia"' (*Sunday Times*, 28 February

1965). This collaboration resulted in MacGowran winning the Best Actor Off-Broadway award and a gold plaque from the Critics' Circle when he performed the show in New York in 1970. He died not long afterwards, a long-standing addiction to 'booze and pills' (*FC*, pp. 175–6) having finally taken its toll. 'Beckett, saddened by the death of his old friend, sent his deep condolences to Gloria MacGowran and their daughter Tara, and did all he could over the years to help the family financially' (*DF*, p. 599).

Donald McWhinnie (1920–87)

As we saw earlier (in the section on Barbara Bray), Donald McWhinnie was instrumental in bringing Beckett to BBC radio, and he directed *All That Fall*, broadcast on the Third Programme early in 1957. Once described as a rather shy, quiet man who could easily pass for a provincial schoolmaster – his obituary spoke of his 'deceptively quiet style which concealed real authority and intellectual power' (*The Times*, 10 October 1987, p. 12) – he told James Knowlson what happened after that:

> I was on the staff of the BBC. Barbara and I thought it would be quite interesting to try and introduce the prose works of this man to a wider audience on the Third Programme – that is what the Third Programme was for. And it seemed to me that Patrick Magee, the Irish actor who had taken a small part in *All That Fall*, had this curious voice, which could somehow speak the words of the narrators in the novels in an interesting way for the audience. We would never have done a straight reading by an Engish actor of *Molloy* or *Malone Dies*; there would have been no point. It wouldn't have meant anything, but when you've got this curious cracked voice of Magee . . . So I said to Sam that I thought that Magee would be awfully good to read one or two bits and pieces from his work: 'Shall we choose them or will you?' Naturally, he said: 'I'll choose a

few bits of them myself.' So he chose about 75 minutes out of *Molloy* and an hour and a half out of *Malone Dies*. And then he said that it would be rather nice to have some music as well. So he said that his cousin John Beckett would be quite good to write some music, and that's how it began.

As is well known, Beckett was so impressed with Magee's readings from his prose works that he wrote *Krapp's Last Tape* for him. What, Knowlson wondered, impressed McWhinnie most when the script of the play arrived?

Well, I have to tell you that the first time I read it, having done extracts from the novels which are so rich, I thought it was a bit thin for Sam. And it wasn't until I started work on it that I discovered how rich it was. This was the beginning of Sam's much more economical style of writing, compared with the more extravagant novels. And it seemed much more accessible. One reason why the first production went so well is that Magee had the entire feeling of when to be still and tender, and when to be violent, without any link or lead up from one extreme to the other. That seems to me the essence of Beckett: violence coming out of nowhere.

(*KLTWb*, pp. 45–7)

After *Krapp's Last Tape*, McWhinnie went on to direct *Endgame* twice, *Embers*, *Cascando*, *Play*, *That Time*, *Ghost Trio* and *... but the clouds ...* with great sureness of touch. He was not always so successful: a 1960 BBC radio adaptation of *Waiting for Godot*, complete with stage directions read out loud, was not to Beckett's taste, any more than a BBC television version of the same play in 1961, about which the author made the astute observation: 'My play wasn't written for this box; it was written for small men locked in a big space, whereas they are too big for this place' (*DF*, p. 488). McWhinnie was deeply hurt, but Beckett was right.

Patrick Magee (1924–82)

Another hard-drinking Irish actor who died relatively young, Patrick Magee had an importance in the production of Beckett's plays, several of which he premièred, that can hardly be exaggerated. Much of that ground has already been covered, so this section can be shorter than would otherwise be the case; this is not to imply, however, that Magee is somehow less significant than other Beckett collaborators. Because *Krapp's Last Tape* was written for that particular gravelly voice, Beckett always maintained his image of Magee as the original Krapp, even if, as a man still in his mid-thirties, the actor was a bit too young for the part, and even if (as we saw) Martin Held's interpretation is, of all those developed in the author's lifetime, perhaps the nearest anyone got to producing a definitive performance.

In an interview with James Knowlson, Magee remembered one difficulty he and McWhinnie encountered in rehearsals:

> That was making the sound of a cork popping [*CDW*, p. 219]. If you merely pull a cork out of a bottle away at the back of the stage behind some curtains, it's not really going to penetrate to the back of the theatre. So I think what we did was to use the sound of a bicycle-pump.
>
> One thing I did develop was the walk. I walked using my left hand as if Krapp were holding on to some invisible rail or rope. It helps the eccentricity of the walk. And it's difficult – at least it is for me – to walk like that, if you don't use your hand.

In this play the actor can either operate the tape recorder himself, as Donald Davis did in Alan Schneider's New York production, or have a technician do it offstage. Provided that to the audience the sound appears to emanate from the machine and not from the wings, this is the safer option, as Magee went on to explain:

> We had a marvellous man stage left; he had a master tape and knew the text very well. When I moved to switch the

machine off, he was poised ready to do it. He got every chance, because old Krapp is not going to turn it off 'bang'. There's going to be some shuffle. That gives the technician one second.

I had enough terror, anyway, of the tape jumping off, or blowing up. Anything can go wrong. There are so many chances, it seems pointless to take an extra one if it can be avoided.

Of his interpretation of the role – never sentimental or resigned – Magee said: 'Sam was very insistent that "not with the fire in me now" [CDW, p. 223] should be firmly delivered, with the emphasis on "fire". Old Krapp, listening to that, needs to keep absolutely still at this point, absolutely quiet, absolutely rigid, to hold the audience's concentration as well as his own' (KLTWb, pp. 43–5).

Jean Martin (b. 1922)

In the French versions of Beckett's plays Jean Martin will for ever be associated with the roles of Lucky and Clov; in the first case he studied patients suffering from Parkinson's disease in order to simulate their trembling and slavering, thereby creating 'a shocking image of human misery that disturbed many spectators and contributed powerfully to the impact of the play' (DF, p. 386), and in the second he adopted a stooping posture that remained a feature of all Clovs subsequently directed by Beckett.

Much of this ground has already been covered, but one or two interesting points remain to be gleaned from interviews with Jean Martin. He told Evelyne Pieiller, for instance, that the first Estragon, Pierre Latour, became very shy when the theatre dresser and her husband roared with laughter during a final rehearsal at the sight of his trousers dropping to his ankles (CDW, p. 87). At the first public performances he refused to do more than lower them slightly. It is well known that Beckett, alerted by his partner Suzanne that his perfectly explicit stage direction was being ignored, had to intervene forcefully with Roger Blin to make Latour let his trousers fall right to the ground. This is important, he said in a letter to Blin, because it must be clear to the audience that Estragon is too preoccupied by thoughts of suicide to notice that removing the cord that serves as his belt has resulted in his trousers slipping down (*DB*, pp. 296–7). Theareafter, Martin recalls, Latour 'put small stones in his pockets so that the trousers would slide down better' (*Magazine Littéraire*, June 1986, p. 36).

In 1970 Beckett directed Martin in *Krapp's Last Tape*, and had some interesting things to say about the work:

> He told me very precisely about the personal [autobiographical] links between himself and Krapp. He worked hard on removing all sentimentality from the play. That was something he insisted on rather a lot. Above all, he stressed that it should be played without too much emotion or regret. 'Krapp,' he said, 'is an old fool, who is rather less of a fool as a very old man than he was, as he listens to the recording of his stupidity of thirty years earlier.'

They decided to go for the riskier option with the tape – that of having the actor operate the tape recorder himself:

> We had a tape-recorder in the wings with an identical tape to mine which could have been used had I got into real difficulties (such as the tape breaking). Playing it with or without the actual tape affects your acting. Because if there is another tape-recorder in the wings connected to a speaker hidden under Krapp's table, no matter how well that machine is operated by someone some distance away, there is bound to be a small delay in response which may not go entirely unnoticed.

One must choose, too, which voice to use on tape and which voice to use on stage; they must, of course, be clearly differentiated. Beckett and Martin went for the more sensible option, in my view: the actor spoke in his normal voice as the thirty-nine-year-old man on tape, and 'made the voice of the later Krapp a little older, a little heavier, and a little slower'. As in other productions, Martin was asked to turn his head to the left, as if someone were touching him on the shoulder; on the final occasion on which his Krapp looked round into the darkness, the look was made to last a long time. 'It is death who is waiting for him there,' Beckett explained; he said: 'Next day, when the play is over, he is found dead at his table.'

Martin's slip on the banana skin (*CDW*, p. 216) was a real slither, 'as on a music-hall stage', which obviously needed careful rehearsal if the actor was not to fall heavily and break a limb. In terms of costume,

> Sam stressed the neglected character of Krapp; he doesn't wash any more; he pays little attention to his physical appearance. His shoes were old, worn-out shoes – things which allow you to walk without lifting your legs and make a shuffling, sliding sound.
>
> I acted in a clumsy fashion for two reasons. Firstly because it goes with the character of Krapp; secondly because it offers the possibility, if one has difficulty with the tape, of putting any fiddling with the tape down to clumsiness. It's not very convenient, you'll appreciate, putting on the tapes when you are afflicted with stage-fright. You mustn't make a mistake in confusing one tape with another, since there is a point where you have to take one tape off and put another one on. So I played him as clumsy and short-sighted.
>
> (*KLTWb*, pp. 81–4)

Madeleine Renaud (1900–94)

As we have seen, this remarkable theatre practitioner will for ever be associated with the part of Winnie, created by her in the French version of *Happy Days* (1963), which Roger Blin encouraged Beckett to envisage with her in the leading role; she also performed in the French translations of *Eh Joe* (1968), *Not*

I (1975) and *Footfalls* (1978). She was a star, one of the great actresses thrown up at intervals in French theatrical history, like Adrienne Lecouvreur in the eighteenth century, Sarah Bernhardt in the nineteenth and Edwige Feuillère in the twentieth.

Her published interviews concern *Happy Days*, which was a great success – deservedly so – but I cannot help feeling that it was one that derived in part from a misunderstanding. Her rather 'gushy' remarks in the Festschrift *Beckett at Sixty* (1967) and in her conversations with André Coutin in *La Déclaration d'amour* (2000) show that she never got close to him. A typical remark is: 'Who knows Beckett? Undoubtedly his wife does. But as for others, for myself? I only know what he looks like. He came to dinner several times at my house, but I have never been to where he lives and I do not possess a photograph of him' (*B60*, p. 82). I suspect that Beckett was – quite understandably – in awe of her, perhaps even intimidated by her, but never really felt that her Winnie was his Winnie. His most successful collaborations in the theatre were either with people who were already on his wavelength (like Roger Blin, Jean Martin, Patrick Magee and Jack MacGowran), or with people who were prepared to submit unquestioningly to his way of seeing things, like Rick Cluchey and Billie Whitelaw. Things were not so easy – on either side – with people like Peggy Ashcroft or Madeleine Renaud, who brought with them the baggage of a formidable reputation. They were less readily impressed by Beckett than lesser-known collaborators, as Renaud indicated to Pierre Chabert:

> I didn't hesitate at all; I wasn't frightened by the character or by her inability to move. I thought right away that Winnie was the role for me. There was never any argument, never any disagreement between Beckett and myself. One day I said to him, 'I'm being indiscreet, but how is it that you are so acutely aware of the importance a woman attaches to her handbag?' He didn't answer.

(*WiB*, pp. 15–17)

He didn't answer because it was a silly question. Winnie's bag, as the text makes clear, is not a handbag, but a shopping bag (*CDW*, p. 138).

As James Knowlson records, the wonderful rapport about which Renaud enthuses did not last. Beckett was 'very disappointed' with her performance as Mouth in *Not I*, feeling that it needed a younger woman to play the part, and he made sure that another actress inaugurated *Rockaby* in French. 'His decision created considerable ill-will with Madeleine's husband,' Jean-Louis Barrault (the great theatre director and actor, perhaps best known for his performance as the lovelorn clown in the classic film of 1945, *Les Enfants du paradis*). Yet the playwright 'was unwilling to compromise on what he thought best for his work'. 'Sadly,' concludes Knowlson, 'Barrault never seems to have forgiven Beckett for, in his eyes, deserting Madeleine Renaud. Equally sadly, Beckett does not appear to have made much of an effort to repair the rift' (*DF*, pp. 689–90).

Alan Schneider (1917–84)

The close, warm, deeply affectionate relationship between Beckett and his American producer is the best-documented of all his collaborations, with the possible exception of his rehearsals with Billie Whitelaw. It began in 1955, when Schneider was preparing to stage the American première of *Waiting for Godot*, and it ended only with the director's death in a road accident in London almost thirty years later. According to Stanley Gontarski, the reason why he was such a good, faithful realizer of the playwright's work was simply that he 'heard Beckett's cadences and saw Beckett's austere, fearful symmetries in his mind's ears and eyes' (*OB*, p. 11). Apart from Schneider's own perceptive writings on the subject, the chief source of information about the collaboration is their correspondence, which has been edited by Maurice Harmon under the title *No Author Better Served*, a quotation from one of Beckett's letters. Schneider directed *Eh Joe*, all of the stage plays in the *Complete Dramatic Works* with the exception of *Act Without Words II*, the *Roughs for Theatre* and *A Piece of Monologue*, and he made the only Beckett movie, *Film*. He was *the* interpreter of Beckett's works in the United States, but he also found time to produce plays by Edward Albee, Harold Pinter and others; in fact, the reason why he was in London on the day he died was to direct a work by a young American dramatist, James Duff.

I met him in 1970 when he visited Norwich, where I was living at the time. Over lunch, I found him splendid company. He confirmed the truth of a much-travelled anecdote about the Miami première of *Waiting for Godot*, in which the famous comedian Bert Lahr (Estragon) told Tom Ewell (Vladimir), 'I'm the top banana in this show, and don't you forget it!' Schneider never really hit it off with Lahr, who, he felt, 'crowded out' E. G. Marshall, the Vladimir in the New York transfer; as he put it to me, 'It's not only Estragon's play,' and said of Lahr's acting (which other people, including Kenneth Tynan, thought a 'triumph', *DF*, p. 422), 'It's a funny play, but not in that way.'

He also told me that, for the première of *Endgame*, in 1958, he did not adopt as décor the cavernous cell of other productions but used the back wall, consisting of dirty bare brickwork, in the theatre building itself. Before the curtain went up someone turned the central heating off by mistake (this was New York in January), causing the radiators, as they cooled off, to click loudly throughout the performance. The critics, and even Schneider's agent, assumed the noise was meant to be part of the production, and praised the originality of the idea. As a result the director had to ensure that the unintended accompaniment was repeated on subsequent nights.

Schneider expressed to me his cynicism about theatre critics. They begin, he said, by slamming Play A as 'awful'. When Play B comes along, that too is awful, not nearly as good as A was. Play C is then dismissed as awful, worse than B, which, though good, was not a patch on A, which in the meantime has become a masterpiece.

Delphine Seyrig (1932–90)

Buried not far from Sam and Suzanne in Montparnasse ceme-
try, Delphine Seyrig was a cinematic icon before she became a
Beckett actress: she appeared in a succession of *nouvelle vague*
masterpieces, and is perhaps best remembered for her performance as the enigmatic *femme fatale* in *Last Year at Marienbad*
(1961). She was perfect in that role, but she was never really
happy playing late Beckett, as she explained, with the intelli-
gent lucidity for which she was greatly admired, to Pierre
Chabert:

> I feel I lacked confidence in *Footfalls*. To play Beckett you
> have to have a real capacity for precision in delivery. You
> have to know how to talk and to act mechanically and pre-
> cisely as if for a Bach partita. It is no use being supple and
> inventing all that you will from within. As for me, I have a
> fluid, undefined, imprecise elocution, which isn't exactly
> bothersome in playing Turgenev, but which is troublesome
> in Beckett.
>
> Beckett is like an orchestra conductor: he sets the tempo.
> He doesn't try to explain what the play means. He says you
> have to do that and that, you have to do it with your body,
> your voice, your lips. I have noticed that great artists only
> say small, very concrete things and not great sweeping gen-
> eralities.
>
> For me, Beckett was an author who wanted step by step
> to create images for what he had written on paper – to cre-
> ate a whole, casting the object in its entirety, rather than
> just describing it. I was strongly affected by my work with
> him: I didn't achieve everything I would have wished; I
> don't have the feeling of having reached the outer limit of
> everything he expected of me. That gives me the feeling of
> wanting to try again and do better the next time.
>
> (*WiB*, pp. 20–21)

Sadly, there was to be no next time. Seyrig was otherwise committed when Beckett wanted her to play the parts of W and V

in the French version of *Rockaby*. A few years later, they were both dead.

Alan Simpson (1921–80)

The Irish theatre director Alan Simpson staged the first Republic of Ireland production of *Waiting for Godot* in 1955. He tells the story in *Beckett and Behan* (1962). The Dublin première had to wait until after the London one for what eventually turned out to be imaginary contractual reasons, but the media furore caused by Peter Hall's production benefited that of his Irish colleague, and since 'the dialogue is more entertaining in Dublinese', the production was a success in Beckett's native city. Simpson says of his approach to the characterization:

> The general reading of the character of Pozzo seems to be of an overbearing, bullying tycoon. Because of my own Irishness, however, I see him as an Anglo-Irish or English gentleman, whose excellent manners and superficially elaborate concern for others conceal an arrogant and selfish nature and a calm, almost unconscious assumption of superiority. As for Lucky, I followed Roger Blin's lead by giving him a sort of old-fashioned footman's coat and knee breeches. There are in Ireland a number of Anglo-Irish aristocratic families who live in grand but excessively delapidated mansions, without nearly enough money to do things properly, so I thought it would fit in with my conception of the Pozzo–Lucky relationship to have Lucky's elaborate livery moth-eaten and tattered.
>
> (pp. 62, 137)

The great thing about this play is that different aspects can be highlighted in different circumstances without denaturing it. Just as the San Quentin inmates recognized themselves in the tramps' familiarity with 'hope deferred' (*CDW*, p. 12), the Dublin audience could relate to social types with whom they were familiar.

Max Wall (1908–90)

To gauge the importance of a particular figure in British life, this is as good a yardstick as any: whether or not a painting of them hangs in the National Portrait Gallery in London. The great actor and comedian Max Wall is there, and in a particularly good likeness, too.

A master of the laconic routine, he was a leading exponent of radio comedy in the 1940s, when the genre was in its heyday. After his music-hall career came to an end he acted in several of Beckett's plays. He appeared, for instance, in a 1981 production of *Waiting for Godot* which, in the words of Michael Billington, 'returned it firmly to its vaudevillian roots': there were moments of 'inspired clowning' from Wall (Vladimir) and Trevor Peacock (Estragon), especially when they 'broke into half-remembered fragments of old song-and-dance routines' and Wall 'did the old trick of spinning a bowler down his arm' (*Guardian*, 11 June 1981, p. 9).

In an interview with James Knowlson, Max Wall agreed that his music-hall background helped him a lot, too, when he played Krapp in 1975 in a production of *Krapp's Last Tape* directed, interestingly enough, by the actor who had first created the role, Patrick Magee: 'It got big laughs from the audience when Krapp is perplexed as to what "viduity" means (*CDW*, p. 219). He had obviously written it when he was 39 but has forgotten what it meant. It was all done with facial reaction which I would use in the music-hall. Having a mobile face and getting laughs from my face, I could utilise that skill to good effect.' Wall was indeed well known as a comedian for the effectiveness of the raising of an eyebrow; and like all good performers, he knew exactly how to 'tease' an audience:

> I knew that they knew that I was going to slip on the banana. This is obvious because of throwing it there. I felt that this must be done in the most natural way and also to get a few little chuckles by not going near it for the first couple of walks and making them wait, wondering when I

was going to trip over it. I did it, then the short-sighted look down, then the slow pushing of the banana skin away – taking a long time to get rid of it, the last shred of it, and especially the last little bit – over the footlights. That got a big laugh. Comedy is derived from sadness and I think that the two go together. It's the old Pagliacci, isn't it? Otherwise Krapp would become too sentimental and spoil it. To my mind, there is a wistfulness about it and a quality where he could laugh at himself. 'How do you manage it, she said, at your age? I told her I'd been saving up for her all my life' [*CDW*, p. 222] is almost a Groucho Marx line, because the comedy is there, the humour is there, in spite of the sadness.

Knowlson referred to the unusual empathy that critics had noted between Wall and Krapp: they praised the understanding of the loneliness, for instance. Was this, Knowlson wondered, something that Wall felt as he played the part?

I would say so, definitely, yes. My whole private life has been a tragedy right from babyhood. I was born a bit sad anyway, and when I listened in that fixed position, I'd lost sight of the fact that I was Krapp – I was listening and going back in my own life. At the same time I have a great acceptance in life and perhaps Krapp has this acceptance too. All this sending himself up by saying 'sold to free circulating libraries beyond the seas – getting known' [*CDW*, p. 222], you know it is that that he accepts. It is all gone, and it doesn't matter. When I read the play through for the first time, I thought, 'Well, this could be my life.' It is not a mysterious play. It is a very pathetic play, with touches of humour in it arising from the peculiarity and eccentricity of Krapp and all the funny things he does.

(*KLTWb*, pp. 112–15)

No wonder the critic John Elsom ranked this 'the performance of the year' (*The Listener*, 25 December 1975, p. 888).

David Warrilow (1934–95)

Athough his name will long remain indissociable from Beckett's later work, David Warrilow was not widely known outside avant-garde theatre circles. He was born in Staffordshire and, after studying French at Reading University, lived in Paris for a while before founding a small company in New York called Mabou Mines to perform experimental drama. He was 'mesmerising on stage, with sunken, dark blue eyes' (*The Times*, 31 August 1995, p. 17). *A Piece of Monologue* was written for him, and he delivered it memorably, in a hoarse, gasping, painfully hesitant voice. He also created the roles of Reader in *Ohio Impromptu*, of Protagonist in *Catastrophe* and of Bom in *What Where*.

From this record of performance in the rather 'dark' late plays, it might be thought that Warrilow was somewhat deficient in a sense of humour. Not a bit of it (in fact, it is hard to imagine how people who took themselves too seriously could possibly have become close associates of Samuel Beckett). He tells a nice story about a lady who approached him after a performance of *The Lost Ones* (a prose text he adapted for the stage with Beckett's permission) to say that the measurements of the cylinder featured in the piece could not be correct. Warrilow checked with the author, who ruefully admitted that the lady was right and that it was 'a most regrettable error':

> I remember being quite shaken. As if I'd been told there was a mistake in the Ten Commandments. Some time later, an attempt was made to do a film version of my performance, and I felt I owed it to the world to obtain a ruling on the matter. And so, as I left Sam one day, I said,
> 'Well, on film, which figure do you want me to say?'
> 'Let me see now,' said Sam, 'which did I say was the correct one?'
> 'Sixteen,' said I.
> 'Then say sixteen,' said he, 'we'd better have the right one.'

We said goodbye, and I set off down the street.

He called after me, with that incomparable delicacy of his: 'After all, you can't play fast and loose with pi.'

(*B80*, pp. 87–8)

In 1989, with Beckett's encouragement, director Antoni Libera and David Warrilow put on *Krapp's Last Tape*, a production acclaimed not least for the intensity of Krapp's facial expression ('mask-like' was the term Eric Prince used to describe it) when fixing the 'fourth wall of audience' at any mention of 'eyes' or 'love'. In an interview with Prince, the actor explained how he and Libera handled the problem of the tape recorder:

The tapes are blank. There are speakers under the table and I switch on, switch off and wind forward according to the script, and the technician in the booth follows me and does it very well. I didn't want real control. I didn't want to have to deal with a machine to that degree. It's not worth it. The risks are absolutely appalling. It's bad enough as it is. The first week a couple of times I suddenly glanced at the machine and the tape was spooling out all over the table. So I had to sit and put that right and then go on with the performance. That's enough to deal with without the other stuff.

(*Journal of Beckett Studies*, Spring 1992, pp. 125–6)

Jean Martin, as we saw, and Donald Davis before him, actually worked the machine themselves. There are clearly good arguments for either procedure, and potential snags with both. This may be a problem that will disappear over time: one day it may be impossible to find an open-reel tape recorder outside a museum, and then, presumably, the producer will have to use a cassette recorder, which raises other issues but at least makes the actor less accident-prone when it comes to manipulating the instrument.

Billie Whitelaw (b. 1932)

In addition to writing her autobiography (*Billie Whitelaw . . . Who He?* [1995]), Beckett's favourite actress has given several interviews about her collaboration with the playwright, including a 'consultation' with Dr Anthony Clare in his BBC Radio 4 series *In the Psychiatrist's Chair* (3 September 1995).

She began by explaining to Clare that her father had wanted a boy, so when registering her birth he got 'Billie' put down on the certificate rather than 'Diana' (the choice of her mother, who was not pleased). Her stage name is therefore her real name. Although she has done a lot of other drama (on radio and television as well as in the theatre), and has appeared in numerous films (such as Philip Kaufman's *Quills* [2000]), it is as the performer of the roles of Mrs Rooney in *All That Fall*, Ada in *Embers*, Winnie in *Happy Days*, Stenographer in *Rough for Radio II*, W2 in *Play*, Voice in *Eh Joe*, Mouth in *Not I*, May in *Footfalls* (which was written for her), V in *Ghost Trio*, W in *. . . but the clouds . . .* , and W/V in *Rockaby* that she will be best remembered. It was, naturally, upon this aspect of her career that Anthony Clare concentrated.

He noted (as have many others, including Whitelaw herself), that Beckett made her 'the ultimate conduit' for his late theatre experiments, which stretch drama, and the performer, to the limit, even – some would say – beyond it. Certainly Whitelaw suffered at his hands, albeit willingly: 'I offered myself as an instrument, as a tool,' she assured Clare when he pointed out to her that what was being sought by Beckett (who once sighed, 'Oh Billie, what have I done to you . . .') was something that the psychiatrist called the 'total elimination of you'. (One critic admiringly called it 'transforming one idiosyncratic human performer into a universal living sculpture' [*Times Literary Supplement*, 14 February 1986, p. 166]).

The *Not I* rehearsals, Whitelaw recalled, were indeed 'frightening', a 'form of torture'. She felt 'disoriented', as if 'tumbling in space'; she was soon 'hyperventilating', and even became 'hysterical'. The strain on her mouth was hard to bear, and her spine and nervous system took a long time to recover. Nevertheless, she persisted with a play which, in a characteristic understatement, Beckett described as 'an outburst' (*JH*, p. 87), and gave one of the great performances of modern times as the hallucinatory pair of lips which, 'gaping like a vagina, glutinous, slimy and weird', form words 'at a tenth of a second, spelling them out like an Olympic clock' (*SG*, pp. 215–16). As Whitelaw perceptively remarked, 'It seemed to me that Mouth was not going *out* to an audience; the audience had to be sucked into this rioting, rambling hole.' Beckett, who was not given to hyperbole, called her interpretation 'miraculous' (*Sunday Times*, 20 August 1995, section 10, p. 12).

Clare asked her what she most admired in Beckett, and she replied his 'integrity', his 'perfectionism': he was for her, quite simply, a 'genius'; and while she made it clear that their relationship was platonic, going no further than holding hands, she admitted that 'he loved me', and that 'it was impossible for me not to love him'. 'His death,' she concluded, 'was an amputation.'

The notion of being his 'instrument' crops up frequently: 'Beckett blows the notes . . . they just come out of me,' she says on the video film of the rehearsal and first performance of *Rockaby* (1981). 'She takes his words off the page and makes them songs,' commented the play's director Alan Schneider (*Time Out*, 10 December 1982, p. 22).

In conversation with Linda Ben-Zvi, Whitelaw drew a sharp distinction between performing Beckett and acting in conventional 'drawing-room comedy'. This is the sort of play where, as the curtain goes up, the telephone rings, a maid enters, answers it, then, turning to the butler, who has just come in with a tray of sherry glasses, announces (in a stage voice loud enough to be heard at the back of the stalls): 'Her ladyship has been detained and wishes dinner to be delayed,' and the audience is all agog to find out what has caused this upheaval in their employer's domestic routine. Whitelaw's comment on this was:

Noel Coward said acting consists of learning the lines, speaking clearly, and not bumping into the furniture. I do admire that kind of expertise in Coward, and I recognise that such acting is more than that. But with a Beckett work, the process is entirely different. It's only by reading it over and over and over, not understanding what the hell it's about, that after a while it starts to take on a music. There is usually a word that gives a clue, that must be emphasised, that becomes a key. When I was preparing *All That Fall*, Beckett used the word 'explosive constipation' to think about Maddy Rooney. She's terribly constipated; she has all these feelings, and wants to explode, to release them, but she can't. In acting Beckett, you actually have to *be* these women, and that is what I think is so difficult and also so great about these plays. It takes courage to go slow, to be unafraid of being achingly boring, reciting like a metronome if need be. I experienced pain in all these roles. With *Footfalls*, it was physically excruciating to maintain the posture required for the part: to stand in that position becomes almost intolerable. *Footfalls* was also difficult in another sense. Just before I did it, my niece committed suicide. I was the last one to speak to her. And her voice, it was without colour, as if she had already done it. She had already left us and was just waiting to commit the act. You see, all that is in Beckett. He is writing about me. Of course he demands such physical extremes of his male actors too. When David Warrilow played in *A Piece of Monologue*, my heart bled for him standing absolutely still.

(*WiB*, pp. 5–10)

'You know how we work,' Whitelaw told Ben-Zvi; 'we sit and look into each other's eyes and say the lines.' No hysterics about metronomes here: one of the most frequently reproduced photographs of Whitelaw and Beckett in rehearsal shows them a few feet apart, she crouching on the stage, he standing on the floor below, their heads at the same height, both looking, as she says, straight into each other's eyes, their right hands raised like an orchestral conductor's beating time as their mouths form the words in unison. This was, truly, one of the most remarkable theatrical collaborations of modern times.

Survey of interviews with, and comments by, those who took an independent line with Beckett's works

Jocelyn Herbert says that 'fewer and fewer people have seen Beckett's productions and they don't know how to do them as he intended – or worse still, they don't want to do them as he intended' (*JH*, p. 79). It is understandable that the practitioners featured in the first part of this chapter consider it sacrilege for people to interpret the plays in a different way – often a very different way – from what the author had in mind; but other approaches, even radical approaches, are not necessarily always invalid. Beckett is dead, and can no more veto perverse interpretations of his work than Shakespeare can. Like Shakespeare, he will have to rely on the common sense of theatre-goers. It is not a bad form of protection. One *can* imagine Hamlet played by an actor in drag or Lady Macbeth portrayed as a transsexual, just as it is *possible* to cast Othello as a modern-day white mercenary in the service of an African régime and Desdemona as the president's black daughter; but I doubt if productions on these lines would run for very long. *The Times* reported on 24 March 1990 (p. 9) that a Broadway production of *Catastrophe* had, no doubt with the best of intentions, substituted a happy ending for 'Beckett's typically gloomy finale', but by then Beckett was dead and others had to protest on his behalf, saying that he would have been 'appalled' by this unauthorized rewriting of his work.

In an era sometimes described as 'post-feminist', one of the most contentious issues where Beckett's work is concerned is the casting of women in male roles; but even Beckett 'loyalists' can contemplate the possibility. In the Channel 4 programme I mentioned above, Rick Cluchey was directing a student drama

group in *Waiting for Godot*, and the part of Estragon was
played by a young woman wearing a bowler hat. At first sight
it looked no more odd than a female infantry officer or a
woman bus driver does; but such appearances can be decep-
tive. The relationship between Estragon and Vladimir, as we
have seen, has often been described as 'semi-conjugal', and the
famous American novelist Norman Mailer (b. 1923) went so
far as to describe the two clowns as a gay couple, 'a male and
female homosexual, old and exhausted' (*Village Voice*, 7 May
1956). Mailer's interpretation has usually been regarded as
silly, since there is nothing in the text to suggest a physical relationship between the two men.

However, it becomes more difficult to exclude unwanted sex-
ual overtones if Vladimir is a man and Estragon a woman. This
is, of course, less of a problem if both players are women: any
suggestion of an erotic relationship then becomes as irrelevant
as it does if the couple consists, as Beckett intended, of two
men. Nevertheless, it is hard to see what – apart from modish-
ness or a desire to make a political point – could lead a director
to choose an all-female cast. Beckett obviously felt this when,
in 1988, he tried to stop a Dutch production that featured four
women dressed as men. Their spokesperson retorted, perhaps a
trifle disingenuously, that the female players were the best people who had auditioned for the roles. A similar argument was
put forward to justify an American production which, in the
same year, chose two actresses to play Estragon and Vladimir.
Linda Ben-Zvi's judicious and balanced comments on this ven-
ture were as follows:

The [male] director did not acknowledge the gender of the
women: all references remained 'he'. More importantly, he
did not play with the possibilities of the gender reversal he
had staged. The dress, the movements, even the look of
Didi and Gogo are masculine, and there is no attempt to
parody male physicality. To have women *disguised* as men –
while not as effective as having men play men – does not in

itself make a gender statement, and in this production gender was not the thing. Therefore, it seemed to me, the integrity of the play was not as threatened as I would have expected.

Nevertheless, she went on, the production made her realize that *Waiting for Godot* is far more a play about *male* experience than she had previously thought. JoAnne Akalaitis made a similar point: '*Waiting for Godot* is basically a buddy story; seeing it once played by women made me realise how much the play is about male psychology' (*DB*, p. 138). The same may be said in reverse about *Happy Days* or *Not I*, which are very much about *female* experience: David Warrilow told Kalb that he would have felt 'somewhat obliged' to tackle the role of Mouth had he been a woman, but since he was not 'of that gender', it was out of the question (*BiP*, p. 231). Similarly, in response to a request from Regensburg in Germany to put on a female *Godot*, in 1982, Beckett himself pointed out that 'Women don't have prostates,' an allusion to the fact that Vladimir needs to leave the stage to relieve himself (*CDW*, p. 35) because he suffers from an exclusively male disorder, enlargement of the prostate gland (*DF*, p. 694). Shrewdly, Professor Ben-Zvi raised the question whether Beckett's abhorrence of tampering with the casting of *Waiting for Godot* was not 'precisely because he intended the actions of the characters to represent male ways of passing time while waiting': 'If anything, the unnaturalness of the two women going through the routines written for men – bantering, bullying, declaiming – made me wonder whether in *Godot* Beckett is as consciously portraying male experience as in *Happy Days* he is doing the reverse. Seen this way, the cry of misogyny, which is levelled at Beckett when he disavows such productions, is undermined' (*The Beckett Circle*, Fall 1988, p. 7). Beckett was emphatically not a misogynist, any more than he was a racist when he objected to the proposal, which I mention below, to cast black actors as Hamm and Nagg. Edward Albee's play *Who's Afraid of Virginia Woolf?*, to which I have already had occasion to refer, features two married couples. The older pair have, over many years, devised vicious ways of humiliating each other in public, but when they are confronted with two smug younger people, they close ranks to deploy against them the weapons honed so effectively in decades of struggle with each other. Albee halted a Texas production in which the couples were cast as homosexuals, not because he is a homophobe, but because the proposal would have turned it into a different play (not necessarily a worse one, just not the one he wrote), and because he felt that it is an oversimplification – one that does not do justice to the complexity of human relationships – to maintain that gay couples are no different from straight couples: there are differences, and it is insulting to both kinds of partnership to claim otherwise.

Apart from the good sense of her conclusion, Ben-Zvi makes an interesting point about *plausibility*. To those who still see Beckett as a master of the absurd, it may seem silly to ask whether his plays ring true or not; but it is clear that *implausibility* – such as casting a man as Winnie and then having to pad his chest out to give him the 'big bosom' Beckett calls for (*CDW*, p. 138), and turning him, as Whitelaw said of herself, into 'quite a sexy little piece in a strapless top, very seductive' (*WiB*, p. 4) – would provoke quite the wrong sort of laughter as the curtain went up, because, as we saw Schneider commenting on another work, 'It's a funny play, but not in that way.'

Beckett spent a lot of time and energy stopping, or trying to stop, productions of which he disapproved. Although he felt he had to, he hated doing it, and as James Knowlson points out in a balanced and judicious appraisal, he was not always consistent:

> In the last few years of his life, Beckett gained something of a reputation for objecting to productions of his plays that deviated radically, at least as he and his friends saw it, from

what he had written. He was often represented as a tyranni-cal figure, an arch-controller of his work, ready to unleash fiery thunderbolts on to the head of any bold, innovative director unwilling to follow his text and stage directions to the last counted dot and precisely timed pause. The reputa-tion resulted from almost saturation coverage in the inter-national press of two or three cases. Yet the truth of his position was more complex and certainly far more interest-ing than this caricature suggests.

One of the most celebrated of these cases was the American Repertory Theater Company's Boston production of *Endgame*, directed in 1984 by JoAnne Akalaitis, to which I shall return. Beckett's objection was to the set: the depot of an underground railway, with a derelict carriage extending across the stage and other paraphernalia that one associates with such workshops. He also disapproved of the use of incidental music by the fash-ionable composer Philip Glass, and the casting of two black actors as Hamm and Nagg, which 'added a dimension to the play that he had not put there'. The company's artistic director responded by asking, reasonably enough, why the author had taken no action in other, more blatant cases of violation of his text and stage directions. This was a reference, Knowlson explains, 'to André Gregory's controversial production in 1973, when American colloquialisms were substituted for some of Beckett's actual words, and to a 1983 Belgian produc-tion (by Marcel Delval), which was set in a Brussels former warehouse that was flooded with water. But whether any action was taken in a particular case depended on some very human factors. As a result Beckett could appear – and indeed was – inconsistent.' One such 'human factor' was reluctance to disappoint a friend, so some people were allowed to do things with his work that would have been flatly refused to others. As I mentioned earlier, David Warrilow obtained permission (with retroactive effect, what is more) for his stage adaptation of *The Lost Ones*, and Jack MacGowran was given a free hand over the use of material in his one-man show; similarly, it was unprecedented for Beckett to invite me to produce a French translation of that compilation without insisting on revising it himself. The inconsistencies were often blatant. Warrilow, as we saw, was a founder member of Mabou Mines, but the unfortunate JoAnne Akalaitis was as well, and so too was Frederick Neumann, who got the go-ahead to stage an adaptation of the prose work *Company*, with music by none other than Philip Glass. As Knowlson makes clear – and as we shall see when I come to the cases of Peter O'Toole and Albert Finney, neither of whom Beckett took to – 'It made a tremendous difference if he liked and respected the persons involved.' He was indulgent over Georg Tabori's 'conceptual' production of *Waiting for Godot*, as we shall see, even if the reports he got about it made him 'squirm'; but it tipped the balance the other way if the 'feelings of shock, horror or dismay of certain close friends whose judgement he trusted were communicated graphically enough'. Then he got angry, and 'once he was angry, he could be very obstinate, determined and unforgiving' (*DF*, pp. 691–3).

Knowlson is correct when he says that Beckett fired off most of his legal anathemas during the closing years of his life, but the history of his disagreements with promoters and directors over productions that he was unhappy about goes much further back. As early as 1963 he expressed regret at a French television version of *All That Fall*; he would have preferred the RTF to commission a specially written work from him rather than adapt a radio play to a medium for which it was not intended. In the same year he let it be known that he was not impressed by a BBC television production of *Krapp's Last Tape* starring the Irish actor Cyril Cusack (1910–93); as we saw in chapter 3, it prompted him to draft his own 'suggestions' for a television version of the play, which firmly excluded dramatizations, recorded on misty film, of such scenes as Krapp bidding 'farewell to love' with the girl in the punt. Cusack's performance did, however, draw praise from the critic Maurice

Richardson, who found it 'uncommonly poignant' (*Observer*, 17 November 1963), and David Warrilow says he was 'overwhelmed' by it as a young man (*Journal of Beckett Studies*, Spring 1992, p. 123).

Likewise, Beckett did not warm to Peter O'Toole's performance as Vladimir in *Waiting for Godot* (Dublin, 1971). He was not impressed by the Irish actor's iconic status as the star of *Lawrence of Arabia* (1962), nor did it cut much ice that the man was married to Sian Phillips, who played Voice in the BBC production of *Eh Joe*, which Beckett had co-directed, and about which Mrs O'Toole had commented wittily: 'I thought it would involve only a few hours' work, but being a Samuel Beckett play it is taking days of discussion' (*Daily Mail*, 24 January 1966). Beckett's coolness may well have had something to with the fact that Mr O'Toole picked a quarrel with Peter Lennon in Paris once, in which the playwright took the side of the distinguished journalist against the actor who will for ever be remembered wearing magnificent Arab robes in David Lean's cinematic masterpiece (*FC*, p. 181).

Beckett was far from being overawed, either, by another distinguished film star, Albert Finney (b. 1936), whose memorable performances in *Saturday Night and Sunday Morning* (1960) and *Tom Jones* (1963) left him cold – or, rather, they would have left him cold, had he seen them: he was notoriously uninterested in modern cinema. His tastes, as we have seen, were restricted to the films of Buster Keaton, Charlie Chaplin and Laurel and Hardy. There is a nice story about this: when the name of Dustin Hoffman (b. 1937), the star of *The Graduate* (1967), *Midnight Cowboy* (1969) and other world-famous movies, was being mentioned in connection with a Peter Hall film of *Waiting for Godot* (a project that never materialized), the great playwright confessed that he had never heard of Dustin Hoffman. Jocelyn Herbert recalls that when, in 1973, Anthony Page directed Albert Finney in *Krapp's Last Tape*, Beckett 'came to a run-through, and after the performance he said it wasn't quite what he had in mind and could he show them?' He then proceeded to 'do the whole play on stage' (*JH*, p. 29). This was not a very auspicious start. Privately, as we have seen, Beckett thought Finney not up to the job, and not surprisingly Finney soon 'became acutely conscious that he was not satisfying Beckett, and tried too hard to compensate', and the result, in James Knowlson's view, was 'disastrous' (*DF*, p. 596). The critic Jack Tinker, on the other hand, thought Finney marvellous. 'I just don't think Albert and Sam got on' was Billie Whitelaw's down-to-earth verdict (*Time Out*, 10 December 1982, p. 22).

As Knowlson says, though, Beckett was not always consistent. A rather pointless sequel to *Waiting for Godot* by the Yugoslav Miodrag Bulatovic was put on at the Edinburgh Festival in 1971. Beckett agreed to accept Bulatovic's dedication of the work to himself, but the critic Derek Mahon wondered 'in what off-moment the strict master had allowed his name to be used' in connection with a play in which Godot, 'a Japanese of Celtic extraction', eventually put in an appearance, only to be greeted with the reproach: 'You're built up as a saviour and you can't even make a decent entrance.' Mahon's apt comment on this was: 'There's always someone to spoil a good joke' (*The Listener*, 9 December 1971, p. 821).

One can only assume that sympathy for the Yugoslav playwright explains what Mahon calls Beckett's 'off-moment'. Certainly it was personal affection that, in 1984, led him, as we saw, to allow Georg Tabori (b. 1914), a Hungarian Jew, to put on a German version of *Waiting for Godot* which, in Jonathan Kalb's words, 'using one of Tabori's favourite devices, stages *Godot* as a rehearsal':

> no illusionistic scenery whatsoever, the actors sitting around a plain table smoking and drinking coffee. At the start of each act Vladimir and Estragon enter languidly in what could be slightly aged street clothes and read indifferently from their scripts (a paperback edition of the play). Then they gradually work up to performance tempo, leaving their

scripts for longer and longer intervals and becoming more and more spontaneous, until at some point – impossible to determine exactly – the spectator realises that they have embodied the characters.

(*BiP*, pp. 91–2)

Beckett did, however, protest when, in 1988, the Comédie Française wanted to stage a French version of *Endgame* with pink walls, twenty mannequins placed around the set, and music to accompany the action. In that instance he was able to get the company to stick to the text; but a *Happy Days* that had been tampered with – to the extent of reducing the two acts to one, dimming down the 'blazing light' and revealing Willie in his underwear rather than 'dressed to kill' (*CDW*, pp. 138, 166) – went ahead in a production by Andrei Serban in New York in 1979, as did a German version by Tabori in 1986 which, among other wilful deviations, replaced Winnie's mound with a bed, all in the hope, Tabori asserted, of 'liberating the text from the dogmatic model which Beckett himself has set or of which he has approved so as to open it to ever-fresh readings' (*Journal of Beckett Studies*, Spring 1992, p. 110).

Since Beckett's death there have been several imaginative (and therefore controversial) productions. It is, of course, impossible to know what he would have thought of them. One that attracted praise from Eileen Seifert in the official newsletter of the Samuel Beckett Society was a performance in 1999 of *Play* by the Thirteenth Tribe Theatre Company in, of all places, the display window of the Right On Futon shop in Chicago:

The actors' voices reached the audience on the street through speakers attached to the exterior of the building. The locale – a shop window – might seem controversial, but director Joanna Settle and her set designer Mark Bello stayed very close to Beckett's stage directions. The window contained a grey cavern-like background with the actors performing in grey classical urns that came up to their

necks, and the lighting supervisor carefully followed
Beckett's detailed instructions.

(*The Beckett Circle*, Spring 2000, p. 3)

So far, so good. But M was performed by a woman, no doubt
once again because she was the best person who auditioned for
the part. The audience soon noticed something odd 'in the tim-
bre of the voice' and began to titter; and once again, too, one
can only repeat Alan Schneider's wise words: 'It's a funny play,
but not in that way.'

Another controversial production was *Footfalls*, directed in
1994 by Deborah Warner (b. 1959), with Fiona Shaw (b.
1958) as May. (Shaw's already distinguished career as a stage
and film actress went stratospheric with her performance as
Harry Potter's aunt in the movie about the boy wizard.)
According to Katharine Worth, Warner's main departures
from Beckett's instructions in *Footfalls* were the use of two
stages rather than the strip, and the choice of May's costume,
'a dowdy, short red dress, drab lisle thread type of stockings,
and flat Start Rite sandals', instead of a 'worn grey wrap'
(*CDW*, p. 399). The Beckett estate was not amused, restricted
performances to one week and banned a tour abroad.
Nevertheless the event won, Worth says, 'a front-page headline on a leading broadsheet, a rare experience for artistic
happenings', and 'nearly four years after the event, Fiona
Shaw still thought of this remarkable stirring up of interest,
often in unlikely quarters, as a valuable outcome of the production', a judgement with which her interviewer was happy
to agree (Worth, 1999, pp. 159–61).

To conclude this section I return to the case of JoAnne
Akalaitis (b. 1937), undoubtedly the most controversial of all
those who have taken an independent line with Beckett's work.
A founder member, as I have said, of Mabou Mines, a New
York theatre company that takes its name from a place in
Canada where they rehearsed one summer, Akalaitis has given
two interviews about her work on Beckett.

In the first, Jonathan Kalb began by asking her what she thought about the scandal that blew up around *Endgame*, which was set, as we have seen, in an underground railway, or as the Americans say, a subway:

> I feel the scandal was sort of made up in a way. There have been plenty of productions which interpreted the design widely, so it was almost an accident that someone decided to make a fuss about it. Frankly, it never occurred to me to write to Beckett and say, 'I'm going to set this in a subway.' In rehearsal every pause was, for me, almost sacred. The actors knew that there was an objective structure that I wanted and that they had to internalise it. It was very vigorous, very mechanical, like 'you take five steps to the left, and then you breathe, then you pause, one two, then you go'. It was not freewheeling, wild and crazy, 'let's play around with Beckett'. It was athletic, strict, and followed Beckett's structure. *Endgame* is probably the greatest contemporary play, I think, and it calls on a lot for an actor to perform. It was really deep work, it was very hard work, and exhilarating. I think a good handle on Beckett is the rhythm of it and also the way these lines just explode; he has these completely perfect, wonderful lines.

The subway décor idea, she explained, evolved gradually in her discussions with Douglas Stein, the designer, and they only arrived at the final conception after 'riding the subway a lot'. As for the musical accompaniment, she said: 'I like, when people come into the theatre, for something to be happening. The use of music inside the play was pretty minimal, pretty sparse, so the music was used in a very conventional way, i.e. to get people in the mood. What I wanted was something threatening, slightly off-putting, intense, repetitive, and Philip Glass did all of those things with that piece.' While she regretted the public row with Beckett, she pointed out that he did not see her production before rushing to judgement, and in any case she felt that 'once you grant the performing rights, you've taken a chance; you don't give the rights and then say, "I'm going to stop the play"' (*BiP*, pp. 166–72).

In conversation with Lois Oppenheim, Akalaitis said that, while she considered Beckett's decision to have been 'wrong-headed', she had only happy memories of the production:

> I look back on it with tremendous fondness. I had an intensely rich time working on it. I'm very, very proud of the work we did. It was grounded in protectiveness towards Beckett, towards the austere. We worked rhythmically a lot; I talked a lot about rhythm, music, and we spent a lot of time just doing it – doing it and doing it. As for the design, you don't just buy the Samuel French edition and say, 'Here's the prop list; here's what the set should look like.' You create the play. The script is the starting point. The script is not the play. The play is an event. Theatre is what happens on the stage. The director is like a sculptor, a shaper, a former, an idea person, a visionary, an artist.
>
> (*DB*, pp. 136–40)

Splendid stuff, and a magnificent note to end on; such a pity that Beckett got angrier over JoAnne Akalaitis's *Endgame* than anyone had ever known him to be. It reminds me of Lear's tragic misunderstanding of Cordelia. Like Lear, Beckett ought to have realized that the one who seemed least responsive to him was his true spiritual daughter.

Select Bibliography

Only major studies are listed here, chiefly those quoted in the text. For other titles, see the bibliographies in these books.

Abel, Lionel, *Metatheatre* (New York: Hill & Wang, 1963) is a ground-breaking study of 'metatheatre', i.e. drama that is self-conscious and reflects upon itself as drama. As I have argued in chapter 2 of this book, much of what Lionel Abel has to say about metatheatre can be applied to the plays of Samuel Beckett.

Aslan, Odette, tr. Ruby Cohn, *Roger Blin and Twentieth-Century Playwrights* (Cambridge: Cambridge University Press, 1988) is the definitive study of the work of a director who, with the possible exception of Alan Schneider, did more than anyone to establish Beckett as a playwright of the first rank.

Bablet, Denis, and Jean Jacquot, eds., *Les Voies de la création théâtrale*, vol. 5 (Paris: CNRS, 1977) contains (pp. 377–455) an in-depth study by Myriam Louzon of Roger Blin's first and second productions, in 1957 and 1969 respectively, of the French version of *Endgame*, followed by an interview with Blin.

Beckett, Samuel, *The Complete Dramatic Works* (London: Faber and Faber, 1986) is the reference text that I have used throughout this book.

Beckett, Samuel, ed. Ruby Cohn, *Disjecta: Miscellaneous Writings and a Dramatic Fragment* (London: John Calder, 1983) is an invaluable collection of Beckett's minor writings; the 'dramatic fragment' is *Human Wishes*, which I discuss briefly in chapters 2 and 3, above.

Ben-Zvi, Linda, ed., *Women in Beckett: Performance and Critical Perspectives* (Urbana and Chicago: University of Illinois Press, 1990) is particularly valuable for the interviews it contains with women who have acted in Beckett, from Peggy Ashcroft to Billie Whitelaw.

Bernold, André, *L'Amitié de Beckett, 1979–1989* (Paris: Hermann, 1992) is the extraordinary story of the friendship between an elderly writer of genius and an academic young enough to be his grandson.

Calder, John, ed., *Beckett at Sixty: A Festschrift* (London: Calder and Boyars, 1967) and *As No Other Dare Fail: For Samuel Beckett on His 80th Birthday by His Friends and Admirers* (London: John Calder, 1986) are uneven collections of accolades and reminiscences, but some of the material is interesting, and where it is I have drawn on it here.

Courtney, Cathy, ed., *Jocelyn Herbert: A Theatre Workbook* (London: Art Books International, 1993) is an invaluable source of information about the work of the great theatre designer who was George Devine's partner in the London Royal Court Theatre enterprise. A close friend of Samuel Beckett, she designed many of his plays.

Cronin, Anthony, *Samuel Beckett: The Last Modernist* (London: HarperCollins, 1966) is a biography that is especially good on Beckett's Irish (and particularly Dublin) literary, cultural and social background.

Esslin, Martin, *The Theatre of the Absurd* (Harmondsworth: Penguin, 1968) is, like Abel's book, a ground-breaking study, this time of the so-called 'Theatre of the Absurd', a term that Martin Esslin popularized; the chapter on Beckett places his work in the context of the wider theatrical movement which, in the 1950s, challenged the traditional 'well-made' play.

Federman, Raymond, and John Fletcher, *Samuel Beckett, His Works and His Critics: An Essay in Bibliography* (Berkeley, Los Angeles, London: University of California Press, 1970) remains the standard work for the period 1929–66. A sequel, bringing the entries up to date, is badly needed.

Fletcher, Beryl S., and John Fletcher, *A Student's Guide to the Plays of Samuel Beckett* (London: Faber and Faber, 1985) has entries on all the plays in *CDW*, to which it is designed to serve as a companion volume.

Fletcher, John, and John Spurling, *Beckett the Playwright* (London: Methuen, 1985). The chapters by John Spurling are of particular interest, since he is a practising dramatist who owes much to, and has been greatly influenced by, the plays of Samuel Beckett.

Gontarski, S. E., *The Intent of* Undoing *in Samuel Beckett's Dramatic Texts* (Bloomington: Indiana University Press, 1985) is a model of textual scholarship. Through a close study of the manuscripts Gontarski demonstrates how the details of Beckett's life are transformed and 'crafted into art' in his plays. There are particularly valuable appendices, one on *Film* (a transcript of preproduction discussions involving Beckett, Schneider and others), and two containing facsimiles of unpublished mime plays.

Gontarski, S. E., ed., *On Beckett: Essays and Criticism* (New York: Grove Press, 1986) is a very useful selection of critical material on which I have drawn extensively, especially the section on theatre (pp. 213–414).

Goodman, Randolph, *From Script to Stage: Eight Modern Plays* (San Francisco, 1971) contains an interview with Barbara Bray (about her work on *The Old Tune*) referred to in Zilliacus, 1976 (see below).

Goodwin, John, *Peter Hall's Diaries: The Story of a Dramatic Battle* (London: Hamish Hamilton, 1983) covers the period during which Hall's production of *Happy Days*, starring Peggy Ashcroft, was being staged.

Harmon, Maurice, ed., *No Author Better Served: The Correspondence of Samuel Beckett and Alan Schneider* (Cambridge, Mass. and London: Harvard University Press, 1988) makes available the invaluable exchange of letters between Beckett and his American director. The first was written in 1955 when the US première of *Waiting for Godot* was being prepared, the last in 1984 shortly before Schneider's death.

Hiebel, Hans H., 'John Calder on Samuel Beckett, London 30 May and 11 June 1988: An Interview with John Calder, Friend of Beckett and Publisher of His Works in England' (*Arbeiten aus Anglistik und Americanistik*, 16, 1, 1991, 67–99) is the record of a wide-ranging conversation.

Juliet, Charles, tr. Janey Tucker, *Conversations with Samuel Beckett and Bram van Velde* (Leiden: Academic Press, 1995) contains interesting interviews with Beckett.

Kalb, Jonathan, *Beckett in Performance* (Cambridge: Cambridge University Press, 1989) contains revealing interviews with JoAnne Akalaitis, Walter Asmus, Klaus Herm, David Warrilow and Billie Whitelaw, on which I have drawn extensively.

Kenner, Hugh, *Samuel Beckett: A Critical Study* (New York: Grove Press, 1961) is one of the earliest and cleverest studies of Beckett's work; this highly readable book was the first to explore Beckett's debt to Descartes and thereby throw light on the thinking underlying the novels and plays.

Knowlson, James, *Damned to Fame: The Life of Samuel Beckett* (London: Bloomsbury, 1996) is the definitive biography, written by an old friend of Beckett's with his blessing and with the benefit of unique access to private papers and to people who knew the playwright. James Knowlson's sympathetic but not adulatory study is unlikely to be surpassed for many decades to come.

Knowlson, James, ed., *Theatre Workbook 1: Samuel Beckett, Krapp's Last Tape* (London: Brutus Books, 1980) is an invaluable source book, covering all the major productions of the play between 1958 and 1977, especially those directed by Samuel Beckett.

Knowlson, James, gen. ed., *The Theatrical Notebooks of Samuel Beckett* (London: Faber and Faber, 1994). The Samuel Beckett archive at Reading University, founded by

James Knowlson with generous gifts from the playwright, contains the notebooks kept by Beckett when he was directing his own plays. They have been superbly edited by James Knowlson and others, and they offer both an indispensable aid to the understanding of the works concerned and a unique resource for serious students of all drama. What would one not give for similar notebooks kept by Shakespeare, revealing the bard's working methods! But alas such valuable documents are unlikely ever to come to light, so we must be grateful that Beckett's have been preserved.

Lennon, Peter, *Foreign Correspondent: Paris in the Sixties* (London: Picador, 1994) is the uninhibited account of the friendship between two Irishmen in Paris, one the *Guardian*'s correspondent, the other the writer of genius.

McMillan, Dougald, and Martha Fehsenfeld, *Beckett in the Theatre: The Author as Practical Playwright and Director*, vol. 1, *From Waiting for Godot to Krapp's Last Tape* (London: John Calder, 1988) is an invaluable survey of major productions, particularly Beckett's own, of the early great plays. Unfortunately McMillan's death, among other difficulties, prevented the appearance of any further volumes.

Oppenheim, Lois, *Directing Beckett* (Ann Arbor: University of Michigan Press, 1994) is a valuable collection of critical essays and of interviews with Beckett directors from which I have had occasion to quote frequently in this book.

Reid, Alec, *All I Can Manage, More Than I Could* (Dublin: Dolmen Press, 1968) is a short, very readable study by an Irish critic and man of the theatre that throws valuable light on Beckett's working methods and is a helpful introduction to his dramatic works. The title is taken from one of Beckett's letters to Alan Schneider (published on p. 24 of Harmon's edition; see under 'Harmon', above).

Renaud, Madeleine, *La Déclaration d'amour: rencontres avec André Coutin* (Monaco: Éditions du Rocher, 2000) is the somewhat 'gushy' record of the reminiscences of the great actress who created the role of Winnie in the French version of *Happy Days*.

Simpson, Alan, *Beckett and Behan and a Theatre in Dublin* (London: Routledge and Kegan Paul, 1962) tells the story of the first Irish performances of *Waiting for Godot*, which Simpson directed.

Wardle, Irving, *The Theatres of George Devine* (London: Jonathan Cape, 1978) is a sympathetic study of the immensely influential director of London's Royal Court Theatre and partner of Jocelyn Herbert; it is a mine of information about Devine's Beckett productions between 1958 and his untimely death in 1966.

Wilmer, S. E., ed., *Beckett in Dublin* (Dublin: Lilliput Press, 1992) is another useful collection of essays on which I have drawn extensively.

Worth, Katharine, *Samuel Beckett's Theatre: Life Journeys* (Oxford: Clarendon Press, 1999) is particularly interesting on later productions of Beckett's plays by such directors as JoAnne Akalaitis, David Warrilow and Worth herself.

Zilliacus, Clas, *Beckett and Broadcasting: A Study of the Works of Samuel Beckett For and In Radio and Television* (Åbo: Åbo Akademi, 1976) is the standard work on the subject, and is especially useful for first making available Beckett's 1969 'Suggestions for TV *Krapp*' (reprinted in *KLTWb*, pp. 70–79).

Zilliacus, Clas, 'Scoring Twice: Pinget's *La Manivelle* and Beckett's *The Old Tune*' (*Moderne Språk*, 68, 1, 1974, 1–10); see under 'Goodman', above.

Acknowledgements

With warm thanks to Rolf Breuer, Edward Beckett, Stan Gontarski, Jim Knowlson and Lois Overbeck.

For permission to reprint copyright material the publishers gratefully acknowledge the following:

APPLEYARD, BRIAN: 'Like leaves . . . remains to be seen' published in *The Times*, 25 February 1984, p. 8. BARBER, JOHN: 'After ordering for us . . . sculpture of himself' published in *Daily Telegraph*, 5 April, 1986, p. 12. BECKETT, SAMUEL: interview in *Transition* no. 48, 1948, pp. 146–7. *Molloy* published by Picador Books 1979, pp. 175–6. BEN-ZVI, LINDA ed.: *Women In Beckett*, University of Illinois Press, 1990. BRAY, BARBARA: article in the *Observer*, 16 June 1963, p. 29. CALDER, JOHN ed: *Beckett at Sixty*, published by Calder Publications Ltd, 1967; *As No Other Dare Fail*, published by Calder Publications Ltd. CIORAN, E. M.: article in *Partisan Review*, 42, 2 1976, pp. 280–85. COFFEY, BRIAN: article in *Threshold* 17, 1962 pp. 28–35. COURTNEY, CATHY ed.: *Jocelyn Herbert* published by Art Books International, 1997. FEDERMAN, RAYMOND and FLETCHER, JOHN: *Samuel Beckett, His Works and His Critics* published by The University of California Press, 1971. FLETCHER, JOHN and SPURLING, JOHN: *Beckett the Playwright*, published by Farrar, Strauss and Giroux, 1985. GOODWIN, JOHN ed.: *Peter Hall's Diaries* published by Oberon Books, 1999. GONTARSKI, S. E.: *On Beckett* published by Pub Group West, 1986. GOODMAN, RANDOLPH: *From Script to Stage*, published by Holt, 1972. HERBERT, HUGH: 'After two hours . . . ambiguous dots', 'there's too much preparation . . . it's inhuman', 'I've never got this . . . bony fingers', 'While he was directing . . . and they made he right sound' published in the *Guardian* 17 May 1980, p. 11. KALB, JONATHAN: *Beckett in Performance*, Cambridge University Press, 1991. LENNON, PETER: *Foreign Correspondent* published by Picador, 1994, pp. 68–70, 216. MAROWITZ, CHARLES: article in *The Village Voice*, 1 March 1962, pp. 1 and 13. MBEBOH, KITTS: article in *African Theatre Review* no. 2, pp. 92–6, 1986. MCMILLAN, DOUGALD and FEHSENFELD, MARTHA eds: *Beckett in the Theatre* published by Calder Publications Ltd, 1990. O'BRIAN, EDNA: article in the *Sunday Times Magazine*, 6 April 1986, pp. 51–3. PINGET, ROBERT: article in *Eonta* 1, 1991, pp. 9–10. SHENKER, ISRAEL: article in the *New York Times*, section 2, pp. 1 and 3, 5 May 1976. WARRILOW, DAVID: article in *Journal of Beckett Studies*, Spring 1992, pp. 125–6. SHERZER, DINA: article *French Review*, 1979, pp. 307–8.

Faber and Faber Ltd apologise for any errors or omissions in the above list and would be grateful to be notified of any corrections that should be included in the next edition or reprint of this volume.

Index